TAKING
COMMAND

GENERAL
DAVID RICHARDS

THE AUTOBIOGRAPHY

TAKING
COMMAND

headline

First published in 2014
by HEADLINE PUBLISHING GROUP

1

Cataloguing in Publication Data is available from the British Library

Hardback ISBN 978 1 4722 2084 4
Trade Paperback ISBN 978 1 4722 2085 1

Typeset in Berkeley by Avon DataSet Ltd, Bidford-on-Avon, Warwickshire

Printed and bound in Great Britain by
Clays Ltd, St Ives plc

Papers used by Headline are from well-managed forests and other responsible sources.

HEADLINE PUBLISHING GROUP
An Hachette UK Company
338 Euston Road
London NW1 3BH

www.headline.co.uk
www.hachette.co.uk

To Caroline, Joanna and Pippa, without whose love
and support much of what follows would not have
happened or been nearly so rewarding.

Contents

Foreword

Great commanders of history, up to and including the Second World War, became household names in their own societies. It was taken for granted that soldiers existed to fight for their nations wherever the bugle called. Today, while the British Army still enjoys the affection as well as respect of the British people, few warriors become celebrities. We inhabit an increasingly risk-averse world in which ignorant people, including some coroners, suppose that if wars are properly conducted, in accordance with Health & Safety Executive guidelines, nobody should get killed. Governments striving to save money – which means all of them – hack away at the defence budget, confident that doing so will not cost them votes, as do cuts in welfare or the NHS. Few prime ministers have much notion of strategy. Most think of the armed forces only when they want to inspect a guard of honour, or to indulge some headline-grabbing lunge into intervention abroad, often without giving a moment's thought to where this might lead them – and Britain.

Thus our modern generals have a tough row to hoe. If they become Chiefs of Staff, sooner or later most face a choice between acquiescing in some folly devised by Downing Street in the later watches of the night, or arguing the toss with the prime minister of the day, and earning a reputation as 'difficult'. David Richards has always been 'difficult', which is why some of us like and respect him so much. In his early career in command, he played a distinguished role in the troubles of Sierra Leone, East Timor and Afghanistan. When he became head of the Army and then

Chief of the Defence Staff, he was obliged to grapple with two prime ministers determined to do foolish things.

Gordon Brown commissioned two giant aircraft-carriers, which some of us – and David Richards – declared from the start were an unaffordable nonsense that would cripple the Royal Navy by devouring a giant's share of its resources. Britain does not engage in political 'pork-barrelling' on anything like the American scale, but it is hard to identify any rationale for Brown's decision beyond that of pumping billions of pounds into the Scottish economy, and preserving jobs in Labour constituencies. I have compared the carriers to the ancient Egyptian pyramids, because they consume enormous labour to produce an outcome of no practical utility. David Richards was courageous enough to fight tooth and nail against the carrier commitment, and I am sure posterity will respect him for having done so. He also, of course, staunchly resisted the Cameron Coalition's defence cuts, most notably the reduction of the Army to 82,000 men. This, again, was a political decision based upon no credible strategic calculation but, instead, upon a back-of-an-envelope guesstimate about what the government reckoned it could get away with.

In this memoir, the former Chief of the Defence Staff describes the immensely difficult arguments between politicians and soldiers, and also between Britain and the United States and other allies about options for intervention in Libya and Syria. It is no secret that David considerably annoyed his political masters by rejecting some of their more schoolboyish ideas, especially those relating to Syria, and by insisting that any British military action should be operationally sound, rather than driven by media soundbite. It may sound trite to say that he is sensible as well as clever, but common sense often flies out of the window when governments decide to play soldiers. David never forgot that the stakes – whether in Ireland or Sierra Leone, Afghanistan or Libya – were the lives of his men by land, sea and air.

He was also sensitive to the need for a local political underpinning for any military action. For Western forces merely to kill enemies and win battles is meaningless unless there is 'something to join up to' in the phrase of the US Army's splendid guru, General H.R. McMaster – a credible polity. Whether in Vietnam, Iraq, Libya or Syria, it is never enough for Western leaders simply to identify tyrants whom they wish to remove, foes they believe should be destroyed; there must also be some local grouping morally and politically worthy of Western support, something to fight *for*. I remember Douglas Hurd saying to me in the 1990s, when he was foreign secretary, 'Your military friends, Max, should grasp the fact that often they won't get the clarity of purpose, the fixed objectives they want. It may be necessary sometimes to take some action simply to avert a humanitarian disaster, and worry later about what comes afterwards.' I understood then, and accept now, what Douglas was saying. But politicians, in their turn, should recognise that commanders' 'obstructionism' – as the Cameron camp viewed the Chiefs of Staff's caution about Syria, for instance – was founded in a prudent consciousness that it would be disastrous to plunge into a morass without some notion about how to get out again.

David Richards is a wonderfully grown-up General, and also the best of company, superbly relaxed even in moments of high stress. I have often taxed him – odd this, coming from me, a journalist – about his indiscretion, his determination to call a spade a spade even in high councils of state, and even when the prime minister of the day is insisting that the spade is something quite different. But a willingness to speak truth to power is a rare gift, and he has it in extravagant measure. His book conveys his sense of fun as well as honesty, courage and professionalism. He has participated in, and often led, some remarkable adventures. Britain will be fortunate if its future Chiefs of Staff, the leaders of the armed forces, match his combination of 'can do' enthusiasm and boring old common sense. David Richards is a remarkable man, and the story that he tells reflects his qualities.

MAX HASTINGS
July 2014

Introduction

Sierra Leone, January 1999. I had been watching a ragged battle across a dried riverbed in the middle of the sprawling capital, Freetown. It was another stifling day in the equatorial heat of the African tropics. I was standing amid the chaos of guerrilla warfare, Sierra Leone-style.

AK47s and rocket-propelled grenades were being loosed off in all directions by the heavily armed irregulars of the Revolutionary United Front (RUF), the feared, brutal thugs whose signature atrocity – the amputation of their victims' hands – had brought the civil war in this small, benighted West African country to the world's attention.

I had gone to see how the Sierra Leone Army was faring as they fought alongside Nigerian soldiers of the West African peacekeeping force and the so-called Kamajor militia – drawn from ordinary people from rural areas who had taken up arms for the Sierra Leonian government. They were having a hell of a battle to prevent Freetown from falling into the hands of the RUF. In the course of it, the RUF were pushed back, with many killed. Afterwards, my protection party from the Royal Marines and I went forward, picking our way through the ramshackle streets and corpses until we came across a hospital.

People often ask me when it was that I made up my mind to do something to help Sierra Leone find its way to peace after eight years of civil war. There was no exact moment, but that visit to the hospital – just over a year before I was to play a part in the country's history – left a profound mark on me.

The hospital was dire – indescribably awful. On the ward where victims, young and old, lay in their own filth, some children came forward to greet us. They wanted to say hello and to thank me. As I went to grasp their hands, I noticed the bandages with fresh blood seeping through and realised that they hadn't got hands to hold with mine. These were children who, only hours before, had suffered traumatic amputation by machete-wielding RUF criminals.

Outside the hospital my five-strong protection team and I stood for a moment in silence. It was time to move on. We crossed to the other side of that chaotic, desperately poor place, following the advance now being made by government-backed forces. Then we stopped at an old people's home where several frail, frightened-looking men lay in bed. They had been unable to get away from the fighting.

One had been in the West African Rifles as a young man and still had his Second World War medals pinned proudly to his chest to prove it. When I walked in, he tried to get up to thank me because he thought I had, single-handedly, pushed the RUF out. In fact, I was only monitoring the battle to see whether or not to recommend that Britain help Sierra Leone. His generosity of spirit and pitiful state made a deep impression on me and I came away resolute in my determination to do what I could to help this country.

Just over twelve months later, in May 2000, and with the RUF on the rampage again, we were back with a small force of British paratroopers and special forces soldiers. We were ostensibly there to organise an evacuation of UK nationals. This time I more or less ignored my orders from London and committed my soldiers to leading the fight against the rebels, a decision that helped to turn the course of the war. We had seen the previous year that the RUF were an ill-disciplined rabble who relied on terror tactics and bravado. I was sure that a well-coordinated response, together with some properly directed firepower, would send them packing.

I sensed then that even though those in the Ministry of Defence in London didn't want me to get involved in the war – my orders made no mention of intervening, let alone committing men to combat – their political masters probably would not baulk at it. But I was a Brigadier; I couldn't exactly pick up the phone and talk to Prime Minister Tony Blair or Foreign Secretary Robin Cook. So it was pure instinct that drove me, combined with my determination not to let Freetown revert to the horrors we had witnessed the year before. I decided to chance my arm.

I do not regard myself as overly ambitious. I know people would say that I must be, otherwise I would not have made it to the top of my profession. But I don't believe I am ambitious in a selfish sense. If I had been, I would have been cautious in Freetown. I would not have risked my whole career. This operation was supposed to be a routine extraction of British nationals. Was I so confident that my initiative was going to come off, that one day a Hollywood film producer would want to make a movie of what we did? I certainly was not. Of course, my actions were not a complete gamble, but I knew it was a very risky undertaking.

To be frank, I didn't give a fig about the consequences for me. I was 5,000 miles from London. I had an outstanding small military command team with me, whom I had trained and trusted implicitly. I knew the Sierra Leonian President, Dr Ahmed Tejan Kabbah, pretty well and his Defence Minister, Hinga Norman. I just sensed that I could make this happen. I remember thinking, 'If this doesn't go well, sod it, I can leave the Army.'

I said to Neil Salisbury, my Chief of Staff and the rock around which my mind worked, 'We're chancing our arm here. I've got no orders for this. But I just can't let it go and I think we can pull it off.' Neil made me laugh when he replied, 'We're with you, Brigadier!' and we just got on with it.

Sierra Leone could well have ended my career, but in many ways it was the making of it. I'd taken a big risk and got away with it. Looking back, Freetown seems more pregnant with disaster than it did at the time. The country had been at war for years and was riven with factional fighting. It was ambitious indeed to think that we could push the RUF out of the capital and back into the interior.

I have always enjoyed risk-taking, not in a physical sense necessarily

– though that isn't bad – but more in the sense of thinking on my feet, having to trust my instincts under pressure. And I have always taken pride in telling it as it is, however unpalatable. In my role as Chief of the Defence Staff (CDS), that trait caused tensions with the government and Prime Minister David Cameron.

Of course, much of the credit for that episode in Sierra Leone – its name was Operation PALLISER – was given to Tony Blair. He cited it – and many lauded him for it – as a successful example of interventionist ethical foreign policy. I don't begrudge Blair doing that, even if at the time he had little or no knowledge of what we were really up to for many days. He set the conditions for what we did, so fair enough.

Taking Command is not only about my days in Sierra Leone. It traces my long career, which started when I was a proud 18-year-old subaltern in the Royal Artillery. By the time it concluded I'd reached the top of the military tree as Chief of the Defence Staff. Along the way I lived in the Far East and Germany, and completed three tours in Northern Ireland. On my last posting in Ulster in 1992, I wrote the Army's first campaign plan for the Troubles.

While based in Berlin, in the mid-eighties, I was responsible for the security of Hitler's deputy, Rudolf Hess, whenever he left Spandau Prison. I saw him three times in his final months and had to play my part in dealing with the ensuing diplomatic stand-off between the Russians and Americans after he died.

As Chief of Joint Force Operations, I travelled to many of the world's trouble spots, in addition to Sierra Leone, deploying to Albania, Indonesia, East Timor and Mozambique among other places. As a Major General, I deployed briefly to Iraq in the days immediately following the toppling of Saddam Hussein. Aside from my role as Chief of the Defence Staff, perhaps the biggest task I undertook was leading NATO's International Security Assistance Force (ISAF) in Afghanistan between 2006 and 2007, where I became the first British General to command American troops at theatre level since the Second World War.

During that posting, I committed my forces to a major battle in

Kandahar, which I still believe was a make-or-break moment for the international project in Afghanistan. Operation MEDUSA in the Panshway district of Kandahar inflicted some of the heaviest casualties on the Taliban of the entire Afghan war. That said, in the course of that command, I fought hard to broaden the scope of the operations of coalition forces away from purely offensive military activity to a wider emphasis on political and developmental goals. I waged vociferous running battles with my NATO superiors over what was viewed as my overly realistic summaries of our progress. On two occasions they tried to muzzle me without success. During that posting I kept a detailed daily journal, which forms the basis of three chapters on my time commanding in Afghanistan.

When I became head of the armed forces in October 2010, I inherited a Strategic Defence and Security Review, which had been largely signed off by my predecessor, Air Chief Marshal Sir Jock Stirrup. While I had influenced the outcome in my previous job as head of the Army, I remain unhappy about the decision to build two very large aircraft carriers, the *Queen Elizabeth* and the *Prince of Wales*. We must make the most of them now but two new ships of the existing class would have sufficed and, vitally, the Royal Navy would have had more vessels overall. The decision to shrink the regular Army to a mere 82,000 personnel is a mistake, I would argue, and the experiment to take the strain using enhanced reserve capacity bold, but I wish it well.

In my role as Chief of the Defence Staff, I worked closely with David Cameron in the newly created National Security Council, which met multiple times during the campaign to support rebels against the ailing dictatorship of Colonel Gaddafi in Libya. One of my first jobs during that campaign was to persuade Mr Cameron not to rush in alongside President Sarkozy of France, who wanted to commit forces to the conflict regardless of whether other allies, including the Americans, joined in or not. My judgement was that, for success, it was vital for the United States and NATO to be involved. It was also essentially my call to make the key decision to switch the effort of the international coalition from eastern Libya to the west.

My other points of focus as Chief of the Defence Staff were the Falklands – my role there was to calm government nerves about another Argentinian invasion, which I never thought likely – the spreading threat posed by Al-Qaeda and its offshoots round the world, dealing with Iran and the potential nuclear threat it poses, and responding to the crisis in Syria. On that issue, I was strongly of the view that Britain should stay well clear of any involvement unless we and our allies were properly committed and mounted a strategically coherent military campaign. I argued this case forcefully to the Prime Minister and others.

I have served during a fascinating period in history. My career far exceeded the expectations that I held as a young officer. I plied my trade from the snows of arctic Norway to the tropics of West Africa and the deserts of the Middle East, from the officer's mess at Larkhill to running NATO in Afghanistan. The common denominator has always been the men and women of the British armed forces. Like all good officers, I like soldiers and hugely enjoy their company. I love the banter and their sense of commitment to each other, through thick and thin. They seem instinctively to feel this and respond to it. There can be no better feeling than knowing your troops will follow you anywhere and that you would do anything for them.

Taking Command is the story of my life in the Army.

ONE

A Typical Army Brat

Boisterous, rebellious at times, quite tough and self-contained, happy in my own company and confident – in short, growing up I was a typical army brat, determined to do my own thing. But I was also sensitive to the general direction in which I ought to be going in life, even if I was going to get there in my own way.

I knew from an early age that the Army was likely to be a very good option for me. My father was a career soldier and seemed to enjoy it; my brother was serving and having a whale of a time.

My father, John Downie Richards, known to all as Jim, was a big influence on me, and his career set the background for a peripatetic and happy childhood during which my brother, two sisters and I chopped and changed schools with his postings. A good-looking Welshman, born in Cardiff and educated at a minor public school in Eastbourne, Jim Richards was a larger than life individual who was great fun and who inspired affection and loyalty among the soldiers under him.

He was a great sportsman. He swam for England and played cricket to a high standard. Were it not for the intervention of the Second World War, he may never have joined the Army and, instead, reached county level. He never tired of the game and played village cricket right through his sixties. He had quite a temper but he was unfailingly kind and patient with me, bowling at me for hours on summer evenings after getting back from work.

Before the war he had worked in banking but joined up even before conscription was introduced and became a sapper – the equivalent of a private soldier. He was sent to France in 1939 as part of the British Expeditionary Force and was eventually evacuated by warship from Calais in May 1940.

He only just got out, though, having been captured by the Germans at one stage. Bizarrely, he made good his escape by walking off, realising that his captors did not have enough men to stop him.

He met my mother, Pamela Reeves, in 1938 in Eastbourne, where he was living before the war. Her family were well-to-do and of middle-class stock from West Kent and East Sussex. Like a lot of people in Britain in those uncertain days, they got married as the war started. My mother was an attractive woman, with a strong and independent streak and she loved the variety of army life. She was utterly devoted to her family and we children – my older brother Nick, older sister Jan and younger sister Sara – knew from an early age how fortunate we were.

Back in England after his evacuation from Calais, my father was selected for a commission and joined the Royal Artillery, a decision that was to have a lasting influence on my own career. He fought at the battle of Imphal in Burma and got malaria twice. In 1946 he was posted to Ceylon as a battery commander, where Jan was born after my mother and Nick had travelled out on a troop ship to join him.

In 1949 as the Army slimmed down, my father decided he wanted to remain a regular soldier and transferred to the Royal Army Pay Corps, the RAPC, known colloquially as the Royal Artillery Pension Club.

It was in that role that he was posted to Egypt as part of the force guarding the Suez Canal and that's where I came along on 4 March 1952. I spent my first year in Egypt, in a little place called Fayed, south of Ismailia, and it has left me with a lasting affinity for the country and people. Whenever I go to Cairo and elsewhere in Egypt today, they still say 'welcome home'. They love that and so do I, and it does give me an entree in that part of the world. I am very much the tailend of that whole era; there are not many British people around these days who were born in Egypt at that time and that connection has given me a head start in my dealings with Arab countries.

When we moved back to England from Egypt, we were housed for a while in a charming vicarage in Bemerton on the outskirts of Salisbury. But after eighteen months we moved to Devizes in Wiltshire and altogether more dismal conditions. Our family – my father and mother and, by now, four children – lived in what were classed as 'married quarters'. In reality, our home was nothing more than a wooden hut with a felt roof. I can still remember how cold it was, and having to break the ice in the glass of water by my bed by poking my finger in it on a winter's morning. It was tough living and it made me quite ascetic – and that was good for soldiering.

I went to a little private primary school just outside Devizes, run by Lady Cowdray. Even at that young age I showed promise in English and history but I was never any good at maths. I was an adventurous five-year-old. I wanted to *do* things, so academic pursuits, such as sitting at home reading story books, took second place to escaping outside and riding my bike to places I wasn't meant to go. I was fascinated by all things military. I remember once sneaking into a tank shed in Devizes and crawling around this huge camouflaged beast of a machine. Somehow I clambered up on to it and then promptly fell off, cutting my head. When I got back and told my mother what had happened, blood was pouring from the wound.

I remember another lucky escape around that time. I was playing in the garden, jumping up and down on a manhole cover, when it suddenly opened, dumping me unceremoniously in the drain; but it closed again above me, leaving me in the dark. Looking back from our health and safety conscious world, it seems quite an astonishing moment. I was playing happily in the garden one minute, and the next I had disappeared. I was terrified and in shock as I tried to make sense of what had happened and started shouting for my mother. But no one could hear me. There was a little ladder and I climbed it, fearful that someone might turn some taps on or flush the loo and wash me away.

My mother, noticing that I had disappeared, came out to find me. I could hear her shouting, 'David, David,' and I was shouting back but she couldn't hear me. I think I was in the drain for about an hour.

Eventually, she must have heard me shouting, 'I'm down here,' and worked out where I was. She panicked at that point and didn't know how to open the manhole, so a neighbour came round to help and they got me out.

When I was seven years old, life changed dramatically. My father was posted to Cyprus, then still a British colony. These were the tense years of the Cyprus emergency when Greek paramilitaries, determined on union with Greece, killed scores of British soldiers in terrorist attacks in the build-up to independence. My sister Sara and I flew there with my parents in a Second World War vintage DC4 aircraft, taking eight hours for a flight that today would take about three. We lapped up the sunshine, went to Army schools under armed guard and enjoyed swimming, water-skiing and learning to sail. It was a fantastic life and I learnt to ride there too – an enduring passion – on a little pony called Susie. We were at school in the mornings only, so the afternoons were just for play. Nick and Jan were, by this time, at boarding school and they would join us in the holidays.

That experience of colonial Army life was definitely a factor in me later joining up. It was fun. We were clearly influential during a very difficult time for people on the island and for our own soldiers. I sensed that what my father was doing mattered. People on the whole were nice to us. They wanted us there, contrary to popular perception. They would say, 'Don't leave, there's going to be awful trouble.'

We moved back to England in late 1960 and after living in north London for a few years, during which time my father commuted to Horse Guards, my parents bought their first proper house. In 1963, when I was 11 years old, we moved into The Platts, a snug, fifteenth-century farmhouse situated in the rolling hills of the Sussex Weald at Bodle Street Green outside Herstmonceux. I loved it.

To get to the house you had to go down a drive and you could barely see anybody else in any direction. We lived in glorious rural isolation. The house had been renovated but was hardly modernised by today's standards; the bathroom could only be described as grotty. There was a huge inglenook fireplace in the sitting room, where I used to sit on the ancient settle and think about all the people who had sat there before me over the centuries, imagining what they were wearing and what they were doing.

Having left a prep school in north London, I now found myself boarding for the first time at Ascham, the prep school for Eastbourne College. My first term there stands out in my memory, chiefly because of an incident when 'Richards' was – typically – breaking the rules and encouraging others in his 'gang' to do the same.

We had sneaked into the gym unauthorised and unsupervised and I was showing off my vaulting ability over the wooden horse. Vault one went brilliantly. Vault two was a disaster. I fell off and heard a horrible crack as I landed. 'I've broken my arm, I've broken my arm,' I shouted to my disbelieving pals, who all scarpered and left me to make my way to matron.

The route involved stairs on which I managed to trip. Without thinking, I extended my broken arm to take my weight and, in doing so, aggravated the break, pushing the broken bone through the skin. Then the pain really hit me. They gave me a couple of aspirin – as they did in those days – and I was whisked off to hospital.

My mother was informed but the headmaster assured her there was no need for her to come rushing down to see her little boy, a decision she felt guilty about for the rest of her life. It was a nasty break and I remember hearing the doctors discussing it. 'This is a bad one,' I heard one say. I was in plaster for twelve weeks and still have a small scar on my left forearm for my pains.

When it came to the all-important Common Entrance exam at the end of my two years at Ascham, I am ashamed to admit that I did a deal with Henry Wooton, who was great at maths but not much good at English or history. We sat next to each other in class and I agreed to show him my history and English answers if he showed me his maths.

I ended up passing with flying colours and was pushed straight into

year two at Eastbourne College. Our creative approach to the entrance
exam was, it turned out, a chicken that came home to roost, as my
performance over the next year failed to live up to the promise I had
appeared to show. They worked me out pretty quickly and I was held
back for a year to help me catch up.

I enjoyed life at Eastbourne. I am one of those boring buggers who
always say that school days were the best days of my life. It was great. I
loved the institution. I liked the order. I had lots of friends and I liked
some of the work. My main interest was sport, something that was
exacerbated by a fairly disastrous decision prior to O-Levels to drop
two of my favourite subjects – history and geography – in favour of
sciences. This came about during an interview with my housemaster –
one Keith Norman-Smith (a good man, known to us as 'Bambi') – in
which I told him I loved horse riding and I was interested in animals.
He concluded there and then that I should become a vet and re-ordered
my studies accordingly.

I was taking a completely wrong turn but that's life. I remember I got
the history prize that term and my history teacher was devastated when
he heard I wasn't going to carry on. So until after my O-Levels, academia
and I were on slightly different planets.

Norman-Smith did, however, have a more edifying influence on the
young David Richards. At this stage in my life I was a bit of rebel and very
much the leader of my own gang. I was a toughie but never vindictive,
and I pushed back against institutional life, even as I rather enjoyed it.
When I was 15, Norman-Smith read me the riot act. If I didn't start
putting my leadership skills to more constructive use, he may have to
ask me to leave.

I think at that moment it dawned on me that it was time to grow up.
Not long afterwards I was made the head of my common room and
eventually ended up being head boy and captain of rugby, playing in the
first XV for my last three years. The rugby master, Robin Harrison, was a
marvellous teacher, serious about his sport and intensely kind. Michael
Birley, the headmaster, was an inspirational figure and even we boys

realised we were lucky to be guided by him. He gave me the shock of my life when he told me that I was to be head boy.

Another important influence was the Combined Cadet Force at Eastbourne. I joined when I was 13, in my first term in 1965, and loved it. I quickly realised that I had a flair for military things. I enjoyed the discipline and order but at the same time I liked the opportunity it gave us to use our initiative. I remember one exercise in particular. Our task was to grab a tin box that was being heavily guarded by a rival platoon. It supposedly contained some secret papers and I was put in charge of the squad with the 'impossible task' of getting hold of them. The master supervising us was convinced we wouldn't succeed, especially since the group guarding the tin was bigger than the one trying to snatch it.

I deployed all the other boys in my team to make a hell of a lot of noise as they attacked in one area while I sneaked in from a different angle and managed to grab the tin. One 'enemy' cadet, Nick Burnett, discovered me, ran after me and was very nearly catching me when I stopped and turned to confront him.

'You don't really want to stop me, do you?' I said to Nick. 'We can get this exercise over now if you let me get away.'

Nick thought about it but refused. So I hit him for his pains and, understandably perhaps, he never forgave me.

I liked leading and I was already thinking of joining the Army. I had a big cardboard display on my wall on to which I had glued cut-out photographs of tanks and guns and all sorts of other kit, and I knew each one. I even wrote mini-pamphlets on military tactics and strategy. These were the 'Richards Doctrine' and covered subjects such as how to attack a position, the art of surprise and how to maintain the initiative. The Duke of Wellington caught my imagination, as did Field Marshal Montgomery, and I read Field Marshal Slim's *Defeat into Victory*, which I thought was a fantastic book. The military life was clearly in my blood.

At home during those years I lived a charmed existence. I would spend hours in the woods around our house, riding my beloved chestnut pony, Skylark, and playing soldiers. Sometimes I would 'ambush' Chilsham

Lane, which ran between our house and Herstmonceux. I would push deep into the bushes in all the kit that I got from my father and I took pride in the fact that no one would see me as I watched the villagers making their way up and down the road.

I was very good – by my own estimation – at patrolling and I would live out in the woods with my dog, Butch, a mongrel who spread his largesse around East Sussex. He was a lovely dog and my partner in crime. I would make my own basha, or shelter, in the woods and sleep in it with him.

The other thing that was a great joke within the family was that I used to practise public speaking in the woods. I would make speeches to the trees and, in particular, I would imitate Winston Churchill. No one really knew about it until an uncle, who was staying with us, went for a walk one day and heard this seemingly disembodied voice declaiming among the trees. My cover was blown.

My speeches were always about the social and political issues of the day. 'The people of this country need to understand that I, and I alone, can bring the salvation they so desperately need . . .' I would intone, adopting my best Churchillian delivery.

But it wasn't always Winston. I gradually developed my own voice as a speaker and I used to practise in the house at school. I would stand on the table in the hall as the boys came in from break. 'Friends, Romans, countrymen,' I would begin and then go off into an Eastbourne College specific issue of no doubt great interest to them, usually delivered in Shakespearean mode.

I was obviously quite confident. I didn't need lots of other people, and although I had plenty of friends and valued them, I never depended on them. I am still a bit like that now. I didn't crave company and I spent most of my holidays on my own.

After A-Levels – I had returned to first principles with English, economic history and history of art – I stayed on for the Oxbridge exams and made a half-hearted attempt to get into Cambridge. They didn't want me. One university that offered me an interview was Bristol where I was

asked by a bearded left-wing lecturer who knew of my interest in the
Army, 'Why should we educate you to be a better killer?' Needless to say,
that was the end of my interest in Bristol. In the end, I settled for law and
PPE (philosophy, politics and economics) at Cardiff. I thought, 'I'm Welsh
and I have never even been to Wales, so why not give Cardiff a try?'

TWO

Learning My Trade

After finishing school, I had planned to have a year off before starting at university, but little did I know that my Army career would start within a few weeks. I had gone to Malta with my mother for a short holiday, to stay with my brother Nick and his wife Carol who were posted there, when my father sent me a telegram asking if I would like to do the Regular Commission Board when I got back. I thought why not? The Board, now known as the Army Officer Selection Board, was a three-day assessment, testing, among other things, intelligence, leadership and physical fitness. And so in mid-January 1971, not quite 19, I attended the Board at Westbury in Wiltshire and was duly selected to be an officer.

A new, nine-month, gap-year commissioning course, designed to fit between school and university, had just started up. I became one of the first recruits. It started with three weeks at the old – now defunct – Mons Officer Cadet School at Aldershot and that was followed by a week's token gunnery course at Larkhill.

I had decided to join the Royal Artillery. I wanted to become a gunner because my father had been a gunner, and although he then went into the Pay Corps, it was clear that his heart was with the gunners. Headstrong as I was, I didn't like what I saw at the time as the pretence of some of the smarter regiments and I took a perverse pleasure in going into a not-very-smart but well-respected and professional organisation with its own *esprit de corps*. The Royal Artillery has old Etonians through to miners' sons commissioned in its ranks and it seemed to fit in with my character. But I had to make a quick decision. People were trying to get me to join other regiments – the Green Jackets, the cavalry or the guards. I stayed with the gunners.

That attitude is one that has stayed with me throughout my career. I like ordinary decent people, without affectation or side to them, so it is not surprising that I like soldiers. I have always felt at home in their company. My father used to say, 'If you're bogus, your soldiers will see through you in minutes and you'll never recover,' and he was right. My parents taught me to be at home with people of all backgrounds. Good army officers instinctively are like this. They don't take themselves too seriously, are competent and professional but natural and friendly. Indeed my own motto has always been 'relaxed but never casual'.

Not long after I attended the course at Mons I was asked to write an account of my first weeks in the Army for the Public Schools Appointments Bureau News Bulletin – presumably to help encourage other leavers to think of joining the Army. Here is a flavour of how I captured my first days of learning to be an officer.

On a windswept Saturday morning at the beginning of February I arrived at Mons Officer Cadet School to start a crash course in officer training. One quickly became accustomed to the life of the soldier, firing rifles and machine guns, reading maps, setting compasses, night patrols, and living in slit trenches. We did not do all these things well, but by the time we left we had somehow acquired enough knowledge of them (and even a grasp of minor tactics) not to let ourselves down when we joined our regiments. After three weeks at Mons, which earned us the name of Three-Week Wonders, we had a small unassuming parade and were officially in Her Majesty's Army.

Then I described the even shorter course I did at Larkhill.

From Mons five of us who were commissioned into the Royal

Artillery went to Larkhill for a week for an intensive course in
gunnery. It was hard work during the day, but good fun. I left
there with a basic grounding in gunnery, I knew which end the
shell came out and could even calculate the data for the simpler
shoots. That week also provided a friendly introduction to the
Royal Regiment.

My goal was to join the commando regiment of the RA, my brother's
regiment, but first I had to win a place. In those days, most young officers
who went on the five week commando course – culminating in the
notoriously tough week of physical tests, that finishes with a thirty-mile
run over Dartmoor – would have done two years at Sandhurst and would
have been preparing for it psychologically and physically for many
months. I went down to Plymouth for the preliminary training for the
course – known as the 'beat-up' – having left school just over two months
earlier. No one seemed to know about the short-service limited commission
I was on. As far as they were concerned I'd done two years at Sandhurst
and I didn't do anything to disabuse them. I must have had instincts
that allowed me to appear more experienced and better trained than I
actually was. I had no choice; it was sink or swim.

I remember that journey to Plymouth. My father delivered me –
he was still serving. I remember going through the imposing gates of
the Royal Citadel overlooking Plymouth Sound and thinking, 'Bloody
hell.' The men I was about to work with were tough. They were
commandos and one or two of the older ones had been in the Second
World War. But immediately I felt at home. I got a cheerful greeting from
the soldiers on guard, and an early word of encouragement from the
Regimental Sergeant Major, one Warrant Officer Class 1 Pat Arber, that
was enough to send me on my way. 'Look after the soldiers and they will
always look after you,' he said. It was advice I soon found to be spot
on and have followed ever since. The commanding officer was Lieutenant
Colonel Nigel Frend. Kind but tough, he was the sort of man I instinctively
liked and respected.

The Citadel is like a castle. Tourists are allowed to visit at certain times of the day. The officers' mess was in an austere and imposing building, the upper storeys of which overlooked Plymouth Sound. The bedrooms were beneath the battlements but the day rooms had views over the Sound where warships lay at anchor. It was an evocative place, and I loved the strong feeling of history and tradition.

You could hardly be expected to try to join the commando regiment without some sort of rite of passage. In Plymouth in those days the requirement was to prove your manhood by picking up a girl at what was colloquially known as the 'Groin Exchange'. During the day this was actually the Plymouth Sailing School but on certain nights it turned into our favourite disco.

There was I, just 19 years old, trying to get fit – very fit – but also having to prove my manhood and my ability to play hard and work hard. We would meet girls and then try to get them back to the Citadel. 'Would you like to come back to my castle for a coffee?' we would ask them cheekily. The soldiers would salute you smartly as you trooped back on your way to the mess. We did days of physical training and basic military training. We did ambushes on Dartmoor and spent countless hours out in the filthy weather in March, getting little sleep – we weren't allowed sleeping bags. It was a tough three weeks but, at the end of it, I was considered suitable to go on the first available Royal Marine Commando course, starting at the end of March.

It was my first real experience of army life and I was pleased to discover that I loved the company of the soldiers, and loved their humour. I was just one of them. Although, when we were not out on Dartmoor, I went back to the officer's mess every evening and they went to their barrack block, in every other respect I was living with them and was treated just as any other soldier.

At the end of March I moved to Lympstone in Devon – the Royal Marine Commando Training Centre. I thoroughly enjoyed my five weeks there. It was bloody tough – lots more training, lots of minor tactics, a lot more time spent on Dartmoor. Then the final week was the test week, including the Tarzan course of ropes, high ladders and beams and an assault course with a task called a 'regain' when you crawl on a rope across a pond while carrying your rifle. You have to drop your body down and then pull up and get back on top of the rope – all the while keeping hold of your rifle – and carry on moving along. There is a technique to doing it and I was good at it. I had good upper body strength. I was like a little monkey. This was followed by a timed speed march of nine miles with all our kit and then an endurance course that included going through tunnels in water and mud and a run back to Lympstone.

The final part was the thirty-mile run over Dartmoor. Officers had to do it in under seven hours with full kit and that was quite something. We actually did thirty-six miles because the Royal Marine captain, who was in charge of our troop, screwed up his map reading – but we passed. I was completely and utterly knackered. As soon as we stopped our limbs froze solid. As I threw my pack down at the finish I felt an intoxicating mixture of exhaustion and elation, knowing that I had achieved my goal.

It had been a gruelling experience but I had made it. The next day was the parade when I was awarded my green beret. I was a fully fledged commando. Less than six months after hanging up my hat as head boy at Eastbourne, I was – as far as those around me were concerned – a trained army officer with the rank of Second Lieutenant. I was on cloud nine. I felt I could take on the world and indeed it wasn't long before I was on a plane. With five months left before university was due to start, and as the next part of the gap-year commissioning course, I was posted to Singapore. I left Lympstone on a Friday and drove home in my Mini. On the following Monday I boarded a VC10 to the Far East.

In early 1971, British forces in Singapore were preparing to leave, following Harold Wilson's decision to withdraw from major military bases east of Suez in the wake of Britain's parlous economic plight of the late 1960s. This policy was partially rescinded by Wilson's successor as prime minister, Edward Heath. I arrived in Singapore with conspicuously white knees and joined 7 (Sphinx) Commando Battery, part of 40 Commando Group Royal Marines, as it was preparing to return home. I was there for four months and it proved to be a hell of an adventure.

I hadn't really had time to get into the military way of life at all. I was still wet behind the ears, to put it mildly. When I arrived, I heard soldiers muttering about how 'they're sending 'em out young now', but I was a commando and I was determined to hold my own. I was given a troop of thirty men to look after, administer and pay. We were gunners so we had guns – the 105mm Pack Howitzer. I was based initially at Dieppe Barracks on the edge of Sembawang airfield in the north of the island, on the way to the Causeway.

We spent a lot of time in the jungle, including completing a jungle warfare training course, but I also played hard in Singapore, indulging in everything from sailing and swimming to officer's mess film nights in the naval base and boys' nights downtown. It was a fantastic life with echoes of Leslie Thomas's comic novel *The Virgin Soldiers*, which was set in Singapore and published just five years before I went there. In short, I went from a schoolboy to a man in six months.

A memorable moment was my first encounter with the Royal Navy. Shortly after arriving, I was waiting in the barracks for the commando group to come back from exercises in the jungle in Malaya. A small troop of naval gunfire forward observers was there, too, commandos from my own regiment. The troop commander, Captain Terry Lyons, asked me if I would like to join them on an exercise they were doing, and I was delighted to accept his offer. The next day, a New Zealand navy frigate took us to Pulau Aur, an idyllic little island in the South China Sea, off the east coast of Malaya. For three or four days I helped them direct naval gunfire on to targets located on a small island just off the main island. We spent the evenings living on a platform in the palm-covered hills overlooking the sea. It was quite a setting.

When we had finished, a Royal Navy Leander class frigate came to take us back. The ship's captain sent a long boat into the surf to pick us up. It was hugely romantic. Here was I, a young officer, wading through the waves of the sparkling blue South China Sea to get into a long boat. I couldn't help thinking of the film *Mutiny on the Bounty* as we made our way into deeper water, a smart rating at the helm. We reached the stern of the warship and, as we walked up the immaculately maintained gangway, we were greeted by the second in command of the ship, holding a tray from the wardroom with silver mugs brimming with cold beer. For the first time – and I saw it on many subsequent occasions – the Royal Navy demonstrated that it knew how to do things in style.

The battery commander in Singapore was Major Tony Bennett, whom I regarded as a bit of a god, so I had little to do with him. The officers who had the greatest influence on me were Lieutenant Phil Wilkinson and Lieutenant Peter Taylor. I shared a room with Lieutenant John Llewellyn, a hard-living son of a Southampton docker. Among the other characters was Sergeant Donegan, a Roman Catholic Ulsterman, who famously said to a local prostitute in reference to me, 'I give you a boy, give me back a man.' I can report that I went in as instructed but emerged, unbeknown to Sergeant Donegan, with my dignity intact. Sergeant Donegan was just one of many colourful soldiers who lived by the motto 'work hard, play hard'. The list of great characters who so generously took this 19-year-old rookie into their midst included Warrant Officer Class 2 Sutton, Sergeants Hanking, Ravenhill and Kelly, Bombardier Wright and many more. There would be many others like them throughout my career.

One of the things we always wanted to do was see the sun come up over Singapore's notorious Bugis Street – the red-light district and home of the famous transgender prostitutes, the Kai Tais. More than once we did that, which meant a particularly hard night on the booze. The next day you could be in the jungle on exercise . . . so it was a tough life.

That period in Singapore sustained me subsequently during many less stimulating and interesting times in my early career. It kept me going and made me loyal to soldiers – my goodness they looked after me.

* * *

Back home in the autumn of 1971, it was time to be a student and to go up to Cardiff where I started reading law and then moved on to PPE. It was quite a shock to be an undergraduate after my early adventures as a young officer but, for the first time, I really clicked on the academic side. I worked harder than I ever had at school and, while I was no Einstein, I ended up with a good 2:1. I suppose I realised I was more able than I had considered myself to be at Eastbourne. I was dealing with subjects I found fascinating – political theory and particularly foreign affairs, comparative history, economic history and international relations. I even did criminology and interviewed murderers in prison.

Before starting at Cardiff I had accepted a university cadetship that guaranteed me a regular commission when I left, and that came with a generous stipend. Now I was a wealthy undergraduate and didn't have to pay anything for university. In return, I had made a commitment to serve for five years after graduating and was obliged to turn up in the summer vacations to 29 Commando Regiment, usually at the Royal Citadel in Plymouth. One summer I completed the parachute selection course and the parachute jumps course. Very proudly, I had a commando dagger on one shoulder and a parachute on the other.

University gave me an opportunity to reflect on the course my life was taking and I came to realise that I could do things other than soldiering. I looked at everything from forestry through to joining the merchant navy, even becoming a journalist, but I felt a moral obligation to do my five years. I had had a hell of a good time in the Army until then and I felt I had to do what I'd said I would do. My father had retired by this time as a full Colonel. He and my mother were running a market-garden business on twelve acres of land at our home. He certainly didn't push me into the Army. Even then he would have been quite happy for me to be a barrister or something else. But I was set on seeing my Army commitment through.

I took a bit of stick at Cardiff, of course, being a young would-be army officer. But I could always handle it and I quite enjoyed playing up to my image. The University of Wales at Cardiff was quite a left-wing place in the early 70s, when students were in a more militant mood than typically they are today. Most of my pals had long hair. My concession to modernity was to grow sideboards, but even that was not for very long.

One moment at Cardiff still brings a smile to my face. Everyone was chuckling and sniggering when I walked into a lecture hall and as I made my way to the back, where my friends were sitting, I noticed, scrawled all over the board, the words 'Dave Richards is a fascist pig'. My fellow undergraduates were all looking at me as if to say, 'F*** off, Richards.' I think I laughed out loud. It was quite an honour. I got a lot of joshing like that.

I got on well with the academics at Cardiff. Professor Paul Wilkinson, who became eminent in terrorism studies, was one of my tutors and we kept in close touch until his death in 2011. My lecturer in foreign relations, Dr Alun Jones, was also a big influence.

It was during my time at university – and one of the best things about it – that I met Caroline. She was at art school in the city and I got to know her through mutual friends. I must have been incredibly off-putting to start with as I tried to bulldoze my way into her affections. Her first year was my last year and when I heard about this very attractive girl, I was determined to meet her. One of my friends, who knew her vaguely, suggested that we go round to her digs after the pub. So one night – and we'd had a few – we found the house and knocked on the door. It was about 10.30 p.m. and, as ever, I was gang leader.

After a few minutes Caroline's landlady opened the door with the immortal words, 'Not too drunk, is it?' which had us falling about.

'No, not too drunk,' I assured her. 'We've come to see Caroline.'

'Oh, she's in bed,' came the reply.

'Get her up,' I said. 'We've come to see her!'

I must have been seriously the worse for wear because there was a dustbin outside the house and I said, 'I'll wake her up,' and started banging on it, making a hell of a noise. Caroline, of course, was hugely embarrassed. The landlady was lovely – she knew the form. Unsurprisingly perhaps, Caroline Bond, as she was, wouldn't play ball for three years but I always kept the hope of a relationship alive.

So that was the sort of bloke I was. Looking back, I can see that I was a bit out of control. The discipline and structure of the Army, where you could channel your aggression, was good for me.

After graduation, I attended a three-month post-university course at Sandhurst where I wore the green beret, which was pretty rare and certainly gave me extra profile. I came second to a cavalryman and friend, Tim Murray-Jones. I mention that because, tragically, he and another friend, who was also on the course, Mark Hunter-Jones, were killed eighteen months later in an avalanche while skiing in the Alps.

After another short, young-officers gunnery course at Larkhill, I was posted back to Singapore. If my first visit there had been an eye-opener, this one was even better. This time I knew the ropes and had a little of my own history in the place to call on. I had a girlfriend – the daughter of the Brigadier – and a clapped-out car to get around in. I joined the 1st Light Battery, known as 'The Blazers', and once again my five-month tour came against the background of pending withdrawal. By that stage, Harold Wilson had returned to power and reaffirmed his decision to leave almost everywhere east of the Suez Canal. So, having taken part in farewell parades once, in 1971, I did so again four years later.

Those days in Singapore, added to the earlier ones, were formative for me. I learnt to live cheek by jowl with soldiers under my command – in fact, probably closer to them than was wise. I would drink with them and so on, but somehow I managed to preserve the relationship that allowed me to lead them without any trouble. I learnt a lot about myself and I learnt a lot about soldiers during those days in the tropics.

Then came my baptism of fire. Returning to 29 Commando, and specifically 79 Commando Battery, we were almost immediately posted to Northern Ireland. I swapped the heat and humidity of Singapore city and the adventure of exercises in the jungle for the delights of Flax Street Mill in the heart of west Belfast. The Troubles were still at their height and parts of the city looked like London after the Blitz. The place had a brooding and tense atmosphere. People hurried about their business without looking at others. After the colour of the South China Sea, this was like a grim black-and-white film.

My battery had responsibility for the hardline Protestant area that surrounded the Ardoyne and the equally hardline Catholic enclave of Ligoniel. These estates were liberally daubed with graffiti – as many of them still are – some of it impressive artwork, although it mostly spoke of communal hatred. The redbrick walls, with their images of men in balaclavas carrying guns, were the 1970s version of the internet, a platform for propaganda where the paramilitaries communicated with their community, inspiring and intimidating them at the same time.

Our main adversaries were the secretive Protestant or loyalist para-military group, the Ulster Volunteer Force. By that stage, they had already made a dreadful name for themselves, targeting Catholics and Republicans in bombings and shootings. We also had Republican terrorists to contend with – mainly the Provisional IRA – who were committed to driving British troops out of Ulster.

This was my first serious soldiering and it was exacting for a young, inexperienced officer. Every time I went out on patrol, I didn't know whether we were going to be shot at, and quite regularly we were. We'd gone from being the saviours of the Catholic population, when the Army first arrived in Belfast six years earlier, to being their enemies. I remember the first time I was spat at by a woman while on patrol and I was genuinely shocked. 'What have I done to deserve that?' I asked her, to which I got no reply, just a look of undisguised contempt.

I started the tour as deputy ops officer, helping to run the operations room in the headquarters at the Mill. Then, very sadly, one of our troop commanders, Richard Hawkins, became ill and had to withdraw and I took on his responsibilities. From then on I was leading routine patrols, and for a while, we were expecting to be engaged every time we left the Mill. But our general training helped because a Northern

Ireland-type environment had often been used as a setting. We got caught up in a couple of riots, but we didn't have a major incident, even though British soldiers were being killed or injured elsewhere in the city.

During that three-month period, we used our weapons probably on four occasions. Single 'cowboy' attacks were the norm, and you could never identify their source quickly enough to retaliate effectively, but there was never a moment on that tour when I thought, 'This is it. I'm dead.' It was my first time on active operational duty and I found I liked it. I liked the challenge and I was good in a crisis. I seemed to be able to think clearly. It didn't faze me. The great thing is you are an officer and you rise to the challenge. You cannot show your fear because you are leading and you know it would be contagious if you did. That obviously helps you to control those instincts that we all have.

I found that I could manage it – I could give orders under pressure and direct soldiers and it all clicked. Although I was never caught up in a major firefight, I had enough experience to feel confident that I could handle it, when it came.

I left Belfast in January 1976 and went on a regular-officers' gunnery course at Larkhill, which almost drove me out of the Army. This was a course designed to turn you into a gunnery instructor. Nothing could have interested me less. It was like maths at school all over again. I saw myself as an army officer – the generic officer – not a specialist gunnery expert. I didn't prosper. In fact, I skipped quite a lot of it, going up to London for parties and leaving my good friend John Thomson to do my work. I'd get back the next morning and he'd show me what I was supposed to know.

Having survived Larkhill, I returned to 79 Battery in Plymouth. After a few months, I was posted back to 7 Battery, with whom I had served in Singapore in 1971. By this time, the unit was based in Arbroath, on the Scottish North Sea coast, and was part of 45 Commando Group, the winter warfare specialists. I drove home to East Sussex and, after a weekend with my parents, drove north for twelve hours in Boris, my orange MG (it was the only one I could afford), stacked to the gunnels with kit.

Our war role was to deploy to arctic Norway as part of the NATO reinforcement of the northern flank. Encouraged by our battery commander, Major Ronnie Young, this was another work-hard, play-hard environment. Autumns were focused on mountain training in Scotland, often on the Isle of Skye. Then, from January until late March, we were deployed to Norway, where I completed the arctic warfare course. I was promoted to Captain during my first year in Arbroath and was allowed to operate independently, running the guns.

I was still pursuing Caroline and invited her up to the 1977 summer ball at Arbroath. It was here that I came up with a winning ploy. I have always been a keen horseman – although I know just one way to ride, which is flat out and undoubtedly bloody dangerous – and while at Arbroath I decided to start a saddle club. The problem was that we had no horses. I asked some friends in the Royal Artillery whether we could have a couple from Larkhill. Caroline was a good horseman, far better than I was, and I asked her if she would help me bring these two animals up to Scotland. That trip revealed her adventurous nature and helped convince me she was the woman for me.

I employed Gunner Stone to drive the Land Rover, towing the horsebox, while I followed in my sportscar. The three of us set off promptly at six in the morning and all went well until the Land Rover broke down on the motorway near Morecambe, in Lancashire, fortunately at a layby. I went off to find someone to fix the engine and when I got back, I discovered a Land Rover and an empty horsebox and no sign of either Gunner Stone or Caroline. The next thing I see is the pair of them riding bareback over the fields and down the motorway embankment. They'd gone off to a nearby village to the pub. I have to admit I was flabbergasted and gave them both a good telling off. But Caroline had made a lasting impression.

Back with 7 Battery, I had great fun on my two three-month trips to Norway. On both occasions I volunteered to be officer in command of troops on board the Royal Fleet Auxiliary (RFA) landing ship that transported our guns and vehicles. This was a three-day cruise across the North Sea and up the fjords. I love being in ships. I had my own cabin and was beautifully looked after by the Chinese stewards who ran the domestic side of RFA ships in those days. We sailed through spectacular, steep-sided fjords, flowing through craggy mountains with snow-capped peaks, and I would stand at the rail and watch Norway go by.

Our destination was the town of Narvik, where we unloaded the ship. The battery was based in Beisfjord, a little village south of the town, and learning to cross-country ski on what were known as 'Pusser's Planks' – named after the logistics officer in the Navy, who issues kit – produced hilarious scenes. The skis were pretty basic by today's standards and the soldiers were generally hopeless to start with. Going downhill, most of them did not know how to stop except by falling over or crashing into trees. Morale was very high and all the laughter and mickey-taking didn't detract from the serious business of learning to deal with the terrain.

We were soon able to ski with packs on our backs, and graduated to skiing long distances with heavy kit on. At night we would build bashas under pine trees the bottom limbs of which were under the snow, so you would effectively have a snow hole that was surprisingly warm. We practised skiing at night, and something called skiawing, when a troop would be pulled behind an over-snow vehicle. That was great fun.

I was commanding the guns and, once we had completed our basic individual training, we'd go on to collective training and take the guns out and fire them. The first year we had the 105 Pack Howitzer; then we upgraded to the new Light Gun, which had a much longer range. We moved the guns under Sea King helicopters. I was paid to have my own snowmobile – the best toy I ever had in the Army – and we would race and do jumps. Army life involves taking risks but it could also be a lot of fun – a word that we used a lot. I spent a lot of time in the company of Sergeant Major Proctor and Sergeant Dixon. Long nights spent in a tent with them and others were some of the most hilarious of my life.

On our second trip we entertained a media party and among them was Peter Hennessey, now Lord Hennessy of Nympsfield, the distinguished historian of government, who was then a leader writer on *The Times*. This was my first encounter with a journalist. I got on very well with Peter – he is a friend to this day and we still chuckle about this – and he remarked on how out-of-date much of our kit looked. I agreed with him – you could hardly not, surveying our ancient skis, guns and vehicles.

A few days later an article appeared in *The Times* saying what a vital role we were fulfilling but pointing out how poorly equipped we were. The hierarchy were not impressed and a big fatwa was issued, demanding to know who had been talking to the media without authority. I kept a very low profile for a few days until it blew over but the next year we were re-equipped. It was an early lesson about the power of the press and how you could circumvent a stubborn chain of command to get what you wanted.

When I was faced with my first posting to Germany after Arbroath, it seemed like make or break time for Caroline and me and I asked her to marry me and come with me. This meant her giving up her new career as a medical illustrator at the Royal Marsden Hospital in London. Despite that, and although we were quite young, she said yes. We were married at her family home at Micheldever in Hampshire on April Fools' Day 1978, just a couple of days after I got back from my final tour in Norway. Many of my Army friends came to the wedding, including a number of my non-commissioned pals like Sergeant Evans and Gunner Stone which made it added fun.

We had five days' honeymoon in a little hotel in Guernsey – that was all the regiment would allow me and I didn't think of asking for more. Caroline, I can confidently report, didn't have a clue that she was marrying the future CDS and nor did the future CDS know that there was any prospect of that sort of thing.

Although everyone knew I was going to Germany, I was posted to Plymouth for four months, to be the commander of half of 79 Battery.

The unit had been facing the axe but there had been a change of mind and I was sent down to try to resurrect it. The appointment was made by Lieutenant Colonel Brian Pennicott, the commanding officer of 29 Commando, who had been in Norway during that winter and must have been impressed by what he saw. This was a key moment for me, when I went from just living for the moment to starting to think that I may have a bit of career ahead of me in the Army. At the age of 26, I had sixty men under my command for four months.

Pennicott (later Major General Pennicott) treated me seriously and set an outstanding example of leadership. He stunned me by grading me as 'excellent' and making me battery commander when there were more senior candidates available. I thought, 'Bloody hell, maybe I'm better at this than I realise.'

THREE

Cold War Warrior

Brian Pennicott convinced me that I was a bit different and might have an army career ahead of me, and so I must go to Germany. 'That's where it's all happening,' he said. It was 1978 and the Cold War was still in full swing as the forces of the Western allies on one side of the Iron Curtain nervously faced those of the Eastern bloc on the other. The Army's focus *was* on Germany. It was where the principal fighting formations were based. And Brian was right – if you wanted a career, you really had to go to Germany.

So I agreed – reluctantly, because I didn't want to go. I fought against it. I wanted to join 7 Parachute Regiment Royal Horse Artillery but there were no vacancies. I had been offered a posting to the ceremonial King's Troop, which would have meant riding every day and enjoying life in St John's Wood. But at the end of the day, you do as you are told and I realised I had to knuckle down. Funnily enough, I have never sought a posting during my career. I have always ultimately done as I've been told and I've never been disappointed.

So I went to Germany with Caroline, posted as a Captain to C Battery Royal Horse Artillery, based at Gutersloh, which was a rather undistinguished place, midway between Dortmund and Hanover. The two big employers in the town were the white goods manufacturer, Miele, and the media conglomerate, Bertelsmann. To be frank, it was quite a boring place that had grown quickly after the end of the war, and we never felt any great affection for it.

People might say that it was all rather arid soldiering in Germany at that time, but actually, at the lower tactical level, I found it exciting. We were out in the field training for much of the time, and for a while I had a troop of six armoured vehicles with about thirty-five soldiers under my command.

Before I arrived, I wrote the traditional introductory letter – known in the Army as a 'bread and butter' letter – to the battery commander, Major Graham Hollands. I told him how pleased I was to be reporting for duty and how keen I was not to be given any job other than troop commander. It was quite necky of me. The point was I was trying to avoid being made BK, or battery captain, a largely administrative role in the battery head-quarters. When I arrived, Hollands informed me that I was to command the Striker troop, affiliated to 1st Royal Tank Regiment, an experienced reconnaissance regiment, but only until Christmas – a busy and enjoyable four months away – and after that I was to take over as BK from the talented but slightly chaotic Barry Winfield, whether I liked it or not. In the end, I made that job my own and came to love it.

Our role, in the event of an east-west war, was to move right up to the inner German border as quickly as we could, into what we called a 'screen position', and observe the Russians as they attacked. We were then meant to roll back into the defensive positions of the divisions behind. My job was to delay the Russian hordes for as long as I could using our Swingfire anti-tank weapons. I used to think I had about a ten-minute life expectancy should war be declared.

I quickly saw that my prejudices about Germany and heavy armoured warfare, which, as a commando, I viewed as ponderous, were quite wrong. The reality was that you had to be fleet of foot and mentally agile with excellent communications. Indeed, if I hadn't gone to Germany at that time, I doubt I would have ended up as CDS. It taught me a higher tempo of operating and how to work, not just as part of a brigade, but as part of a corps, even an alliance. This was a different type of soldiering with much greater demands on my intellect than hitherto. With this type of warfare and in this setting, you had to *think*.

We went up to the border regularly, often in plain clothes, to have a close look at where we would deploy. We could see what axes Soviet forces would be attacking us on and design our defence accordingly. (In 1990, after the Cold War was over, I visited the East German Army's bunkers in Potsdam. A big map on the wall showed many arrows pointing towards West Germany and I couldn't help noticing one in particular – a bloody great arrow pointing right at the area where I would have been if war had started.)

We used to conduct exercises in the field whereby the whole division would deploy within a certain period. Just occasionally, the whole corps – and indeed the whole NATO alliance, including Americans, Germans, French, Dutch, Danes and Belgians – would deploy. It was as impressive as it was ambitious. We would not manoeuvre in designated training areas but over open countryside and you would see tank after tank trundling through villages, and sometimes we would find ourselves staging mock fights inside villages.

We took it seriously and I became a great advocate of the military strategy that lay behind what we were doing. It was the Chinese military strategist and philosopher Sun Tsu who said that the height of military skill is to defeat your enemy without firing a shot. Ultimately, the West and NATO did just that and brought the Soviet Union to its knees. Moscow began to realise that they could no longer afford to compete and this was, in substantial part, because of the presence of the British Army of the Rhine and the other allied armies that were deployed in Germany. The Russians couldn't match us as their economy faltered. Afghanistan obviously played a big part, too, in the downfall of the Soviet empire, as did Margaret Thatcher and Ronald Reagan, but I always feel resentful on behalf of the generation who won the Cold War. Not many medals were handed out, and yet it was a highly effective military strategy, the execution of which placed continued pressure on the crumbling Soviet system.

Once or twice a year we would practise live firing. The Swingfire was a wire-guided missile that you had to steer, with a range of 4,500 metres (5,000 yards). It took real skill to hit a target, especially a moving one, so we had to train our soldiers intensively. Officers certainly didn't get much of a chance; it would have been too wasteful. I think I fired one missile in my entire three years. Eighty per cent of the missiles functioned properly but occasionally a rogue one would fly all over the place before it could self-destruct. Pylons and power lines were another problem. Did you steer under or over them? We had to practise all of these eventualities.

Today, more advanced weapons are available, such as Hellfire missiles. You simply put crosshairs on the target and the system does the rest. I must say if I had gone to war with our Swingfires, it would have been quite difficult. Although, as I said, we wouldn't have lasted long, we still believed we would have taken out a good few Russian tanks first.

At troop level, my responsibility was to decide where the weight of fire should be and allocate priority targets. These were powerful missiles – they could take out a tank with ease – and we carried fourteen of them in each vehicle. We were vital to the whole NATO battleplan in the event of a Soviet push west.

On the big exercises, I worked closely with Brigadier Brian Kenny, the brigade commander. A calm, good-looking cavalryman, I noticed that he never flapped, always had time for people and showed great courtesy. At the end of an exercise, most of the hierarchy couldn't wait to get home to their wives and their quarters. Brian never did that. He stayed out in the field and went round every unit, thanking them for what they had done. Everyone knew that he wasn't rushing off. That was an example I tried to follow if I possibly could. Kenny ended up as a full General and was NATO's Deputy Supreme Allied Commander Europe.

Life was quite different in Germany compared to our former existence in the UK. We were part of a community of well over 150,000 British soldiers and their families, plus a further RAF contingent. In England, people tended to go home at the weekends. In Germany, you stayed where you were, so there was a great 'patch life' and a lot of parties. In those days communications weren't so good, so you focused on the people and the community around you. But our life in Germany was a British microcosm and some of us got out as much as we could.

When we first arrived, Caroline and I lived in a flat over a garage in the village of Spexard on the edge of Gutersloh by the autobahn. It was hardly the most salubrious accommodation and after a few months we moved to a house in Avenwedde Bahnhof, a village about five miles from the base. We lived there for three years. We had a car, but I used to take it most days so Caroline would spend much of her time in a village where nothing much was going on. She was wonderful. She started a business doing pen and ink drawings of the local area as well as of children, dogs and horses. I was away quite a lot, sometimes for up to six weeks on exercise at the border.

The British Army in Germany was living a self-contained existence abroad. We had our own sailing clubs, our own ski centres and our own adventure training programmes. My battery had the onerous task of organising the divisional ski meeting every winter, which grew into the British Army of the Rhine's cross-country meeting. For two years in succession, I found myself running an army restaurant in the Alps, providing cheap meals for the soldiers competing. For five weeks in that first winter, we were stationed in a little place called Oberjoch in the spectacular mountains of Bavaria, living in a lovely guesthouse. My sole job was managing this tented restaurant, which was actually run by my quartermaster sergeant. I had to turn up once or twice a day to check everything was going smoothly and Caroline and I had lunches there. The rest of the time, we skied for nothing. The second year we did it all over again in the equally charming resort of Ruhpolding.

The sailing was at Kiel, four and a half hours up the autobahn from Gutersloh. I bought my first boat when I was with C Battery. I'd always sailed and had a romantic notion about boats and being out in the wind and the waves. In that first summer of 1979 we went up to Kiel – to the British Kiel Yacht Club (BKYC) – and Caroline and I went on a one-week course so that I could qualify as a 'Baltic skipper' on a four-berth yacht. We sailed for three days around Kiel and four days around the Danish islands. It was varied and challenging sailing with some lovely creeks and estuaries to explore – the perfect foil to our sometimes claustrophobic life at Gutersloh.

I got my skipper's ticket and in a rush of blood to the head decided to buy a boat. We could get it tax-free, so I went for the biggest, best-value yacht I could find – a Robert Clarke-designed thirty-footer, a Verl 900, that we named *Bonaventure*. To get her, I swapped my BMW for a clapped-out Fiesta and borrowed £10,000 from my father. We were doing it the unglamorous way and used to victual the boat with leftover army rations given to us by the soldiers. The restaurants of the Baltic seaside towns and villages were beyond my captain's salary.

I spent weeks sailing, often with Caroline but I also invited some of my soldiers on board. That proved rather useful because I chartered *Bonaventure* to the Army and got paid – not a huge amount, but it covered the cost and I enjoyed sailing with my soldiers. We cruised around the Danish islands, as far north and east as Finland, and made it to Gothenburg twice. I also sailed Army boats and skippered one in the Tall Ships Race. Although my days in Germany are long gone, I retain strong links with Kiel and am proud to be the Admiral of the BKYC.

In C Battery we were doing major Cold War exercises but the skiing and sailing were a significant part of life. It was a bit like living in Singapore again. Patch life, regimental life – it was a wonderful life if you liked it. Some people would have wanted to be in London or back in Britain, but if you were a self-contained person and collectively happy with your lot, it was a good lot. We were all good friends and you knew everyone. People jarred occasionally but we somehow got round it. You felt you were doing something that was worth doing – protecting the free world and all that stuff.

Towards the end of the tour, in the summer of 1981, the battery was deployed to Aughnacloy, a sleepy little village in Co. Tyrone, Northern Ireland. This section of the border with Co. Monaghan in the Irish Republic was fairly quiet, although, in previous years, there had been considerable IRA activity in the area. Aughnacloy was a typical border village. A farming community, it was divided almost equally between Catholics and Protestants and you could feel the underlying tension between the two sides. On the whole, we were treated by the locals with what I might call a rather curt civility.

Again I was lucky on that tour. I never got shot at. I was the ops officer but, whenever I could, I went out with the soldiers on patrol in the lanes and the fields around the village. In between patrols we lived in the heavily fortified military base on the edge of the village. The sanger, or fortified checkpoint on the border, half a mile from the centre of the village, was fired at three or four times. There was the odd attack elsewhere and we found concealed bombs – now known as IEDs (improvised explosive devices) – in the area. But, despite being there when the IRA prisoner, Bobby Sands, died following a hunger strike, which heightened tensions for a while, we had a rather uneventful tour doing important but routine constabulary work.

By then, the police had taken primacy in the fight against terrorism, so we were in a supporting role alongside them. I got on well with the local police. As the ops officer it was my job to go to all the planning meetings with them and I used to play tennis at a local school once a week with my opposite numbers.

The battery commander by this time was Major Barry Stevens. He had been awarded an MC in Northern Ireland on a previous tour. We knew we had not been scheduled to go to Ulster and the strong suspicion among us was that he had volunteered the battery. He was quite ambitious and he knew Ireland, whereas he didn't know soldiering in Germany that well. Despite this, we all enjoyed our time in Aughnacloy and I even managed some sailing with Caroline on Bonaventure during my four days 'R and R'.

As soon as we got back to Germany, Stevens was posted on promotion (he ended up a Brigadier). His nominated successor, the charismatic Billy King-Harman, was not available until Christmas, so I wondered with some trepidation who would be brought in temporarily as our boss. To my surprise, Colonel James Templer, our notably tough artillery group commander, decided I would take over from Stevens with the challenge of retraining 150 soldiers, post-Ireland, back into their war role in Germany.

I took command when we got back and found myself running the battery in Gutersloh for four months. This was a big, high-profile job. Those batteries were like the divisional commander's own personal weapons systems and, at 29, I had to take this seriously. Going from Northern Ireland-mode to war training sounds easy, but it is not. A totally different mindset is required. On a personal level, I had to impose my will in a different way now that I had command, and one or two soldiers tested me.

I remember, during one exercise, we had the whole battery out and Sergeant Bob Lodge, a great character from the East End of London, who has since apologised to me – in fact, we have laughed together about it – came on the radio to question orders I had given. I knew that if I failed that test, my authority with the whole battery was finished. And I didn't fail it. I got a grip of Sergeant Lodge and told him to report to me *now* and that I did not want to hear anything like that ever again on the battery radio net. I got the message across and, from then on, I *was* a battery commander – I had moved on to a different plane of authority. Up until then I had led through influence and by trading on the soldiers' affection for me. Now that wasn't going to be enough. I was getting older and was being given more responsibility, so I had to get on top of it. I was still relaxed with them, by which I mean relaxed but never casual, my motto again. There is a big difference.

As I rose up the ranks, I identified a line beyond which I would never go. I would have a laugh with soldiers but they were never really certain whether I was serious or not. It's quite a disarming skill and sometimes it can go wrong. They're not quite certain whether you're being serious when you call them a f***wit, which happens to be a favourite term of mine. Officers would say to me that now they had been called a f***wit by me, they had made it. 'Until you've been called a f***wit, you are nothing,' they would say; or until you have been teased by the General you aren't anybody in his mind. So being teased is good, they reasoned; being ignored is a problem.

I had a lot of friends who were soldiers but I always called them by their rank and they always called me 'Sir'. To me, and my father was an influence here, you can have great friends who are warrant officers, corporals and sergeants and I do. But they never call me by my Christian name. They always call me 'Sir'. Occasionally, if I was being guarded by a close-protection team, I would slip into nicknames, but never for anyone other than those in the team, and it was always 'Sir' back to me. I think it helps. With the very best of soldiers it doesn't necessarily matter but most of us need boundaries within which to work. If soldiers know, ultimately, that you are still 'Sir', then psychologically that means there is a point beyond which they cannot go. I despair when I hear soldiers and officers calling each other by their Christian names. Where does it stop? Come a battle situation, suddenly you might not necessarily obey someone because he's just another pal, whereas an officer has to be instantly obeyed.

During those four months I wanted to turn the battery into the toughest and best trained in the Army, and I had precious little time to do it. When we had our annual live-firing exercises on the Bergen-Hohne ranges in northern Germany – the big NATO training area – I invited Major General Martin Farndale, the divisional commander, to come along to watch. Farndale was quite a character – a gunner who knew his own mind and was seen as a very professional soldier and an innovative tactician. In retirement, he wrote a four-volume history of the Royal Artillery.

This time the series of exercises was particularly demanding, on a scale that had never been attempted before – live firing with realistic battlefield effects, including smoke, simulated incoming artillery, the need to move regularly and 'casualties'. We really put the soldiers through it. I took Farndale to watch the firing as far forward as we could go and we ended up venturing into the impact area. He loved it.

There we were, in my armoured personnel carrier, bouncing around, watching incoming fire reach its targets, when I got a message on the radio to say that all firing had been stopped because of a 'rogue' vehicle in the middle of the ranges. 'And who the hell was in it?' I could hear a voice asking. I had to tell the General that we had to go back and that I was going to be reported to my divisional commander (which was him).

'I think I'd better tell you now that we're breaking all the rules by being here,' I said. He thought it was highly amusing and I was just using my initiative.

There is no doubt that in those four months the battery became bloody good and I left on a high, having learnt that with the right leadership and the right team I could set and achieve very high standards. I learnt that people responded to being trusted, almost invariably rising to the challenge. I was helped by some outstanding soldiers, including the tall, imposing Jeff Smith, who went on to make a fortune in business, and the physically tough yet diminutive Rich Drewett. Rich's dynamic personality more than compensated for his height. In due course he was to become my Regimental Sergeant Major and later he was commissioned. Bob Lodge also became a successful businessman and Paul Sherrell, who, like Drewett, was to serve with me again, achieved senior commissioned rank and universal respect across the Royal Regiment of Artillery. Then there was Taff Kalies, a brilliant sportsman and one of the most natural leaders I have had the privilege of working with. By the time I retired, he was a Lieutenant Colonel. His great mentor in C Battery was Jimmy Michie, a quietly spoken Irishman who, in some respects, was the most gifted of a very talented group. Domestic travails held him back while, in the very generous-hearted way of the Irish, he watched his pupils slowly overtake him. There are too many more to mention them all by name but they know who they are and I will always be in their debt. The close bond we enjoyed, which is not uncommon in the Army, allowed us to weather the bad times, including, sadly, the occasional death, as well as the good. Not surprisingly, we still have a thriving old comrades association.

After C Battery I was posted to 11th Armoured Brigade at Minden, south of Hanover – my first staff appointment – but before I took up my duties I attended the Junior Division of the Staff College at Warminster in

Wiltshire. This was my first formal staff training. Initially, I had a pretty dismal term under a rather uninspiring Major and my morale suffered. We were taught basic staff duties, the rules of the staff office, how to do movement planning, how to write properly in military style and how to write orders.

My second term was led by Philip Trousdell, then a Major (later a Lieutenant General and General Officer Commanding Northern Ireland), and an effective communicator and leader whom people naturally liked. A thoughtful, empathetic man, who seemed to understand my frustrations, he pushed to one side any lingering doubts I retained about staying on in the Army. I had done the civil-service exam and thought about being a diplomat. 'You have a future as a soldier,' Trousdell confidently predicted.

In the second term we spent a lot of time doing TEWTS – Tactical Exercises Without Troops. The idea is that you and your fellow students are positioned on a hill and set up with a fighting scenario. Your enemy is coming along this valley or that valley, with a second flank to your right. The instructors tell you where your reinforcements are and how many troops you have and their capabilities. You are then given forty minutes to prepare a plan for your defence and set out how you might organise a counter-attack. We did a lot of this and you always dreaded being the one called upon to make the presentation on behalf of your colleagues.

The three-month course at Warminster completed, Caroline and I moved to Minden and I took up my job at headquarters 11th Armoured Brigade. This was one of the brigades within 1 British Corps in the British Army of the Rhine. Still a captain, I was the staff officer Grade 3 G2, with responsibility for intelligence. On major exercises, in addition to my intelligence role, I worked on operational planning and the execution of orders. It was a small headquarters. The brigade commander was Brigadier Garry Johnson who went on to be a four-star General and retired as NATO Commander in Chief of Allied Forces Northern Europe.

In order to take on this new job I had to go on a month-long course at the headquarters of the Intelligence Corps at Ashford in Kent. This turned out to be a classic case of a one-week course squeezed into four. It was while I was preparing to start the course, staying with my parents in East Sussex, that my family was struck by tragedy with the unexpected death of my older sister, Jan, at the age of 36. She was by far the brightest of the four children but had never really settled down professionally or personally and had struggled, at times, with anorexia. She had done a variety of jobs in Britain and abroad – everything from a trainee patent lawyer in Hamburg to working as a clerk in Eastbourne – and had never married.

On the night Jan died she had been out with friends to celebrate the imminent start of a new job and arrived home after Caroline and I had gone to bed. We were tired after a long drive from Germany. Jan's apprehension about the next day, and a determination to get a good night's sleep, seemed to have combined to cause her to double-dose on some sleeping pills she had been prescribed to ensure she was on good form for the new job. It was all desperately sad and her death came as a terrible shock, especially to my poor parents who discovered her the following morning. It was a harrowing experience for all of us and Caroline was terrific with my mother and father in the days that followed while I was away on my course.

Every corps commander or army commander wants to be associated with a tactical innovation. It is good for his career and for everyone serving under him; otherwise you can get stale. This was particularly so in the days of the British Army of the Rhine. A wonderful man, known to us as 'Ginge' Bagnall, was Commander of 1 Corps at this time (Sir Nigel Bagnall, later Chief of the General Staff). He was a radical military thinker, renowned for coming up with new ideas, and known as Ginge because of his generally peppery nature as well as the red hair of his youth.

Nigel Bagnall formulated a plan whereby instead of just sitting there and absorbing a Soviet advance, we would do it more cleverly. The idea was to suck them in and then hit them with a big flanking counterstroke.

We would do it at the tactical level – at brigade and divisional level – while the Americans would do something similar at the operational level in a massive counterstroke involving a number of divisions. It sounds simple but this was demanding, a lot of fun to execute, and 11th Armoured Brigade were given the pioneering task, under Garry Johnson. I'm not sure why – perhaps we just happened to be available when plans were being laid. We put a hell of a lot of effort into it.

I used to run the Brigadier's tactical party, a mobile HQ of three or four armoured vehicles, and got to know Johnson very well. A tall, cadaverous individual with greying fair hair, he didn't talk a lot – unlike some Generals. When he did speak, in his slow, deliberate way, you tended to listen and you didn't mess around. He had great warmth of character and a mischievous sense of humour. This was not immediately obvious but I saw it because I was living cheek by jowl with him during those exercises.

My job on manoeuvres, including the counterstroke training, was to make sure we got the map reading right, do the routine radio stuff and also – and most importantly – keep feeding Johnson oatmeal blocks. His quiet but penetrating voice would ring out: 'Another oatmeal block, Richards.' 'Yes Sir. Oatmeal block coming up.' And he'd be good for another half hour. We were under great pressure to get the counterstroke right and demonstrate it could be done. General Ferdinand von Senger und Etterlin, a Second World War German hero and renowned expert on tank warfare, who was commander-in-chief of NATO's Allied Forces Central Europe, came to observe what we were doing, as did Bagnall. So there was big pressure on Johnson and on me, but Johnson didn't flap at all. He was another man from whom I learnt a great deal about taking it in your stride. He had an ability to get the best out of people without making them feel under pressure. If things went wrong, he never panicked. 'Don't worry about it, just find a solution,' he would say.

With Bagnall and Senger und Etterlin watching, we had to put two tank regiments through thickly wooded countryside on a ridge at night to get them on to their start line, ready to attack at dawn the following day.

People told us we couldn't do it, but they got through. The two regiments involved, the Life Guards led by Lieutenant Colonel James Emson, and the 3rd Royal Tank Regiment under John Woodward, were just brilliant. Surprise, seizing the initiative, coming from an unexpected direction and hitting Soviet forces hard in the flank were what we were about.

At this level, I did a lot of the planning and the recce-ing to see if the manoeuvres we wanted to pull-off were feasible. It was then usually my job to control those moves. The decision when to launch an attack would be Johnson's and I would advise him, telling him whether everyone was in position or not. 'The Life Guards won't be there for another half hour, Sir,' I would tell him. 'What the f*** . . . we've only got half what we need,' he would reply. 'Right, don't worry Brigadier, we'll have to roll them straight through.' It was exciting. We didn't sleep – it was like being at war. We were constantly on the move. Imagine Rommel in the Western desert – well, we were playing that role in every respect other than it wasn't live firing and it was on the north German plain. The enemy didn't know where they were going to be attacked and we took them by surprise – it was professionally very satisfying.

On that counterstroke exercise, or a later one, an amusing episode occurred when we were defending positions along the banks of the River Leine. Central to our plan was a bridge at Alfeld, south of Hanover. As the exercise developed, the 'enemy' began to threaten the bridge and it became a race against time to get our remaining assets – men and machines – back over the river before the bridge was attacked. I had gone off to grab a couple of hours sleep while my colleague, Major Nick Mangnall, a lugubrious, urbane Green Jacket with a great sense of humour, had gone off to recce our next location.

That left Ian Talbot in charge. He was the Chief of Staff and would not normally run the detail of a battle. Ian is a good friend of mine and an impetuous character at times. When Nick and I returned to our posts, we discovered that Ian had ordered the Alfeld bridge to be blown. He had been worried that it would fall to the enemy and that our opponents would force their way across the river and then penetrate into our rear areas. But a lot of our own forces were still on the far side and the demolition could have waited another thirty minutes. Garry Johnson was not impressed. In fact, he was angry, and there was an extremely tense atmosphere in the headquarters. I remember saying to Ian, possibly winding him up a touch, 'Eh, the bridge has gone. Who authorised that? There's still a lot of kit over there.' He said something under his breath, words to the effect of 'Just get on with it, will you.'

When the exercise was finished, Nick Mangnall decided he couldn't let this pass without ribbing Ian about it, and he had some ties made, decorated with an image of a collapsed bridge. We started wearing them around the headquarters. Poor old Ian came in one morning and asked, 'What's that tie?'

'Ah, well, it's the BBA tie,' said Nick, with a straight face.

'What's the BBA tie?'

'It's the "blown bridge at Alfeld" tie,' replied Nick as we all – Ian included – laughed uproariously.

While I was at 11th Armoured Brigade I was selected to go to Staff College at Camberley. Again I did not much want to go but Malcolm Watson, the eccentric, amusing but wise Major in the headquarters responsible for our administration, who had become a great friend, explained in his unique and rather comical way that I would bloody well do as the Army told me.

In the spring of 1983, I went to see Ian Talbot, and told him I'd been selected for Camberley in the autumn. I explained that I was keen to have one last good sail on *Bonaventure* in the Baltic before I went back to the UK, and asked him if there was any chance of having more than the basic two weeks leave that was all we were allowed.

At that time 80 per cent of our troops had to be available for active duty at a moment's notice. We were regularly tested to make sure we could be out of barracks and in preliminary deployment positions in four hours. If we failed, we would be deemed incapable of fulfilling our role in NATO's war plans, a big black mark no one could afford. Talbot said he didn't think I had a chance and, in any case, it was above his pay grade and one for the Brigadier. By this time, this was another equally impressive officer, Jeremy Blacker. A large, physically imposing, clear-thinking individual, he had kind eyes and a genuine concern for people. He also had a fearsome reputation. So I went to Blacker, not rating my chances with what was quite a cheeky request.

'Sir, you know I have been selected for Staff College?' I said. Of course he knew.

'Yes, very good Richards. What's this about?' he replied.

'Well, you know I sail a lot?'

'Yes, can't understand that.'

'I have my own boat and I was wondering if I could have a third week of leave because it's my last chance and then I have to go to Camberley.'

Blacker said no. And that he was sorry.

'Oh, OK, Sir. I thought it was worth checking.'

'No,' he went on, 'don't take three weeks, take five.' He said I would never have this opportunity again.

'You're going to go places if you want to, and you're going to have to work hard, and you'll never get long leave again. Take five weeks, go and enjoy yourself and then hunker down for a long haul.'

I knew then that he had identified I had something going for me. On our subsequent voyage, Caroline and I went up to Finland and got caught in a full gale, an experience she in particular was determined never to repeat.

I eventually turned up at Staff College in January 1984 and I loved it. This was an opportunity to learn about tactics, history and staff duties. I worked hard and I came out of it as one of the top seven graded officers. It was a memorable year for another reason in that my sister Sara met and fell for one of my greatest Army friends and fellow Gunner, Nigel Cooke. Nigel was on the same course as me and had been the Royal Artillery rugby team's scrum half when I was their hooker. They were married the following year. During my time there, I was promoted to Major and afterwards I was posted to command a battery. The normal route was a staff job after Camberley but I had already done that before I went there.

By coincidence, it was back to Gutersloh to command what was really an undistinguished but old battery – 3 Battery RA.

I took over from Nigel Harding Newman, whom the soldiers – always alert to a pun on words – good-naturedly nicknamed 'Hardly Human'. This was a battery that was down on its luck and the soldiers were nothing like the C Battery soldiers or the commandos. They were pretty average guys but their hearts were in the right place and they wanted to do well. Initially, I was disappointed because I had done well at Staff College and was one of few people at Camberley who had been a staff officer in Germany. So I thought maybe I had taken a wrong turn. In fact, it was the best thing that could have happened to me because it brought me down a peg or two. I rationalised it very quickly and, skilfully guided with much good humour by my commanding officer Lieutenant Mark Douglas-Withers, I got stuck in.

I could see that turning 3 Battery round to become the best in the regiment would be a great challenge, but by the time I had finished, I was told 3 Battery was the best in the *division* by some margin. I ended up being recommended for an outstanding grade in my confidential report. That was important because it is your performance in command that matters most from a future career perspective. Without a really good report as a battery commander I had little chance of commanding a regiment in due course and I was beginning to think I would enjoy that challenge, if it ever came my way.

One of the ways I instilled pride in that group of men was by reminding them of their history. The battery had been founded in 1716 and had fought all over the world but there was no board in the battery offices recounting that history, as you would always find with other units. I felt it was important to engender a sense of their heritage in my soldiers and the battery Sergeant Major, Ian Wright, felt the same way. Between us we spent weeks researching the history and compiling a list of battery commanders. Before the Army, Wright had been a coffin-maker, so he had rudimentary carpentry skills and he knocked up a couple of boards – they looked a little bit like coffin lids – and Caroline and I used Letraset to list all the deployments and the names. And then we varnished them. We put them up in the offices and the soldiers came to have a look and you could see them thinking, 'Wow, so we go back to 1716.' I said, 'You've got a bloody good lineage and should be very proud of yourselves.'

I had two years commanding that battery, two years in which we did a lot of exercises and I had a lot of fun. Caroline and I were set a marvellous example by Mark Douglas-Withers and his very supportive wife Josie, and we were fortunate to be in a brigade commanded by Brigadier Roger Wheeler. Roger set very high standards and ensured we met them. It surprised no one when he subsequently became the Chief of the General Staff. As with C Battery, I learnt again that most people rise to the challenge when given clear direction, when trusted and when they feel that they and their families matter to their boss and the boss's missus. The latter is most important to the maintenance of morale in such an environment, something that, sadly, is increasingly lost on the politicians and the bean counters who refuse to recognise it. It was with particular pleasure that I handed over to my new brother-in-law Nigel Cooke, confident in the knowledge that he and Sara would look after everyone in the way Caroline and I had.

FOUR

Berlin

In the autumn of 1986 I took over as Brigade Major of the Berlin Infantry Brigade. At that time, the city was still deep in the Cold War. Although the dramatic events of 1989, the 'year of revolution' when the Berlin Wall came tumbling down, were only three years away, no one could see them coming and the old certainties still ruled our lives. The British, French, Americans and Russians had carved the place up at the end of the Second World War. But the reality of the Iron Curtain, which cut the city in half and surrounded its western portion where we lived, was still the dominant theme in everyday life and in our military planning.

Berlin was at the front line of the Cold War, which made it a fascinating place to live. It was a hotbed of intrigue and rumour, the espionage capital of the world where spy scandals played out on the most atmospheric of stages. The iconic Checkpoint Charlie at the corner of Friedrichstrasse and Zimmerstrasse, and the Glienicke Bridge, connected the western part of the city to Potsdam in the east. Berlin was a fun place and a vibrant city where we could enjoy high culture in both the east and west sectors, especially opera and classical concerts, and the outdoor life in the forests and along the lakesides. Indeed, we were fortunate to live right on the edge of the beautiful Grunewald forest, an amenity we made the best of.

Just seven years before I was born, Berlin had been the final setting for the collapse of Nazi Germany and one relic of those days was still a prominent feature when I arrived. Rudolf Hess, Hitler's deputy and the man who had tried and failed to sue for peace with the Allies when he flew secretly to Scotland in 1941, was still a lone inmate in Spandau prison. He was ailing and in his nineties and, little did I know, had less than a year to live when I took up my post, which included responsibility for the external security of the prison.

Looking back from the second decade of the twenty-first century, with the West having to deal with the unpredictable and multiple threats posed by Islamic extremists, the Cold War seems attractively simple and stable. Yet in those days we lived under the shadow of the threat of MAD, or Mutual Assured Destruction by means of nuclear weapons, and Berlin was the cockpit of that battle of nerves with Moscow. The French, Americans and British were there for a purpose – to defend the city and to try to stall a Soviet ground attack on the West.

The Western Allies had three brigades in the city – Britain had about 3,500 troops, the French slightly fewer and the United States, around 5,000. We were loosely coordinated and had a common defence plan. This was wrapped around defending the British sector, which sat in the middle of West Berlin, with the French to the north and the Americans to the south, and was where most of the institutions of city government were based.

Our plan assumed the enemy would come in from the north, the west and the south. (For some reason, we regarded it as a remote possibility that they might come at us from the east, the shortest and most direct route. Perhaps that was just too horrible to contemplate.) The plan was based on modelling of the Soviet attack on Berlin in 1945 and acknowledged that we were effectively surrounded. We were living in a salient in the middle of their armed forces, which left us with a very difficult hand in the event of war.

During my time in Berlin, we put a lot of effort into looking at how we could interdict the Soviet lines of communication, and the idea of attacking outside the city to disrupt the westerly progress of Warsaw Pact forces. We hoped we would be able to hold out for three to five days and that, in that time, something would happen; the war would stop or we would be captured. We knew where our final redoubt was. These were massive buildings in the centre of the western sector that would be difficult to capture, as had been demonstrated in the final weeks of the Second World War.

We had emergency plans for evacuating our families in a crisis. They would leave by air or in buses if the corridor from East Berlin through East Germany to West Germany was still open. But there was always a risk we wouldn't get them out. Obviously, this was a big issue. If our families were stuck with us in Berlin, the question was would our soldiers fight hard, as we were being paid to do, or would we be thinking about looking after our loved ones? I like to think we would have fought and fought hard. Would we have been told to surrender by those above us? I don't think so. The whole Cold War effort in the West was predicated on giving an impression to the Russians that we meant business and that if they did attack us, it would be more painful and much more costly than they might think. Our troops in Berlin played a critical role in getting that message across.

The theatricality and elaborate routine of the Cold War confronted you every time you travelled the corridor from West Germany to West Berlin, as I did for the first time in October 1986. First, you would arrive at Helmstedt in West Germany on the inner German border and report to the British corridor control room. You needed a pass that you would have already obtained from the orderly room in your regiment. You would go in, present your pass and it would be stamped, so you were authorised to travel up the corridor.

Then you would arrive at the Russian checkpoint, a drab, single-storey hut, surrounded by watchtowers and wire, and with a solitary soldier standing watch in front of his guardpost. You would get out of the car, go to the guard, show him your papers and then head into the waiting room in the hut. This was like a railway station ticket office except that you would never see the officials when you presented your papers because they always worked with the blinds drawn down over their windows. They could see you, though. This probably made it easier for them needlessly to delay stamping your papers – their stock in trade.

Then you had to wait. Depending on what mood the Russians were in, you could wait thirty minutes or more. This was just to annoy you because all they had to do was stamp the papers. If relations were bad between Russia and Britain at the time, they'd make you wait longer. Of course, there would be treatises on Lenin and communism for you to read, to pass the time until your papers were returned. Once you had them, you'd go back outside, show them to the guard, and get in the car.

You would then have two hours to transit the 100-mile corridor. You had to go at a steady pace – you couldn't get there too early or too late. If you hadn't arrived at the Allied and Russian checkpoints on the edge of West Berlin after two hours and fifteen minutes, the alarm went up. Under protocols that had evolved over the years, there was a bizarre situation whereby the East German police and military, who patrolled the corridor, were not allowed to stop you or interrogate you. Only the Russians, who had a right to regulate the movement of allied troops up to their respective sectors in West Berlin, could do that. This used to annoy the East Germans.

The great thing was that, as you got bolder and became a bit of an old hand, you could barter with these people. What we all wanted in those days were furry Russian winter hats or the little red and gold hammer and sickle badges that soldiers wore on their caps. There were two currencies you could use to pay; cash in the form of Deutschmarks or pornography. I never used the latter but my soldiers told me that was what the Russians really wanted. I got a couple of badges – we all did. Normally, the one to ply with cash was the sentry. You'd give him your papers and underneath you'd have your Deutschmarks. When you came back out of the hut he would have a hat or badge. So there was a glimmer of humanity beneath all the formality, the studied contempt and the process.

When I first arrived in Berlin, I lived in the mess at the British headquarters at the old Olympic stadium, while we waited for our quarters to be vacated. Caroline stayed in Gutersloh with our two children; Pippa had just been born at that stage and Joanna was two.

While I was busy getting to know the ropes, it was left to Caroline single-handedly to pack up in Gutersloh and make the six-hour journey to Berlin with the girls. After a brief stay in temporary quarters, we finally moved into our new home – a detached modern house on the edge of the Grunewald in a cul-de-sac occupied entirely by British officers. We got in just after Christmas.

About two days after we moved in, a telephone engineer came unannounced to the house to 'put right a problem on your line'. Caroline let him in after checking he had a pass and thought little more of it. From then on, every time we used the phone we would hear a mechanical click. On one occasion we heard singing. Subsequently, after the Wall fell, I was informed that it had become clear that the phones of all the key officers – including mine – had been monitored by the East Germans throughout our time in Berlin. We used to talk about being under surveillance. It was definitely on our minds and we were conscious of spying in general. To amuse ourselves we used to tap the furniture, or surrounding accessories, in meetings – a lamp for example. 'Are you listening, Fritz?' we would say; or, 'Are you ready, Vlad? The meeting is about to start.'

For most of my time in Berlin, my boss was a fiery Welsh Guardsman known to have the most explosive temper in the British Army. Brigadier Richard Powell was a well-turned-out and highly capable officer with a narrow face, a large nose and piercing eyes, who could suddenly detonate in an explosive outburst of fury. He was one of those people who was outstanding for 80 per cent of the time, but 20 per cent of what he did could be quixotic at best. I tended to focus on the 80 per cent. He was my brigade commander and I was his Chief of Staff, so I had a duty to remain loyal to him. I think I was the only officer in the whole of the Berlin Brigade with whom he never lost his temper. He would be grumpy but he never actually lost it with me. As strong a personality as he was, I think that was because subconsciously even he needed one person to work with whom he had not pissed off. But you could get in a car with Powell and travel for two hours and he'd literally say nothing. You'd say, 'Good morning, Sir,' and he'd say nothing. You'd sit there in silence, twiddling your thumbs.

One of the highlights of our year was the Queen's Official Birthday parade, the second biggest of its kind in the British armed forces. This was staged on the Maifeld, a vast green expanse next to the old Olympic stadium where May Day parades were held in Hitler's time.

Each year we had this extravagant parade and there was a lot of pressure to get it right because a few years earlier a brigade commander had got the orders wrong and the three main battalions each did something different at a key word of command. One stood fast (Guards), another marched forward with their weapons at the trail (Gloucesters), while the Parachute Regiment did what they were meant to do and shouldered arms before stepping off. 'Remember the Berlin f***-up,' was the order of the day. Richard Powell, Deputy Chief of Staff Bill Bailey and I rode horses in the parade, animals loaned by the mounted branch of the Berlin police. We used to undergo intensive coaching for three months beforehand, mainly in an indoor school but sometimes cantering and galloping through the Grunewald and along the side of the Havel river. Not a bad way to spend a few hours of the working day.

Now Powell was a Guardsman so he knew about drill and he very much took personal charge of the parade. On one occasion, we were in the middle of a rehearsal, not long before the big day. The band was playing and the Brigadier was looking increasingly unimpressed. Standing in front of them, he suddenly bellowed at the top of his voice, 'Stop!' Then he tore into them in front of hundreds of their fellow soldiers. 'If you don't start putting some wind into your instruments, I'm sending you back to the zone,' he thundered in a reference to West Germany. By the time he had finished the band was shaking to a man. This had never happened before. Officers, especially a brigade commander, just didn't do that – stop a whole parade and give people a public bollocking.

On another occasion, we had just got back to headquarters after a rehearsal and the Regimental Sergeant Major started to say something along the lines of 'if I may, Brigadier, I think we need to improve this or that . . .' at which point, Powell completely flipped. 'IN-SUB-ORD-IN-ATION!' he roared as we stopped in our tracks. Then there was another diatribe, which ended with a flourish. 'If I hear any more comments like that Regimental Sergeant Major, you'll be in the bloody clink,' he roared. The Regimental Sergeant Major, who was a big man, was quaking in his boots as Powell strode off.

The brigade consisted of a number of famous regiments, including the 1st Battalion the Black Watch, commanded by Alistair Irwin (later Adjutant General and one of the Army's foremost thinkers). Powell and I were invited to a regimental guest night and after the meal the dining room was cleared to make room for Scottish country dancing. A good-looking young officer approached Powell to ask, as was the regimental custom, if he would like to dance. 'Preposterous,' he roared. 'I have never danced with a man before and I'm not starting now. Richards, we're off.' And off we went.

Powell went on to become Director Army Training at the Ministry of Defence and then retired as a Brigadier. He was actually a very decent man and a highly cultured individual. I grew to like him a lot but you had to see through his fiery and brittle facade to get to what was underneath.

As Chief of Staff of the Berlin Brigade, the orchestration of all tactical military activity came under me and that included the defence of the city, or our part of it, coordinated with the Americans and the French. It also included routine security in close cooperation with the Berlin police. One of my responsibilities in that regard was for Spandau Prison, because it was within the British sector. My job was to look after its external security; anything outside the prison perimeter was my business and that included a check on Rudolf Hess whenever he came out of the prison.

That event occurred for one reason only – when he was ill, or pretending to be ill – and he'd be taken to the British Military Hospital, just over a mile from Spandau. Quite often these visits to the hospital coincided with the Russian month in charge at the prison – the four allied powers rotated control of Spandau – when the Russian governor would take Hess's television away. The Russians hated Hess and opposed any suggestion that the then 92-year-old should be released on humanitarian grounds, an idea gaining currency in the West. Deprived of his television, Hitler's former deputy would request a hospital visit, where he knew one was on hand.

As soon as a 'Hess leaving prison' operation was ordered, I took responsibility for his security and retained it for as long as he remained outside the prison. This effectively meant sealing off the hospital, where he had his own floor. While he was there, I had armed soldiers concealed in the hospital grounds in a standard security matrix. It was a big routine.

During my time in Berlin, Hess made this journey three times, twice alive and once dead. Was he actually Hess or the world's most famous doppelganger, as the conspiracy theorists would have us believe? All I can say is I saw him and I had no doubt it was him. I would get the code word and a car would come to pick me up within two minutes. It was well rehearsed. I had to beat the ambulance to the hospital in order to be there when Hess arrived. There was no doubt we all wanted to impress him with our own version of Teutonic efficiency. The soldiers driving him always left a time lag to give me a chance.

On his arrival, one of my tasks was a tick-job on a form to confirm his identity. I had to be sure that the grey, frail and shrunken figure in front of me was Hess. This never caused me undue trouble. First of all, I trusted the people who brought him from the prison – they were British military guards. Then I would have a good look at him. I can tell you, unless there was a perfect double, it *was* him. I had looked at plenty of photographs, so I knew what I was supposed to be seeing.

Still, the first time I saw him was quite a moment. You were confronted with this old man who, in his pomp, had been at the heart of Hitler's tyranny, a living reminder of how recent the Nazi era had been. I remember thinking, 'F****** hell, it *is* Hess,' and being struck by that cadaverous look. He was old but I wouldn't say I viewed him as pathetic. There was definitely something about him, even then. I went back home and said to Caroline, 'Bloody hell, I've just seen Rudolf Hess – it was

Hess.' I am a keen historian so I knew everything he had done – his role in the Nazi party, his relationship with Hitler, his bid for peace – and there he was. It was a pinch-yourself job. It did make the war feel very real, the Second World War come to life. Here was the guy who had fled to Britain to try to sue for peace and there I was saying, 'Guten abend, Herr Hess.'

The British Military Hospital was run by a rather overweight British Colonel. After the first time I signed Hess in, he and I agreed that the way Spandau's only inmate was being manhandled out of the ambulance and on to a trolley was none too clever. The Colonel decided he would design a new system and immediately set about it. The key to it was a pair of rails that would extend out of the back of the ambulance and rest on feet on the ground. The stretcher with Hess on would then slide gently down ready to be picked up by four soldiers, who would transfer him to a trolley.

When the second hospital visit on my watch occurred, the Colonel was very proudly ready to demonstrate his new system, both to us and to our prisoner. The trouble was, there had been no time to practise it. As the rails came out and they put the little legs down, I was watching and thinking, 'Is this going to work?' All went well to start with. The rails came down and down came the ever-silent Hess on his stretcher. The four soldiers stepped forward to lift him on to the trolley but then disaster struck. Try as they might, they could not lift the stretcher clear of the rails at one corner. It was stuck fast.

Watching this with increasing embarrassment and anger, the Colonel stepped in and said to the hapless soldier at the offending corner, 'I'll do it, you obviously don't know what you're doing.' The Colonel was a big man and he wrenched at it with all his strength. As the stretcher broke free, Hess jerked upwards and nearly fell off on to the pavement. The man who used to introduce Hitler at the Nuremberg rallies and who held the second highest rank in the SS looked at me, because I was the only other person watching, as if to say, 'What a farce.' We both sort of shrugged and, in that instant, it was as if he was saying, 'How the hell did you lot win the Second World War?' A smile came over my face. I couldn't resist. I think I detected the glimmer of a smile in his eyes.

Everything about Hess was controversial, including his death. From my own perspective, I had no reason to doubt the official account and still don't doubt it, despite the protestations from Hess's son Wolf and others that he might have been murdered. What happened, as I was told it, was that Hess had asked for a summerhouse to be built in the garden at Spandau because he liked to sit out when he could. The four powers agreed to his request and a white shipping container was moved into the garden of the prison with one of its long walls cut away and turned into a big glass window. At the time of his death, the structure was still being prepared and German electricians had been inside fitting sockets and the wiring to go in them, which they had left either rolled up or hanging from the wall. At this point, Hess requested a walk in the garden and the electricians were cleared from the area.

Hess went out into the garden, saw the summerhouse and, out of natural curiosity, went across to have a look at it. When he got inside he saw the flex, tied it round his neck and managed to strangle himself with it. He didn't hang himself. Having tied the flex round his neck and then to a window handle, he sat down hard, pulling against the weight of his body, and managed to kill himself. It was strangulation rather than breaking his neck. The naysayers doubt that, at the age of 93, he had the strength to achieve this. I don't see why he could not have done it. After all, he was strong enough to walk around the garden on his own and, at that age and in that frail state, it was probably quite easy for him to kill himself. In any case, no one I knew at the prison, including the governors, had any doubt that it was suicide.

This all happened during the Americans' turn to run the outside security of the prison for a month. But none of their guards saw what happened from their watchtowers on the prison wall because of another bizarre Cold War rule that the Russians had insisted upon. This forbade guards from looking inwards at Hess. They were there to secure the prison, not the prisoner. Nevertheless, the Americans were sensitive about the fact that this had happened on their watch. Whether they were responsible or not, it was quite clear that standards within the prison had become routine and slightly lax. You could understand why. This was a massive prison with six hundred cells, almost all of it deserted. Hess, a nonagenarian, was the only inmate.

The internal security of the prison was the responsibility of a small number of full-time warders – prison guards drawn from several nationalities. The four governors – American, French, British and Russian – turned up occasionally as they rotated shifts, but four deputy governors actually lived there. In the end, it was one of the American warders who raised the alarm.

I got the code word to say he was coming out of the prison, and a bit more information than usual. 'We think he might be dead. He is certainly very ill,' I was told.

So, once again, Hess travelled to the British Military Hospital and I was there, but this time it was not such a happy atmosphere. I looked at him – I had to check it *was* him – 'Check Hess; Hess dead,' I said to myself. I could see he was dead. More importantly, the doctor said he was dead. Anyway, he was taken in, they did a post mortem and he was declared dead. It was another big moment. Our routine was based on the fact that Hess was there and had been for years. It was part of our lives and now suddenly he was gone and the media were all over it in a frenzy.

The question then was what to do with Spandau prison? The four powers most certainly did not want it to become a shrine to Nazism, a view shared by the German Federal Government in Bonn. As it was located inside the British sector of the city, it was decided that we would now have sole responsibility for it and it was our job to erase it from the face of the earth.

The governors went to the British sector commander, Major General Patrick Brooking, and he called in Richard Powell. 'Brigadier, we've got responsibility for Spandau and I'm delegating this to you,' he said. 'We've got to raze the prison to the ground with not one brick left – we've got to get rid of all these bricks.' Powell then called me in and said, 'Right,

Richards, I am delegating this to you.' Of course, being a lowly Major, I couldn't delegate it to anybody.

I will never forget going to the prison after Hess died. I went there to meet the governors, who, along with the warders, all looked a bit shell-shocked. They took me round, and I saw where Hess lived – it was a typical Victorian-era prison landing with cells off it, all of which were empty and hadn't been occupied for years. Aside from Hess, the last prisoners to be incarcerated at Spandau – Albert Speer, Hitler's chief architect, and Baldur von Schirach, the former head of the Hitler Youth – had been released in 1966.

I remember the high prison windows. Hess had two cells. At some point a wall had been knocked through so he had a bigger space, but he was still living in a cell and was still locked up every night. He had a small library and the TV. It was basic – a bed, a chair. I don't think he had a lavatory from what I remember. The warders showing me round were quite embarrassed, especially the American, who was still touchy about Hess's death. After the tour, I went to the officer's mess and they gave me lunch. We talked about how it had happened and the American didn't want to discuss it.

The others, especially the Russian, were needling him about how Hess had died 'on your watch'. 'How did that happen?' he demanded. Answering his own question, the Russian declared that it was as a result of lax security and lack of vigilance by his erstwhile ally. He was giving it the full works through an interpreter. The British governor, Tony Le Tissier, who went on to write prolifically about the war, and his French counterpart were really rather relishing it.

After lunch, the prison was signed over to me and I was given the keys. I was told I had to get it demolished and every brick had to be buried. It was not easy to find a site in Berlin to bury a vast redbrick prison complete with its own chapel, but in short order we found one in the southwest of the city at the RAF base at Gatow. I gave the task of demolishing Spandau to my Royal Engineer officer, Major Andy Harris, and he did a good job. It took about six weeks. Lorry after lorry transported the bricks and rubble to a huge hole in the ground. Afterwards, the site of the prison was redeveloped as a car park and a new NAAFI shopping centre, the Britannia Centre Spandau, nicknamed Hessco's.

People did turn up at the prison in the weeks after Hess died, trying to get hold of bricks, and some of our own soldiers attempted to squirrel some away, but it wasn't a big problem. Actually, it was an impressive prison, a classic, German nineteenth-century building, and I think it was a bit of shame it went. The chapel was lovely, even if it was full of pigeons and there were droppings everywhere. Death row was still there, and the place where they hanged inmates – I'm not sure there wasn't still a guillotine there. You could still see the cells where the condemned would have spent their last days. They had double-barred doors and were very small. They were really cruel.

There were, of course, lighter moments during this time in Berlin. In 1987, big celebrations were held to mark the 750th anniversary of the founding of the city. The British contribution was to send the Royal Ballet over for two performances at the Deutsche Oper. At that time, I had two captains working for me, one of whom, Roddy de Norman, was a tall, angular and rather languid cavalryman. Now Roddy was very interested in history and in his intelligence work but I think found the routine of brigade life rather wearisome. I liked him and he had his heart in the right place, but this sometimes meant that he tried to get through his in-tray rather too quickly and I asked him to check things through with me before taking any decisions. One day, during my first six months in Berlin, Roddy came into my office and said, 'Right, Sir,' – he was actually quite well-spoken – 'I've got this request from the Royal Opera in London. They want us to provide extras for their performances here. I'll tell them to f*** off, shall I?'

'Roddy,' I replied, 'you will not tell them to f*** off and furthermore this is a great idea. We'll open it up to the garrison. It's the sort of thing we need to do and I'm going to be one of the extras myself.'

'Oh, right, Sir,' said Roddy, somewhat taken aback.

I duly opened up this unusual and remarkable opportunity to the garrison and when audition day arrived, thirty-six of us lined up. They wanted extras, not ballet dancers, fortunately, and they decided it would be easier to recruit a load of soldiers than try to work with local Germans and deal with the language barrier. We were to appear in the background during the closing scenes of Stravinsky's Firebird Suite at two performances on the Saturday and Sunday night. The first of these, incidentally, was in the presence of the Prince and Princess of Wales whom Caroline and I met at a reception earlier that day.

At the audition the inevitable jokes surfaced about guardsmen and sappers performing the pas de deux. We had to walk up and down and someone looked at us and gave us a tick or a cross. I didn't pull rank – I would have been quite happy to be a peasant – but I was selected to be a boyer, a Russian nobleman. I wore a big tall hat and a long red tunic. At the first rehearsal that afternoon, I remember the director saying that, at the end of the ballet, when the dancers go forward to take their bow, we were not to take part in this. I thought, 'I'm not happy about this at all – I'm *performing* here!' But I kept that to myself. So off we went to get our costumes.

I was keen on opera – we used to cross into the east to attend the Berlin State Opera – but didn't know much about ballet, and there I was, at the Deutsche Oper, standing in the wings watching some of the finest ballet dancers in the world at close quarters, and my opinion was transformed. As a professional soldier, I could appreciate that this was a highly disciplined organisation. The dancers were hard working, committed and, physically, tremendously fit. It was the best type of tactical military operation you could think of and I saw it in that way. I loved it. I actually thought about leaving the Army and becoming an impresario there and then. I was impressed by the men and I loved the girls. They were, of course, petite and generally very pretty.

When my moment came on the boards, all I had to do was go on from one wing at the back, turn left, turn right, stop, turn in and stand there. That was my role. And not long after that the ballet finished. As I say, we'd been told to stand still and stay like that as the applause rolled in and the curtain came down. I thought 'bugger that' and said to one or two of my friends, 'We'll take a bow, too.' So, contrary to orders, when the company started doing their bows I walked forward at the same time and bowed. I was given a bollocking by one of the director's staff afterwards but I did it on the next night, too.

I'm not sure what would have happened if the Russians had invaded on one of those two nights. I would have left the theatre very quickly and we would have gone into our drills. I'm not sure if I would have had a chance to change back into my uniform, so I might have taken on the Soviet Army dressed as a nineteenth-century Russian nobleman, which would have been a nice twist.

About a year later, Roddy came in with an even more exotic request.

'I've been asked whether we can provide bodyguards for Joan Collins,' he said in his matter of fact way. 'I'll tell them to f*** off, shall I?'

'No Roddy, you tried to do that last year and we all had fun with the ballet,' I said. 'Tell me more.'

Well, it turned out that Joan Collins, who was then at the height of her fame, had been invited to present the Best Actor award at the Berlin Film Festival but she was worried about attending without bodyguards. On a previous visit to Europe she had been jostled and did not want that to happen again.

The army connection was through Major Harris, who had done so well disposing of Spandau Prison. His wife Niki knew an American woman who was involved in the festival. Strangely, there was not a single company in Berlin that offered bodyguarding at the time and she had asked whether Her Majesty's Armed Forces could help. Once again, I stopped Roddy in his tracks.

'We'll do it and, what's more, I'll be one of them,' I said.

At lunch with the organisers, I told them, 'We'll do this, but we'll have to keep it under the radar. It might not go down very well, having army officers acting as bodyguards to film stars.'

Of course, it quickly got out. Major General Patrick Brooking, the sector commander in Berlin, who was the big white chief and a very nice but quite strict man, somehow heard about it. Fortunately, Brooking had a Major working for him, Chris Guthkelch, who was my sidekick. Chris rang me slightly mischievously.

'You're for it this time, Richards,' he said. 'They've found out about your bodyguarding skit.' He said he thought the General was going to come down and talk to the Brigadier about it in half an hour. I was glad of the tip.

I thought, 'Oh shit. I should have told the boss about this,' and went to see Powell, treading rather lightly it has to be said.

'Brigadier, you remember at the last O Group [orders meeting] we discussed the problem with your welfare fund and the lack of donations?' Powell had a fund that dispersed money to help units look after their families and so on.

'Yes,' he said.

'Well, I've come up with a rather unusual way of getting some money for your fund. We're going to be paid about 5,000 Deutschmarks [about £1,600] each for bodyguarding.' None of us were in it for the money but I took an instant decision to volunteer our fee. With six of us on the roster, he was going to get the equivalent of £10,000.

'Bodyguarding?' Powell replied with more than a hint of a raised eyebrow. 'We don't *do* bodyguarding. Bodyguarding who, exactly?'

I told him it was Joan Collins.

'Well,' he said, 'this *is* unorthodox, David, but I suppose we could manage that.'

With a 'Thank you Brigadier, it is after all for charity,' I left while the going was good.

When I got back to my office, which had a glass wall, I could see a figure striding purposefully towards our part of the building. It was Brooking and he was obviously intent on talking to Powell. After he went in, I heard slightly raised voices. Five minutes later he came out and popped his head through my door on his way past.

'I'll get you yet, Richards,' he said with a good-humoured twinkle. Then my phone rang. It was Powell.

'Ummm, yes . . . sailing close to the wind, David, but it's a very good cause. You'd better keep a low profile; we don't want this in the newspapers.'

On the day of her arrival, we turned up in civvies at Tegel airport to meet the one and only Joan Collins. We didn't have a clue about what we were supposed to do. We didn't have weapons, obviously. We didn't even have proper communications. We had, though, found some rather antiquated walkie-talkies in the field stores. We each had one but they didn't work properly and we hadn't rehearsed.

We got to the foot of the steps leading up to the plane, and down came Joan looking regal and being met by her flunkies. She looked at us with a slightly disbelieving air.

'HHHhhhello, Joan. We're the bodyguards,' we said.

Behind us someone curtly corrected us. 'Miss Collins to you.'

There was a big, smart car waiting for her and we jumped into a Ford Transit. We drove off to the city following her, trying to keep up, as she made her way to the smartest hotel in Berlin. When she got there, she still hadn't really logged that we were there, so we trundled up, Keystone Cops style, trying to get in front of her, trying to do what bodyguards do.

'Right, form a phalanx round her,' I said. So we formed a phalanx and tried to protect her from about 300 people swarming all over her – fans, cameramen, photographers and journalists. We managed to get her into the hotel lobby and then up to her room but it was an amateurish job. People had certainly got between her and us. She was angry.

'Who got these bodyguards?' she demanded.

'Er, me, Miss Collins,' said Major Harris.

'Well you're bloody useless. I got hassled there. You'd better improve or I'm off.'

She was tired and like Alexis Carrington, her character in the television soap *Dynasty*, she was ordering new pillows, different tea, different lamps and the flunkies were coming in and out. Then she went for a rest.

That gave us a chance to get our act together before the press conference in the afternoon. We were much better there and enjoying ourselves by then, standing behind her, pretending we had weapons in our jackets.

Then we took her round Berlin and this time I was in her car and I began to break the ice with her. We showed her Checkpoint Charlie and some of the other sights and I took over as her guide. By the time we arrived at the film festival drinks reception that evening, she was calling me 'David'. But I wanted to preserve a certain formality and stuck to 'Miss Collins'.

At the theatre for the awards ceremony, she joined other stars including Gina Lollobrigida, Richard Attenborough and Anthony Hopkins. She asked me to warn her when she had twenty minutes to go until she was on and, in the meantime, I rewrote her script, because, as I pointed out to her, it was rubbish.

'You can't say that,' I told her.

'What shall I say then?'

I got to work, putting a bit more oomph into it, and she was very grateful. When she came back from getting herself ready, I realized for the first time really how strikingly good looking she was. I took her down to the stage, through the backstage area where all the cables were, and she went on and did her thing.

'That was really good. Fantastic, Miss Collins,' I offered.

I took her back up and we had a drink together. I really got to know her a bit. I asked her what it was like, living her sort of life. She said she found it rather artificial; her body and her face were her future and her income and people were always after her for money.

Afterwards we went to the reception ball. All the actors sat at adjoining tables while lowlife like me sat nearby keeping an eye on them. I took my bodyguarding duties seriously though, to the point of asking Joan if I could have a dance with her, to which she graciously agreed. Then it was time to go back because she was flying the next morning.

'I'm very sorry,' I said, 'I'm not going to be here in the morning, and I really must go back to my wife now.'

'Why aren't you going to be here in the morning?' she asked and I told her I was on duty. At that, she rang a bell and in came the secretary. 'Get a photo for David,' she instructed. I still have that photograph with the legend: 'David, thank you for all your assistance. Joan Collins.' It's in the downstairs loo.

The next morning Andy Harris turned up with four others when it was time to take her to the airport.

'But we're not all here,' she said.

'Yes, we're all here,' replied Harris.

'But where's your sergeant?' she asked. From then on I was known as Sergeant Richards throughout the brigade, or at least to those in the know. We raised £10,000 for the welfare fund, had a fun twenty-four hours and learnt a lot about showbiz life along the way.

In the autumn of my second year in Berlin, Caroline and I received, out of the blue, an invitation to join Sir Brian Kenny, then Commander in Chief of the British Army of the Rhine, on a visit to Potsdam, just over the Glienicke Bridge. Among other hats that he wore, Sir Brian commanded an organisation known as BRIXMIS – the British Commander in Chief's Mission to the Group of Soviet Forces Germany – which mirrored the Russian organisation, SOXMIS – the Soviet Group of Forces to British Forces.

This role gave Sir Brian the right to visit the East whenever he liked, including Potsdam, which was out of bounds to regular soldiers. We were allowed into East Berlin only through Checkpoint Charlie. The soldiers of BRIXMIS were basically uniformed spies. They could drive anywhere in East Germany to observe. There were certain constraints – for example, they were not allowed on trains – but they could go and monitor new equipment as it came into East Germany from the Soviet Union and elsewhere. The BRIXMIS soldiers spent their whole lives in cars being followed. It was a game they played with the East Germans and many went on to become full-time intelligence specialists.

I was puzzled about being asked on this trip. I remember saying to

Caroline that this was way above my pay grade. In the event, we had a thoroughly enjoyable day, visiting the rococo splendours of Sanssouci, Frederick the Great's summer palace, and also the Cecilienhof Palace. This was the setting for the Potsdam Conference, where President Truman, Joseph Stalin and Winston Churchill – and his successor, Clement Attlee – met in the summer of 1945 to decide the future of Germany and post-war Europe.

I hadn't spoken to Sir Brian since I was a captain back in Gutersloh, so it was good to catch up with him. What I did not know was that we had been included on the trip so that he could get to know me again to see whether, in his judgement, I merited an 'outstanding' grade in my confidential report. In the end, I did get an 'outstanding' for that tour in Berlin, which was the perfect way to lead into my next posting as a member of the directing staff at the Staff College, Camberley.

We left Berlin in January 1989, the year in which the Wall fell, and I am certain that no one, and I mean no one as far as I am aware, had any inkling of what was going to happen later that year, or indeed of how the perceived and actual role of the Army would change in the coming years.

FIVE

Regimental Command and a Final Tour in Northern Ireland

I arrived at Staff College in January 1989, newly promoted to Lieutenant Colonel, to become a member of the directing staff. I had an outstanding grade in a key job behind me and, on reflection, something of a growing reputation. But I was soon to discover that I still had a lot to learn about the business of soldiering.

The prospect of teaching at Camberley appealed to me and to my sense of history. I liked the fact that people I admired, such as Viscount Alanbrooke and Field Marshal Montgomery, had filled the same role at Staff College as I was now taking on. I was not ticking off the moments to when I was going to become a General, far from it. I just liked to be on the cutting edge and do the best job I could, and one that seemed to have some sort of historical relevance.

Every moderately ambitious officer seeks to command his regiment, and rightly so; it's a challenging but enormously rewarding job. As my confidence grew, I was no different, and a job as an instructor at the Staff College was a recognised route. That said, I never assumed anything, unlike some of the other so-called 'pre-command' directing staff at Camberley.

These postings were highly sought after and prestigious. There was a cosy assumption that anyone who was lucky enough to become a Staff College instructor was inevitably destined to command a regiment.

Indeed, many of my fellow directing staff officers had come to Camberley from commanding regiments. They were known as 'post command' directing staff. It was customary to be greeted with the question, 'Are you pre-command?' I would delight in puncturing the general air of complacency by saying pointedly, 'I really don't know.'

After my first year at Camberley, the Royal Artillery postings branch suggested that I was in the running for command. I was delighted and hinted that 47 Field Regiment, then based on Thorney Island in Chichester Harbour, would suit me. I had commanded 3 Battery, one of the batteries in the regiment, a few years earlier in Gutersloh, so this seemed a natural progression. The more important reason was the prospect of spending two and a half years in a house beside the sea with a tied mooring for a small yacht, if I could afford one, which I was determined I would. However, the postings branch clearly saw through my eagerness and I was told to expect to have to wait at Camberley for quite a while before a regiment became vacant.

Some of my friends moved on quickly and I had the odd pang that I might miss the boat altogether, but I was not overly concerned. I was thoroughly enjoying the ethos and ambience of life at Staff College and I was not having to work too hard, either. I was also conscious that I was learning much more than those I taught. Camberley was often referred to as the Army's 'brain'. Some of the brightest officers of their generation were there and one, Brigadier Rupert Smith, who went on to become a four-star General, having commanded operations in the First Gulf War and Bosnia, was especially influential. I was fortunate that from the beginning of my second year I became part of what was effectively his 'think tank'. Three of us were based next door to his office and we would be called upon when the Deputy Commandant of the College, as he then was, wanted to discuss new doctrine or concepts.

I also spent time looking into the application of computer war-gaming in army training, a role for which I was spectacularly ill-qualified. Smith taught me much, as indeed, in different ways, did his successor, the taciturn but ever wise Brigadier George Kennedy. I benefited from the fact that I had time to pursue my profession relatively untroubled by many other responsibilities.

We spent three happy years at Camberley. As well as being professionally content, I ran the offshore sailing club, organising a number of small regattas with other staff colleges, and had time to refurbish a small wooden sloop I had bought cheaply through some friends. We lived in a pleasant married quarter in the woods between Staff College and RMA Sandhurst, from where it was just a short walk to my office. Joanna and Pippa went to an excellent local primary school in nearby Bagshot. All in all, we could not have felt more fortunate.

At the beginning of 1991, it was confirmed that I was to be given command of 3rd Regiment Royal Horse Artillery. This was a huge privilege, doubly so because as an RHA regiment, it was regarded as the most prestigious of the commands within the Royal Regiment of Artillery as a whole. We moved to Colchester, where the regiment was based, in early December 1991, and I took over from my old friend Freddie Viggers (later a three-star General and Adjutant General before he retired and was appointed Black Rod). We were made to feel welcome by everyone there and we knew quite a few from our time in C Battery a decade or so earlier. It didn't take me long to work out that, with the notable exception early on of two of my battery commanders, who it seemed to me did not have their soldiers' interests at heart and whom I sacked or moved on prematurely, I was once again fortunate in the people I now had to lead.

My Regimental Sergeant Major was the irrepressible and highly efficient Richard Drewett, who had been a bombardier in C Battery. We are close friends to this day. My second in command, Matthew Sykes, went on to become a Major General, as did the Adjutant for most of my tour, Richard Nugee. My two quartermasters were outstanding, too. Bob Harmes, who had spent most of his career as a soldier in 7 Parachute Regiment RHA, was superb, one of those rare people who start as private soldiers and go on to become Lieutenant Colonels. The other, Terry Worster, who had been too much of a miscreant in his youth to emulate Bob's success, was loyal, effective and had a wonderfully mischievous sense of humour.

My self-appointed task, building on Freddie's legacy, was to turn 3 RHA into the best regiment in the Army. I made it clear to everyone that this was the job in hand and we set to with a will. With Matthew's help, I designed some innovative training schemes that put the emphasis on the development of leadership and initiative, as well as technical excellence. These culminated in a demanding series of dry and live-firing exercises in Norfolk and on Salisbury Plain. In the middle of one exercise in Thetford in Norfolk, I was called to a phone to be told that there was a possibility that the regiment would have to deploy at short notice to Northern Ireland. A few days later this was confirmed. I decided not to tell anyone until the end of the final big exercise.

When the whole regiment was gathered together in a hollow square on Salisbury Plain, I stood on the bonnet of a Land Rover, Monty-style, to pat them collectively on the back for an outstanding three weeks of training, and to tell them how pleased I was. But, I added, there is a downside to being viewed as the best regiment in the Army – we might be asked to do things no one else would do. I then told them that we would be deploying to Ulster in about three months' time – a unit would normally expect to be given a year in which to prepare – and that we would immediately move on to a Northern Ireland footing and start training. But first, I said, you can have a long weekend off. It was the best I could do. Initially, this was greeted with stunned silence. Then someone started cheering and everyone followed suit. To feel the effect of such high morale from a powerful team of committed professional soldiers was intoxicating.

At that time 3 RHA was part of 19 Infantry Brigade, commanded by Evelyn Webb-Carter. He had a lovely way with soldiers, enjoyed their company and they his. Although he came from a well-established Guards family, and his wife Celia was the daughter of a peer, there was no side or pomposity to him. He was everything you would expect from a first-rate officer and I admired him hugely.

In mid-1993, just after we returned from Northern Ireland, Evelyn

decided he should take the key officers from his brigade on a battlefield
tour, or 'staff ride' as they were known. The aim was to study historical
battles at first hand and to place what happened in them in the context
of the modern day. In his typically colourful way, Evelyn decided we
would go to Epernay in north-west France, the main purpose being to
spend twenty-four hours with Moët & Chandon at the Chateau de
Saran – the elegant house used by the company to entertain clients
and invited guests. The trip's official objective was a serious study of
battle, but for many, Epernay perhaps unsurprisingly, became the main
talking point.

I had never stayed anywhere like the Chateau de Saran in my life. We
had a sumptuous lunch during which our hosts brought out a pre-1900
bottle of champagne. I managed to stagger through until mid-afternoon,
when I thought, 'I've got to sober up for the evening's activities.' The
prospect of more of the same led me to decide I had better take some
exercise. I was told later that I was seen weaving through the vine-
yards very much the worse for wear, determined to finish my run. We
had a bloody good evening, de-corking the bottles with sabres in the
traditional way.

Moët's man in London, Rupert Lendrum, a delightful ex-Household
Cavalry officer, was running the Chateau, and I told him that if ever I
became a brigade commander, I would love to visit with a party of my
own.

'Yes,' he replied, with an air of disbelief, 'if you ever make it.'

Three years later, when I had made the grade, I rang him.

'You're not!' he said.

'I am, and when are we booked-in?'

And so we did it all over again and it was just as much fun. On that
occasion they ran out of vintage.

'Zut alors,' said our British host, 'we will have to go to normal.'

'That'll do, crack on.'

On a more sobering note, I took the opportunity on this trip to visit
Verdun and the experience hit me unexpectedly hard. It is one of the

most sombre and tragic places. This was where more than 260,000 French and German soldiers died and at least another 450,000 were wounded. Casualties ran at an average rate of 70,000 per month of battle. A building there contains the unburied bones of some of the dead. Walking among the rows and rows of graves and sensing the sheer extent of the slaughter, however understandable the causes, I was overwhelmed by the stupidity of war on that scale. After our tour I went into the little shop in the museum and bought something to remember Verdun by. It's a family tradition in the Richards household that every Sunday morning we have boiled eggs, so I bought myself a wooden egg cup with Verdun written on it.

When I got back, Caroline asked me, 'Why have you bought that egg cup?'

'So that if ever I'm a General in command of thousands of people, I don't make the same mistakes as those Generals did in not standing up to the politicians who put them in such a hopeless situation,' I replied.

It will always remind me to dig deep, to question my politicians and to think of my soldiers. I still have that Verdun egg cup and every time I use it, it makes me think through my priorities.

After two months of training we deployed to Northern Ireland in early September 1992. By that time there had been a false dawn or two in the slow march to peace in Ulster and more violence had occurred, particularly in the south of the province in Armagh. My regiment, 3 RHA, became the heart of what was termed the Drumadd Battalion, so called because we were based in Drumadd barracks in the historical city of Armagh. I had responsibility for the north of Armagh county. This was not as dangerous as the southern part of the county but there were some unpleasant people there and the Army dealt with regular IRA operations in the area.

We were kept on our toes during that tour but we did not lose any soldiers. J (Sidi Rezegh) Battery, stationed at Bessbrook Mill, just north of Newry, was under a lot of pressure and was attacked a couple of times by the IRA, and C Battery on the border was mortared. I was fortunate to miss a massive IED planted in a hedge on the route I would have taken to a conference. Fortunately, I changed my plans and the officer who took my place chose to go a longer way round. No military vehicles went past it and the Provisionals eventually detonated the bomb themselves, fearing that they might end up killing some of their own supporters if they left it any longer. I went to see the crater and realised what a lucky escape I had had.

During my days in Armagh, there was a dramatic moment when I confronted the local IRA commander after coming across him purely by chance. We knew from our intelligence that this individual was responsible for the deaths of several British soldiers and I wanted him to know that we knew who he was and that we were waiting and watching for the moment to get him. On a number of occasions I made it my business to go up to where his house was to see if I could find him, but he always eluded us. Then one day, when I was patrolling with my soldiers in the city centre, we spotted him, walking through a shopping area. I strode up to him.

'I know who you are,' I said, 'and I know what you've done. We're watching you, following your every move, and if you step one inch out of line, we'll take you out.'

He told me that we didn't have a shred of evidence to pin on him.

'We have all the proof we need,' I said, bluffing, 'and, by the way, my name is Richards and I'm commanding the Area of Operations here.'

He said nothing, just looked at me and walked off. Of course, he was right, we couldn't 'lift' him, to use the local parlance, because we didn't have enough evidence. My intention in confronting him was to try to get into the mind of my opponent and make him understand that we were different, we meant business and we would get him in the end. I'm not sure if we did, in fact.

Another episode that sticks out in my mind concerns conversations I had with a terrified woman from a hardline IRA family who wanted out. I was asked to talk to her and give her encouragement to turn her back on her own community, a difficult and dangerous thing to do. The IRA punishments for 'touts', or informers, were notorious. She told me the most frightful stories about what would happen to her if she did turn and how she would need to be looked after. It brought it home to me how brutal the IRA could be with their people.

While not for one minute countenancing the Provisional IRA's tactics and the misery they inflicted on the people of Northern Ireland and mainland Britain, I could not help but respect them from a purely professional perspective. They were cunning, clever, ruthless and a difficult enemy, who often came up with new tactics while we, the bulk of the Army, were relatively ponderous. The question was how could we, a conventional Army, outwit and outmanoeuvre them at the tactical level, playing our part intelligently within a wider strategy? That was the challenge facing me and my fellow officers.

Overall, I think the Army showed enormous strategic patience in what it did over those thirty years in Northern Ireland, and acquitted itself generally superbly. What the regular, uniformed Army did was part of a much greater campaign, which included special forces, police, political initiatives and economic development. The Army created opportunity for politicians and bureaucrats by holding the ring, suffering a lot of casualties in the process. Soldiers behaved largely honourably under terribly trying circumstances and under major constraints on what they might naturally have wanted to do. They managed to do that because they understood the political context in which they were working. I think the Army can be proud of its service in Northern Ireland and the country should be proud of the Army for what it did.

For much of the infantry in particular, Northern Ireland dominated their lives for three decades. One consequence of this was that, to some extent, we lost the edge in conventional war fighting, although troops in Germany worked hard to keep up their skill levels. But for many, life revolved around Northern Ireland tours. Expertise in counter-insurgency developed as a result of some excellent training in that field. Since large sections of the Army were so Northern Ireland focused, it was all the more impressive that the forces conducted themselves so well in the Falklands in 1982 and in Kuwait nine years later.

Critics say that our long experience in Ulster made us complacent about tackling insurgency elsewhere – a case of 'we've done this in Northern Ireland, so we know what to expect and how to deal with it.' As a result of our experience in Ulster, we certainly had a feel for the requirement to keep people with us and to work within a political environment. But I think in Iraq, for example, too many British officers would, without realising what they were doing, slip into a Northern Ireland mindset. Very early on that was an appropriate response when the efficient administration of law and order along the Northern Ireland pattern was what was required. But once things escalated, we needed to think in new and innovative ways in order to deal with a complex and unique insurgency amid the collapse of Iraqi society. That did happen but maybe it took longer than it should have done.

Northern Ireland accelerated our expertise in other ways. A good example is the dangerous and skilful business of IED detection and clearance. We were miles ahead in that area until the Americans put their energy into catching us up on an industrial scale. We gifted that expertise to them and to many other countries – we had all the robots and experience; they had nothing like that.

My role in Armagh came to a premature end in early 1993. The experienced and colourful Sir John Wilsey had been succeeded as General Officer Commanding Northern Ireland by the more orthodox Sir Roger Wheeler. I was immensely lucky. Whilst quite different, they were both inspirational and likeable leaders. Wheeler decided to restructure the Army's command arrangements in the province. He allowed me to carry on until February, because he could see that I was enjoying myself and he genuinely wanted to give me the experience of command on operations. Knowing I was handing over, I was looking forward to a more relaxing few weeks at Drumadd when Wheeler called and asked me to take on a completely unexpected project. This was to research and then write the Army's first formal campaign plan for Northern Ireland, a mere twenty-three years after British troops first arrived on the streets of Belfast.

A well-educated and forward-thinking officer, Wheeler had come in and said, more or less, 'Well, where's the plan?' There were various plans but no single, coherent, theatre-level campaign plan. I had majored in this subject at Camberley so I understood strategic and theatre-level process and what was required. It was about the linking of ends, ways and means. The ends and ways mean defining an objective and how you go about achieving it; the means are what you have available to do it. They all have to be in synch; you could have a great plan but it could be completely impractical because you haven't got enough troops or enough money or time to execute it. I understood this theory and had taught it at Camberley, and Wheeler, who knew of my probably undeserved reputation as being a bit of a guru in this area, wanted me to do it.

It was hell. There was I, thinking I was going to have two easy months and then go back to Colchester. Then, all of a sudden, I was presented with the worst essay crisis of my life – far worse than anything at Cardiff or Staff College. I went up by helicopter to HQ Northern Ireland at Lisburn, outside Belfast, and set about it. I had two months to do it. I looked at the development of the campaign, its long history, our failings and our successes. Much of it was going right by then; it just hadn't been formalised or codified. So I felt that we knew roughly what we were trying to do as the peace process trundled on, even if a breakthrough seemed a long way off.

I was given my own office at Lisburn and I did most of the work there. Whenever I wanted to go anywhere, I was provided with a helicopter. I went to visit all the brigade commanders and made sure I understood their up-to-date views on the campaign. I went to see Anthony Palmer, the brigade commander in Londonderry, who seemed slightly resentful to begin with about the whole project and my responsibility for it, but was then very helpful. I also discussed it with 3 Brigade commander in Armagh, Douglas Erskine-Crum, who had been my commander at Drumadd, as well as Alistair Irwin, who by then was commanding 8 Brigade in Belfast and had been a post-command instructor at Camberley with me. All three were generous with their time and had many excellent ideas.

The most important point in the plan was that, ultimately, this was a political problem that would require a political solution. The role of the military was to facilitate that. This would mean sometimes doing things that tactically were frustrating or didn't appear to make much sense. When you were trying to encourage a political process, you might have to be very hard on certain IRA terrorists in order to reinforce the fact that you meant business until they came to the table. Alternatively, you might not do things that militarily made sense in order to induce constructive behaviour.

The requirement to remain strong was a key principle – there was a temptation to reduce troop levels at that time, which would risk showing weakness. The economic dimension was important. The people of Northern Ireland had to see that their lot was improving. Cross-border cooperation and the role of special forces were other elements. My blueprint remained within the general parameters of what we were already doing. It wasn't terribly innovative – the innovation was having a plan at all, to bring it all together.

During my months in command at Drumadd, I came to the view that some of our tactics were rather arid. Even before Wheeler commissioned me, I had been looking for innovative tactical solutions. One tactic I came up with was the concept of Dynamic Unpredictability, which I rather cheekily christened the 'DUP' principle. Of course, DUP was the acronym for Ian Paisley's Democratic Unionist Party.

We had become predictable in the way we went about things and, I concluded, we could do more to keep the IRA guessing and on their toes. For example, once a patrol had been through a village the opposition would know we wouldn't be back for three days. They knew they had that period of grace. Under my approach, you would put another patrol in three hours later, or the original patrol would double back. When you were deploying a vehicle checkpoint on a road, the Army tended to do it in one place and hope for the best. I came up with a model whereby you would simultaneously deploy a large number of checkpoints over a thirty-mile stretch. Normally, if IRA members were driving a car bomb to Belfast, for example, a spotter car, travelling ahead of them, would warn them of any checkpoints and they would change their route accordingly. Doing it my way gave us a much better chance of trapping the car with the bomb in it. It was a case of trying to avoid patterns in our own behaviour and exploiting the element of surprise in order to seize and retain the initiative. Standard principles of war applied to the routine business of Northern Ireland operations.

I went to a combined military and police seminar at that time, in the south of the province, and met an amazing character, who was reputedly held together with wire. A tough Northern Ireland policeman, he was a long-serving special branch officer, someone who had devoted his life to what he believed in. He'd been blown up at least twice and we lesser mortals were all in awe of him. I was asked by the brigade commander to comment after my first couple of months in Armagh and so I mentioned my new concept and how I had christened it the DUP principle. Then I heard a laconic voice coming from the front row: 'I think you'll find, Colonel Richards, that we have a different meaning for that term here.' That brought the house down and helped break the ice.

When I had finished my work on the campaign plan, I went to discuss it with Wheeler and he was grateful. To be frank, I don't know what they did with it. I was told that they used it as the basis for what the staff produced from then on. All I know is that it was a huge weight on me, because it was my responsibility, and I was relieved to get it finished.

When we got back to Colchester after Northern Ireland, we had a hell of a party. Everything we did and tried to do in 3 RHA was the best and that went for letting off steam too. The ever-resourceful Bob Harmes had saved up £10,000 in regimental funds during the tour in Ulster, and we had enough for a free party for all ranks. We had the 1812 Overture played by the band of the Royal Artillery – complete with our own guns firing blanks on the conductor's cue – there was a funfair with dodgems, and a sumptuous display of food and booze. At the parade two days later,

John Patrick told us that, in his mind, there was no question our regiment was the best in the British Army. In a way, I felt we *were* the best regiment and I was very proud of what we had achieved.

Just a few weeks after getting back from Ireland, the regiment moved to our new base at Topcliffe in North Yorkshire and began the process of re-equipping, swapping the wheeled FH70 gun for the new tracked AS90, which posed a fresh set of technical and tactical challenges. There was no let-up in my last year in command and I found I thrived, loving everything that was thrown at me. It included a parade in front of the Queen marking the 200th anniversary of the founding of the Royal Horse Artillery – during which I introduced to Her Majesty a soldier by the wrong name who proceeded to ignore her and correct my error, much to her amusement. 'Now you've been told Colonel Richards!', she quipped. The year included a series of big exercises, finishing on Salisbury Plain in the early summer of 1994. The regiment took all this in its stride and consistently achieved the highest standards in all we did, which is much more a testimony to them than to me, but I played my role and loved them for it.

After just under three years in command of 3 RHA, I was promoted to Colonel Army Plans, based at the Ministry of Defence. I didn't want to go to the Ministry of Defence but Evelyn Webb-Carter had convinced me that it was the right thing to do and Colonel Army Plans was reputed to be the best Colonel's job in the Army. And, of course, I could put red tabs on my collar for the first time, so it was a big step.

In that role I was responsible for the size and shape of the Army at working level, which sounds quite onerous. In fact, I had a relatively easy time of it, coming to the post in the wake of the John Major government's Options for Change defence review. It was an influential position. For the first time I was attending meetings with the Chief of the General Staff (CGS) – General Sir Charles Guthrie, as he then was – and I was the main Army representative on a number of tri-service committees. I also had responsibility for the Army in NATO. It was another one of those jobs where I learnt more than I gave, and it was to prove a useful grounding for later in my career when I became CGS and then CDS.

The tri-service aspect of the job was an interesting new challenge and I am sure I defended the Army's interests robustly. I worked alongside – and often competed for resources with – my opposite numbers in the Royal Air Force and Royal Navy. My job was to represent the Army, but I had studied war and military history and was beginning to have a real feel for my profession, so I was well aware that defence is a tri-service team effort.

The move to the MoD required yet more upheaval for the family – we were to move twenty-nine times in total during my career – and once again Caroline bore the brunt of it with her usual uncomplaining efficiency. On this occasion, we were so rushed that we sent Caroline's devoted stepmother, Algar, to look at a house for us in East Grinstead, just east of Salisbury, and we bought it without even seeing it. When we got there from Topcliffe, it turned out to be a lovely house where I based myself at weekends. During the week, I lodged with True and Gordon Maxwell in Chelsea. Gordon was a charming and distinguished retired Colonel in the London Scottish Regiment who had fought in the Second World War. The girls meanwhile started at another new school in Salisbury.

In the spring of 1995, I was selected to command 4 Armoured Brigade before I'd had a report as a Colonel. Before I took up that role, as a newly promoted Brigadier, I attended the Higher Command and Staff Course at Camberley. This is another big filter as you move up the ladder, designed to train and educate the most senior officers-to-be in all three services. We focused on campaign planning, military history and the practice of theatre-level command.

After the course had finished, in June 1996, we all piled into the car and headed once again to Germany, this time to the lovely town of Osnabruck, where I was to take command of 4 Armoured Brigade. As we set off, we all felt 'here we go again', but this was a marvellous job and an enormous privilege. I was taking command of one of the two 'Desert

Rat' brigades that had previously been led by such illustrious people as Charles Guthrie.

I had two garrisons under me, one in Osnabruck and one in Munster, and I shuttled between them, doing my best to combat the sense that Munster was the poor relation. About 5,000 soldiers were under my command, two armoured regiments, two armoured infantry battalions, an artillery regiment, an engineer regiment, a field ambulance unit and intelligence sections – all the elements that make up a fighting brigade. And of course, I had responsibility for the welfare of the soldiers' families, a role Caroline and I took very seriously.

We also found ourselves enjoying the challenge of playing a quasi-diplomatic role with the local German community, led by the Mayor of Osnabruck, Hans-Jurgen Fip. Caroline and I were guided through this process by a wise retired military policeman and his wife, Jock and Ann Smith. They introduced us to some generous and kind Germans to whom we owe much. On top of this, although the Cold War was quite self-evidently over at that stage, we prepared, through intense training and exercising, to be a fine manoeuvre brigade within the Army's order of battle.

Osnabruck is a beautiful old place and we had one of the best army quarters there. Talavera House is one of the grandest houses in the town, built by a rich industrialist in the 1920s. It was undamaged during the war and was used immediately afterwards by British officers doing de-Nazification work. They used the cellars to hold suspects before interrogation.

The girls had started boarding at St Mary's School on the outskirts of Shaftesbury in Dorset, so they were with us just for the holidays. The job was almost two years of fun. I was beginning to discover that I loved command at every level. As I became more senior, I found that in many respects it got easier. As a battalion or regimental commander, everything ends up on your desk from the most trivial upwards; as a brigade commander you are one step removed from all the detail and can focus on the things that arguably really matter – morale, high standards, long-term planning and so on. Very rarely, maybe once or twice in a command

In the garden of our family home in Sussex –
Colonel Jim Richards OBE with his newly commissioned son.
I had just passed the commando course and
been awarded my green beret.

Left: Ceylon 1947 – Major and Mrs Jim Richards, my parents, with my brother Nick, sister Jan and house staff.

Above: Egypt 1952 – mother Pam holds on to me in my christening garb.

Left: Egypt 1952 – my first sight of the Suez Canal came at a very young age.

Below: Egypt 1952 – family portrait. I'm sitting on my father's knee, aged nine months.

Clockwise from the top: Eastbourne College Combined Cadet Force annual inspection 1970.
I present my company to the inspecting officer. Major Forbes Wastie, a good friend to this day,
looks on approvingly; Backpacking in the summer of 1970; Captain of Eastbourne College rugby
team, Roehampton Sevens, 1969.

Above: Malaya 1971 – Second Lieutenant Richards and Second Lieutenant Peter Taylor (right), jungle training.

Left: Singapore 1971 – outside the Officers' Mess.

Above: Singapore 1975 – on a visit to the war cemetery.

Left: Arctic Norway 1978, writing up my orders.

Opposite top: Flax Street Mill, Belfast 1975 – about to go out on vehicle patrol.

Opposite bottom: The Bone, Belfast 1975 – loyalist graffiti.

Below & right: Our wedding day, Micheldever Church, 1 April 1978 –
Captain David and Mrs Caroline Richards (née Bond) and the honour guard.

Above: Berlin 1987 – at the Queen's birthday parade. From left:
Me, Brigadier Richard Powell (late Welsh Guards) and Major
Bill Bailey RE. I was the Brigade Major.

Right: Germany 1981 – Sergeant Jimmy Michie, C Battery
Royal Horse Artillery, talks to Colonel James Templer,
Commander Royal Artillery, 2 Armoured Division.

Below: Germany 2001 – HQ Allied Rapid Reaction Corps
on exercise in simulated chemical warfare conditions. I'm in
the foreground.

Opposite page: Joanna aged seven and Pippa aged five –
a favourite photo.

Photograph: (c) 1988 GARY BERNSTEIN

Above: I was one of Joan Collins's bodyguards in Berlin in 1988.

Right: Rudolf Hess – I was the Brigade Major of the Berlin Brigade when Rudolf Hess died in Spandau Prison in 1987.

tour, one of your battalion commanders would bother you with their issues. If they did that too often, I would question their motives and wonder about their capacity to command.

To start with I had a tricky hand to play as a result of my attendance at the Higher Command and Staff Course. This had been delayed – I should have been on an earlier course – and it meant that I arrived in Osnabruck later than planned. As a result, I missed the chance to take elements of the brigade to Bosnia, a considerable challenge that fell to my predecessor, Brigadier Richard Dannatt. A clever, meticulous and hard-driving officer who was already a notable communicator and leader, Richard went on to become Chief of the General Staff immediately before I took the post.

The delay in my arrival was frustrating. While I was disappointed not to have gone to Bosnia, I had to put it down to happen-chance. The upshot was that when I got to Germany, most of my senior officers were still away. As they returned to duty, I had the challenge of establishing my authority over a brigade that had just done well in Bosnia, and try to get them to re-focus on conventional war fighting.

I had another fantastic team, including some talented newly arrived officers. My Chief of Staff was a scruffy but highly competent cavalryman, James Everard, who is today a Lieutenant General. He was succeeded by Piers Hankinson, another top officer, who is currently a Brigadier. One of my battle group commanders was the gifted Adrian Bradshaw of the King's Royal Hussars, who deservedly went on to become a four-star General. Another, James Bucknall of the Coldstream Guards, could have been a four-star but chose to leave the Army as a Lieutenant General. He was to work for me later in Afghanistan. One of the other battle group commanders went on to become a Brigadier and another a Major General, so I had some outstanding people under me. They would say – politely – that I helped bring them on and added to their chances of success but I'd say it was absolutely symbiotic in every case.

During our second summer in Osnabruck, we returned to the UK in early August for a great family party at the Platts to celebrate my father's

80th birthday. Although he joined in manfully and enjoyed it, it was clear that all was not well. He had been diagnosed with cancer two years before and had been given a maximum of two years to live. Tough and physically fit, he had lived every day of that precious time to the full.

Caroline and I had paid for a holiday in Greece with the girls and my father was determined we should go. Looking back, I'm not sure either he or we realised how serious his condition was. Two weeks later we returned home to find him gravely ill and five days later he died peacefully in his bed, with his three surviving children round him and my mother holding his hand.

While he could be something of a rogue, the loss of this larger than life character who was a formative influence on me and for whom, subconsciously, I did much of what I achieved, left me feeling quite lonely. I had lost not only a father, but also a mentor and friend to please. He did not live to see me reach the top of my profession but he knew I was en route to doing quite well when he saw me take command of an armoured brigade. He knew this was a rare step for a gunner officer and he could not conceal his pride in it. Along with Caroline and my daughters and, in her own way, my sister Sara, my elder brother Nick has since replaced him as the person who is most evidently proud of what I have got up to, sending me the same congratulatory letters and making the same phone calls that my parents did.

In the end, I had just under two years in Osnabruck. I loved every moment of the job and left at the end of March 1998 much against my wishes. I had been promised another year because of missing the Bosnia deployment at the start of my tour, but then I was told I was to be the first in a new appointment – Chief Joint Force Operations, running the Joint Force HQ. This turned out, in many respects, to be the best job I ever had.

SIX

Small Wars and Escapades

Much as I was disappointed to leave Osnabruck early, it didn't take me long to grasp that I had been given a terrific new job, even if its title and acronym took service nomenclature to new heights of long-windedness. I was to be Chief Joint Rapid Deployment Force Operations, a position summarised by the indigestible collection of letters CJRDFO.

What this actually meant was that I was to command a new headquarters staff drawn from all three services whose task was to prepare for quick deployments at short notice anywhere in the world. Not only was I going to lead it, I was also tasked with expanding the concept that underpinned its creation, something called the Joint Rapid Reaction Force (JRRF). In retrospect, this looks like the military's response to Prime Minister Tony Blair's advocacy of an ethical and interventionist foreign policy with an accent on human rights. It was as if the Chiefs of Staff were saying to themselves, 'If we have to intervene in a hurry, we'd better be ready.'

My job was to build up the headquarters staff and create a reconnaissance team from officers of all three services that would be sent to assess crisis situations and determine what response, if any, Britain could provide. Before any of that could happen, I decided to sort out my title. Luckily, my request to simplify it fell on fertile ground and I was cut down to a mere Chief Joint Force Operations, or CJFO.

My first proper task was to flesh out the more ambitious concept of the JRRF – who should be in it, what its state of readiness should be and how its command structure and headquarters would function. I put together a small team of five officers, one from each service plus a coordinator, and within six months we had worked up a plan. Midway through the process I was asked to present an interim report to the Chiefs of Staff. This was an important moment for the whole concept of joint force deployment – I had to show that we could make it work properly. What I recommended would have far-reaching implications for each of the three services.

In my new job I was based at the Permanent Joint Headquarters (PJHQ) at Northwood in Hertfordshire. Caroline and I had moved with the girls to a quarter just outside the base after getting back from Germany. I had made the trip from there to the Ministry of Defence in Whitehall several times and on this occasion, knowing who would be at the presentation, I sensibly allowed an extra half hour on top of the usual maximum journey time. But then I got stuck in the most horrendous traffic jam. I was due to present to the Chiefs at 11.00 hours sharp but at 10.45 I was still many miles away, stuck in traffic with my blood pressure rising. Standing up the Chiefs of Staff was a complete no-no for any officer, let alone someone with hopes of further promotion. I managed to put a call through to Group Captain John Ponsonby, Deputy Principal Staff Officer to Charles Guthrie, by then the Chief of the Defence Staff. He tried to calm my nerves and said not to worry. He was sure I'd soon be there and he would schedule me as the last item at 11.30 hours. But by then I was still an hour away.

Guthrie apparently was not a happy man, saying that this had never happened in the history of the Chiefs. Fortunately, Admiral Sir Peter Abbott, the Vice Chief of the Defence Staff, who had been based at Northwood himself, soothed his boss's anger by saying that he had been stuck in a traffic jam on the route I was on and that they really should be more understanding (or words to that effect). Either way, the top echelon of the armed forces were so distracted by my failure to appear that they nodded through my report without amendment. This is not a tactic I would bank on or recommend to others. I saw Charles Guthrie later and apologised. By then he was back to his customary charming self and had forgiven me. As CDS myself, I tried to be relaxed in situations like that. As someone remarked of a good officer: 'If he's late, we know he's got a good reason.'

In the late 1990s, joint force deployment at short notice was becoming the next big thing in terms of British military doctrine and I was the one charged with delivering it. As we emerged finally from the Cold War, there was recognition that what was known colloquially as 'out of area operations' was going to become a more common requirement. This was in the wake not just of the warming of relations between the West and the former Soviet countries but of the NATO intervention in Bosnia, the ill-fated attempt by the Americans to intervene in Somalia, instability in Indonesia, a collective shame over the West's failure to intervene in Rwanda, and evacuation operations of foreign nationals from Sierra Leone and Albania in 1997. A repeat of the Falklands War would have been a classic role for the JRRF and, while the Iraq war of 1992 rapidly came into another category by virtue of its scale, initially even that would have been a JRRF task.

The key to the JRRF concept was assembling what was termed a 'golf bag' of capabilities from each of the three services. The commander of the day could then select whichever 'clubs' were most appropriate for the task at hand. Not only that, all the various units on the joint-force roster would be at graduated states of readiness. So units at Readiness State 1 (R1) were on standby to deploy anywhere in the world within forty-eight hours; R2 units were on forty-eight to ninety-six hours notice; R3 was at seven days' notice, and so on.

In the R1 category, the Army, for example, would have a nominated lead company of up to 120 men, followed by its lightly protected parent battalion at slightly lower readiness. Heavier elements – an armoured battle group with tanks, infantry fighting vehicles, mortars, anti-tank weaponry and artillery – were available at thirty days' notice. The RAF had an air-defence squadron of fighters, a close air-support squadron (ground-attack aircraft), Hercules transport aircraft and helicopters in the roster. The Royal Navy had a number of frigates and destroyers as well as a submarine and an aircraft carrier within the JRRF, all at different states of readiness. Special forces were another important club in the bag, most of them at very high readiness.

In the first months, we did a lot of development work on the scale and staffing of the headquarters for this capability. Though the comment probably originated with General Robert Barrow, it was US General Omar Bradley who, after the Second World War, wisely said that amateurs talk tactics, professionals talk logistics. He was right, of course, but I was already of the view that if you did not get the command and control right, it did not matter how good your logistics or fighting soldiers were, it would not work. To start with, the plan had been for a compliment of twenty-four people at Northwood. I expanded this to fifty-five, something that our training and experience on exercise was proving necessary. In the headquarters, we were all on high states of readiness. I always had a bag packed and ready in the house. Caroline knew about it and, if I was unable to get home before deploying, this could be picked up and taken to the airport for me.

Initially, the single services were reluctant to embrace the JRRF concept. Then they saw the advantages of it and I had to fight them off. I went round briefing them on what we were doing and you could see their eyes open. 'Bloody hell,' they'd say, 'we need to be part of this.' Suddenly, I was getting more offers of help and assets to be included than I knew what to do with. This was partly because a large chunk of the military training budget was devoted to elements within the JRRF, so if you weren't in it, you didn't do the same level of training and you were in danger of missing the boat when it came to deployment.

In my meetings with the Chiefs, I explained the concept that under-pinned what we were doing, how it would be used and what the key requirements were. At those meetings, the three single-service Chiefs each wanted to have more assets in my golf bag than I thought was required. I think they were thinking about the advantages from their particular service's point of view at a time when defence cuts were making it ever more important to justify what capabilities were left. That was quite understandable and provoked useful thought and discussion. My job was to ensure that we ended up with a balanced tri-service force that could be tailored to need.

Our first big test was an exercise in the West Indies called YTRIUM MERCURY in the early summer of 1998. I set up headquarters in Jamaica, having flown out with my team in an RAF BAe 146 aircraft used, among others, by the Queen. The 146 has a limited range, so we had to stop in Iceland, Newfoundland and North Carolina on the way. The long journey on this rather smartly fitted-out aircraft gave us time to prepare and we hit the ground running.

The exercise was more demanding than a simple Non-Combatant Evacuation Operation, or NEO, that was to be our bread and butter in crisis settings. It posited fighting between two rival ethnic groups and our job was to recommend to the government at home how we could help. It became even more complicated when we got caught up in the fighting and I was given command of troops sent out to help to stabilise the situation. It was a demanding scenario and we ran it from the ruins of a house on Errol Flynn's plantation in a gorgeous stretch of country below the Blue Mountains on the north coast of the island, near Port Antonio. Part of the exercise was based in Belize so we could practise communication drills over long distances between the different elements brought together on a joint operation.

All in all, it was a successful trip and morale among my team was high by its end. We were ahead of the game in many respects, so I was confident about completing the concept paper for the Chiefs, and in the fact that we would have a headquarters staff who could deliver the goods in terms of command and control. In that respect, I was already realising how lucky I was in my staff, in particular my slow-speaking, caring and experienced Royal Marine Chief of Staff, Colonel David Hopley. Attentive to detail, as any CoS should be, he organised twenty-four hours R&R for us all at a not very smart, inclusive resort in Jamaica just before our departure from the island. These things are important for the maintenance of morale and to give very hard-working people a bit of a break. The outcome of the 'Mr Reggae King' dancing competition, in which I was entered, will however remain our secret, although I did better than I expected. Hopley's successor a few months later was another Royal Marine, Jerry Thomas, who was equally good if not better. Like all marines, they both knew how to enjoy life while being highly professional.

That autumn we staged our next big exercise, deploying my headquarters to the aircraft carrier HMS *Invincible* off the north coast of Scotland. This was another sophisticated scenario when we tried to test the limits of exercising command and control of a large joint force fighting a war at considerable distances from the UK. Our mission was to recapture and stabilise a friendly nation that had been invaded by a hostile neighbour.

Under the concept I had developed, once an operation was beyond a certain scale, I, as a mere Brigadier, would become Deputy Commander or Chief of Staff to another more senior officer from one of the three services. In this case, command had been assumed by an Air Vice Marshal who had been personally selected for the job by the Chief of the Air Staff. Part of the point of the exercise was to trial that transfer of command upwards. The exercise was high-profile stuff. The Chiefs of Staff were monitoring it, as was everyone else in the three single services, because this was an important proving ground for the joint-force concept and for their roles within it.

When I got aboard the carrier, a little later than planned, having been finishing work on my paper for the Chiefs, I found that the atmosphere was not what I'd hoped it would be. The Air Vice Marshal didn't seem to have a feel for the theatre level. He was tactically focused, wanting to get into the detail all the time and not thinking enough about the bigger issues, as he should have been as a theatre commander. The theatre level is the vital gearing between tactical activity – dropping bombs, manoeuvring armoured forces and firing artillery – and the strategic level at which politicians and Chiefs of Defence operate. It is the level at which campaigns are run and where political intent is analysed and turned into military effect; it is where wars are won or lost and it is demanding stuff.

I had an awkward moment when a very senior RAF officer – a four-star – came to visit the exercise and asked me about the Air Vice Marshal. He had heard rumours that all was not well. I had to tell him that I didn't think that he was right for this sort of job.

The officer in question wasn't sacked but his cards were marked. I was told that he subsequently blamed me for blighting his career, believing I had somehow manipulated the outcome, as an Army officer, to prove that an RAF officer wasn't up to it. He alleged that he was the victim of a single-service conspiracy. Nothing was further from the truth. A decent man, he just wasn't trained or temperamentally suited to the job.

There is a broader point here. Perhaps controversially, in my view neither the Royal Air Force nor the Royal Navy prepare their officers as well for high command of a joint force as does the Army. This is partly a consequence of the way their careers tend to progress. RAF officers don't actually exercise field command. Army officers do from Second Lieutenant upwards. They are almost always commanding soldiers, and very often under pressure, whether in the field or in an intense operational staff environment. The Navy is somewhere between the two. Their officers command ships but today they never do so on any scale and rarely with the intensity of their Army contemporaries. Whereas a senior Army officer will lead a battalion of 600 or 700 people, then a brigade of 5,000 and then perhaps a division and a corps, with all the moving parts and synchronisation that entails, a senior naval officer will run, at most, a ship or a few ships. Although a ship can experience short periods of intense activity, its well-honed crew is essentially a single highly responsive unit. This contrasts with a battalion, for example, which has lots of points of command with all the friction this generates. So people come to a joint-force headquarters with different backgrounds and experience; some rise well to the complex challenges and often austere conditions involved, but, on the whole, the Army officer is better prepared. This problem is now maturely recognised, and excellent training programmes, such as the Higher Command and Staff Course, seek to address it, but more needs to be done. Talented officers from the Royal Navy and Air Force are too often not as comfortable or competent in joint-command appointments as they could be, through no fault of their own.

In the case of the Air Vice Marshal, he was moved on to a different career path but not sacked, which I think was the right decision. The tradition in the British armed forces is that if you are removed from a job, it is usually terminal and is viewed as such. It rarely happens because the officer's superiors are usually decent people who know there is a family to consider. The officer will have expectations and will probably have worked hard, so they will do everything they can to avoid sacking.

I am of the view that removing an individual from a job in the interests of the greater good is something that we should be prepared to do more often but that it should not necessarily be regarded as terminal to his or her career. It could be that the officer is just ill-suited to a particular job and that the appointments board got it wrong. For example, my predecessor as CDS felt he had to sack a three-star officer in a key appointment. The officer got another job, but everyone knew it was effectively the end of what, until then, had been a fine career. Many of us felt he would have prospered in other demanding posts, but he was never given the chance. When I was CDS, having usefully learnt my predecessor's lesson, I felt I had to move on a two-star officer in a key appointment in the Ministry of Defence operations branch. I actually moved him into a good job that I felt he would be much better suited to. I explained to my fellow Chiefs that if someone fails in a particular job, we should not view a decision to move him on as a terminal act on our part. One or two were reluctant. They wanted it to be seen as an immutable sanction that would mean the end of a career and that would encourage others to do better.

As 1998 drew to a close, the civil war in Sierra Leone began to loom large on my horizon and I made two trips to the capital, Freetown, in early 1999 to see what help we could give the embattled president, Ahmad Tejan Kabbah. Those visits formed the build-up to perhaps the defining point in my career, Operation PALLISER in May 2000. This was when I liberally interpreted my orders, some would say disobeyed them, to conduct a restricted non-combatant evacuation operation in Freetown and instead unilaterally decided to intervene in the war. This is dealt with in detail in the following chapters.

Sierra Leone aside, we were very busy in 1999. My team was commissioned to write an invasion plan for Kosovo, followed by one for Macedonia. Charles Guthrie and others were impatient with NATO's failure to devise a coherent and workable plan for Kosovo and so I was tasked to come up with one. It was our first large-scale campaign design. An illustrative solution, it set out the broad themes of how an invasion and occupation might work. It did not, for example, go into what each unit would do on any given day; it was a proposal at theatre level, which seemed, at that time, to be beyond NATO. We did it over five manic days, getting virtually no sleep. Colonel Paul Newton (later a three-star General, rightly viewed as one of the most capable officers of his generation) was central to me being able to do it. It was well received by Guthrie and then carefully slipped into the NATO planning process so that it did not appear to have UK hands all over it.

Subsequently, it was deemed so useful that when NATO was contemplating the need to sort out Montenegro, Guthrie directed that I should come up with an illustrative plan for a putative invasion. At one stage, this looked a real possibility. So we did it again. We never stopped. Living at Northwood, I could walk up a little hill to my office from our home – a redbrick married quarter that was far inferior to our house in Osnabruck. When under the cosh, we all worked long hours. I saw the children mainly at weekends or other times when they were out of school, and I tried to make as much time as I could for them in the school holidays, but I was away a lot, including trips to places as far afield as Japan, Indonesia, Singapore, the Gulf, the US and Ghana.

On Montenegro, I ended up briefing not only the Chiefs but subsequently the Ministry of Defence ministerial team. One was Baroness Liz Symons, whom I recall questioning why she and the other ministers had not been told about this 'very impressive' planning capability. I do remember that Guthrie told me not to include a section on my concerns about the legality of the operation when I briefed ministers. Somewhat to his rather obvious annoyance, I decided I should leave it in.

My hard-working team was really coming on. Weeks of demanding training and some vital operational experience were paying off. With occasional reinforcement by some talented single-service officers, such as Paul Newton from the Army, the Joint Force Headquarters seemed to make light work of every challenge thrown its way. Then came a crisis on the other side of the world.

In the late summer of 1999, the Australian government was coming under intense international pressure to intervene in East Timor. The long and bloody struggle by the East Timorese for independence from Indonesia had moved into an acute phase, following a UN-supervised referendum on autonomy, which was rejected by an overwhelming majority.

The *de facto* vote in favour of independence was followed by an orgy of punitive violence and looting by pro-integration militias backed by elements of the Indonesian Army. At least a thousand people were killed, hundreds of thousands fled or were deported to West Timor, and towns and villages – including the capital Dili – were ransacked. The UN responded to the violence by deploying troops on the island less than a month after the referendum, and followed up by introducing a transitional administration as years of occupation came to an end and independence dawned.

The Australians were anxious to avoid an escalating conflict in their backyard, featuring their ally, Indonesia, and agreed to lead the UN force, rapidly named the International Force East Timor (INTERFET). This was a UN-mandated deployment by national contingents working to Australian command that would hold the ring until the UN could take over in a more conventional peacekeeping role as soon as was practicable. It was regarded as the only way that an effective response to the crisis could be developed fast enough amid fears of further blood-letting. In any case, the Australians, under Prime Minister John Howard, were not prepared to go 'blue beret' from the outset, privately concerned that they were about to

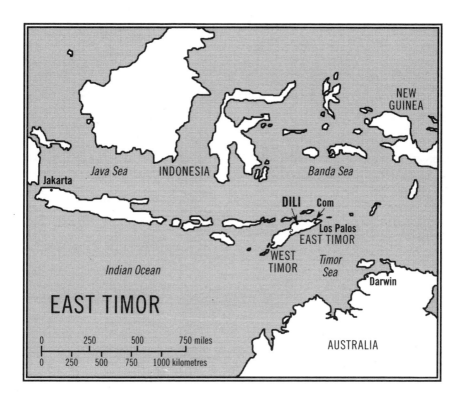

enter a war, not a peacekeeping operation. The fear in Canberra was that Australian troops would end up fighting either the Indonesian Army or their proxy militia in East Timor. These were men who had prosecuted a reign of terror in much of the country and fought against the East Timorese freedom fighters or Falantil in a low-level conflict that had scarred the community for decades. In fact, we now know that the Indonesians had decided they were not going to make a stand over East Timor after the referendum, but they were going to teach the people a lesson in the process of leaving.

I was scrambled at short notice to Australia, initially only to see how we could help our old ally. I don't think for one moment the people in London who sent me thought we would end up putting British boots on the ground. It was, most probably, to be a case of offering logistical help – mainly air-transport assets – to the Australians. Given our recent experience of similar operations, I was to advise them on how to go about it, if they felt a need. I arrived in Sydney on 7 September and spent a hectic few days shuttling between Sydney and Canberra, seeing key Australian military leaders and visiting their equivalent of our Permanent Joint Headquarters (PJHQ). I also briefed Robin Cook, the Foreign Secretary, who flew into Sydney and was keen to know my thoughts on what we could do.

I am one of the few people in Whitehall, and certainly in the military sphere, who have a high regard for Cook. I know he must have been difficult to work with at times, but I found him down to earth and thoroughly focused on the issues at hand. In fact, he rang me when I was in Dili two or three weeks later, which caused great panic in my headquarters. The cry went up: 'The Foreign Secretary wants to speak to the Brigadier.' Cook was at the UN in New York but he had bothered to make the effort to speak to me directly to find out how things were going and did not rely on his staff to do it for him.

During this preliminary phase, I met Major General Peter Cosgrove for the first time. 'Cos' was the epitome of an Australian General – a large, stocky, strong-jawed individual, who wore a slouch hat and displayed a no-nonsense attitude. He had won a Military Cross in Vietnam. A few years earlier, he had been a member of the directing staff at Camberley. He is now Governor General of Australia and, while I know I am biased, I cannot think of a better person for such an important job. Back in 1999, Cosgrove was slated to command the Australian contingent and INTERFET, and was the man to whom I would find myself reporting in East Timor as British national contingent commander.

Cosgrove was understandably cautious and focused on the security of his force until he was absolutely certain there was little risk to it. Although I fully understood his concerns on that score, I rapidly came to the conclusion, once we had deployed to East Timor, that the threat level was low and fast declining. In my view, it was imperative that we moved quickly on to the humanitarian phase – helping thousands of displaced people and rebuilding the infrastructure. Although there were some tense moments and sporadic attacks on us by the pro-integration militias in the first few days after we deployed, it was clear this was not Vietnam all over again. This was a disagreement about timing between Cosgrove and me, not about principle, but we were to cross swords over it before my tour in East Timor was over.

As capable as the Australian command team was, it quickly became clear that they were feeling their way in terms of how to carry out their mission under acute time pressure. By their own admission, they had little experience of command of an intervention of this kind. Their embryonic joint-command capability was much more limited than Britain's and weighted towards the Army. Their officers were still learning the ropes in terms of theatre-level planning, which was another cause of tension in our relationship, because my small team and I were a long way down the curve in this area. Wrongly, I suspect at times I showed my impatience. But the Australians needed us, politically and militarily, to come in alongside them, in part to ensure that this did not end up looking like an Australian-only intervention.

As so often was the case, no one else, even from within the region, was ready in time to deploy alongside the Australians. So Britain, from 8,000 miles away, stepped into the breach. Not for the first time, I clashed with my superiors at the Ministry of Defence, on this occasion over whom we should deploy. London was adamant, stubbornly so, that this was a job for the Spearhead Battalion, which would have to fly out from Britain. My view was that we had a capable battalion in the region, already acclimatised and ready to move at short notice. For them to deploy would take a quarter of the time it would take an equivalent coming from Britain. This was the Second Battalion Royal Gurkha Rifles, based in Brunei. I had visited them earlier that year and had been impressed by the soldiers and their commanding officer, Lieutenant Colonel Mark Lillington-Price. In the end, I resorted to leap-frogging the Brigadiers and the Generals at the MoD and lobbied Charles Guthrie, who as usual saw the sense in what I was saying.

Once the decision was taken to send the Gurkhas, preparations gathered pace. I continued to shuttle between Sydney and Brisbane before moving up to Darwin from where we would fly to Dili. A small group of us – five or six – joined Cosgrove's headquarters to help develop their plan and focus on getting the British element ready. The MoD allocated us two RAF Hercules, and the Type 42 destroyer HMS *Glasgow*, which was in the region, was placed under my command along with a small special forces detachment from the Special Boat Service.

While I was in Darwin – sharing digs with the BBC TV correspondent David Shukman (Darwin was full of soldiers and media and you had to find accommodation where you could) – I met John Howard to discuss the crisis, and Admiral Chris Barrie, the Chief of the Defence Force. He described the East Timor intervention as the most significant military undertaking by Australia since the Second World War.

I gave one of my first television interviews in Darwin, to Australia's ABC Television, and I used it to try to smooth any ruffled feathers. Asked why I was there, I replied, 'I don't know, but you have come to our help repeatedly this century, so maybe it's time we did a little bit to help you.' That went down well with the Aussies. I asked the ABC journalist for some tips on doing live television. He said, 'You're doing fine. Just have a conversation. Forget there's a camera in front of you, forget the sound man, just talk normally.' It was the best bit of advice I was ever given on that score.

Another task in Darwin was to convince the MoD that I should deploy to Dili myself – the view in London was that I could do my job perfectly well from Darwin, which was patently absurd, given the distance involved. Once again, I used my contacts in Guthrie's office, in particular Group Captain John Ponsonby, his outstanding Deputy Principal Staff Officer, to break the impasse.

Three weeks to the day after the referendum that had sparked the crisis, Cosgrove and I flew into East Timor along with around 1,000 Australian troops, and 240 Gurhkas. We found a devastated country and a terrified people. Large areas of Dili were in ruins; the roads were deserted and homes were still burning after the looting and vandalism of the past few weeks. The acrid smell of burning hung over the whole city and many streets were littered with the detritus of mass looting. The harbour was full of small Indonesian craft, taking everything they could off the island. Outside the capital, much of the forest had been cut down and the towns were again deserted and smoldering. Driving around, you would see nothing except the odd Indonesian Army vehicle, with the locals nowhere to be seen.

Despite the bleak setting, I immediately sensed that the Indonesian Army was going to be compliant, although there were suggestions at the time of our arrival that their move to leave East Timor was a con. Their officers and soldiers didn't welcome us but they didn't stop us, either. They were smart and well turned out even if resentful of our presence. In our first meeting with them, we agreed where we would take their place, and our zones of responsibility. The British were given the area to the north of Dili and the district around the UN compound on the edge of the city, backing on to the hills. This was high profile because the looting of the compound by an Indonesian-backed mob had featured in TV coverage a few weeks earlier. Those scenes had been instrumental in convincing the wider world and the UN Security Council that something had to be done about the crisis.

I went straight up to the compound to negotiate its takeover with the Indonesians. I stressed to the Brigadier General in charge that they should stop destroying everything. The eyes of the world, and especially their fellow soldiers globally, were on them. It was all over for them in East Timor, but I suggested that it was not too late for them collectively to salvage something of their professional reputations and come back into the international fold. I know Peter Cosgrove was playing the same tune at his level. It seemed to resonate and, on the whole, I think it worked. In my case, the Brigadier General heard me out and was courteous as we began the handover.

The second time I went into the compound I took Ian Martin with me. He was the UN representative for East Timor. It was a very emotional moment for him; he couldn't believe what they had done to the place and all their vehicles. Thousands of pounds worth of white Toyotas had been destroyed and only one or two rooms were still functional. For the first few days, this was where we established our headquarters.

Then we set to, securing key ground and installations, setting up vehicle and personnel checkpoints to intercept any movement by the militias or the Indonesian Army, establishing field clinics and getting out on the streets on regular patrols. We encountered almost no resistance. There was only one notably threatening encounter that I recall, when two lorries loaded with pro-integration militia fighters drove towards a Gurkha checkpoint in Dili – an amazingly smart sandbagged one, something the Gurkhas took great pride in – but then deliberately turned off down a side-road, so no shots were fired. Those lorries were found in the docks where the militia were taken off in boats by the Indonesian Army.

Scenes like that convinced me we could move quickly to a hearts and minds operation. I became concerned that the uncompromising posture of the Australians could make things more difficult than need be. At one point, they stopped even controlled traffic movement in one part of Dili, something that was guaranteed to annoy the locals. Peter Cosgrove soon resolved such inconsistencies but for a while it just baffled the people, who thought we had come to help them.

It was a tricky situation because Cosgrove was the overall commander and I was the British national commander, there to support him. I was very careful to ensure that the Gurkhas operational tasking came from the Australians. I didn't want to interpose myself between Cosgrove and our troops. I could have vetoed orders – London had given me red-card authority if I needed it – but I was working with the Australians and made sure I knew what they were trying to do.

Looking back, it was more instinct than anything that told me how things were panning out. Through hard training and growing experience, I must have been developing a much better grasp of the link between the tactical and the strategic. It is what a German General would call *fingerspitzengefuhl* or finger-tip feeling. You can have it at battlefield level, and like most decent soldiers I have some of that but I was also developing it at the operational, or theatre level. As Clausewitz's aphorism suggests, war is an extension of politics by other means; you win by deploying a multiplicity of weapons systems, only one of which is military. My time in East Timor under Cosgrove, not least observing the ease with which he switched from the tactical to the operational to the strategic, and communicated so well at all three levels, was to serve me well in Sierra Leone and Afghanistan.

The short-term difference of emphasis with my Australian comrades in arms was graphically captured for me during a conversation with Cosgrove, whose intelligence officers had been talking up the threat, while we were on board HMS *Glasgow*, shortly before she was due to set sail from Dili after ten days there. We were on deck, leaning on a rail discussing progress while waiting to do some media interviews. The bay was flat calm and in the distance we could make out the smoke from fires still burning in the capital, although by then things had quietened down.

'This is really going very well,' I said.

'David, don't be naïve,' he replied. 'They are *still* out there, they are very dangerous and we're going to have to get them.'

'But General, where are they? I don't think there are many left and the Indonesians are on their way out.'

Not long after that conversation I went up a windy road into the hills to a village just inside our area of operations where hundreds of internal refugees from Dili were sheltering, fearing for their lives. Australian special forces were near the village, all camouflaged up, ready for action. We drove straight in, in a couple of Land Rovers, and I went and found the local tribal elders and explained what was happening. Speaking through an interpreter, I stood in the small square and told that fearful and suspicious group of people that it was now safe to return to their homes.

'The Indonesians are going,' I told them. 'Dili is waiting for you to reclaim it.'

And I got cheered. It was the first time anyone had told them what was going on.

'How many of you want to go back?' I asked.

All of them put their hands up. Later that day, we started doing ferry runs up to the hills, transporting people back to their houses.

Eventually, the tensions between myself and the Australians boiled over. They had put together a small force to go out to the east end of the island where there were reports of a humanitarian crisis involving thousands of displaced people. I was pleased that the Australians were going. In my view, this was exactly the sort of thing we should be doing. This was also the reassuring view of my outstanding New Zealand counterpart Brigadier Martyn Dunne (later a highly regarded New Zealand High Commissioner in Canberra).

Each evening, Cosgrove would hold his Orders Group meeting. By that stage, it included not just us but also Americans from Pacific Command. At the meeting that night, the Chief of Staff – who appeared not to like my influence over Cosgrove, if I had any – went through the orders for the next day and finished by saying abruptly that the humanitarian relief operation to the east had been cancelled. Were there any questions?

'Why has the relief operation been cancelled?' I asked, feeling the hostile attention of Australian officers on my back. There were no resources to do it and no real sense it was necessary, I was told. I explained that I thought we had agreed the day before that it was very necessary; it was a dire situation and we needed to do something about it. The Chief of Staff looked at Cosgrove and he looked at me.

'David,' said Cosgrove, 'we haven't yet got the resources for that sort of task on top of everything else we're doing.'

'But that's one reason why we're here,' I replied.

'Do *you* want to do it?' Cosgrove continued, clearly irritated.

I said that I thought the Gurkhas had the capacity to take it on.

'OK, David. Fine. Let's see if that's possible,' replied the General.

As the meeting broke up, I could see the Chief of Staff having an earnest conversation with Cosgrove. Suddenly, the General, at the top of his booming voice, intoned, 'Gentlemen, clear the room, clear the room. Brigadier Richards and I have got to have a little discussion, just him and me.'

I thought, 'Here goes, I'm for it now.' We stood facing each other, alone.

'David, is it time I told your people back in London that your time here is over?' he said.

'General, you tell me why you're saying that.'

He replied with words to the effect that I was being difficult and that I was second-guessing his headquarters staff. I could feel the bile rising and I certainly was not going to take this without standing up for myself. Given the Indonesians' largely helpful stance, it was time to encourage Cosgrove to re-address his priorities, something that no one else around him seemed prepared to do.

'Right General,' I said, swallowing hard. 'You have got a bunch of officers beneath you who rightly worship the ground you stand on, but as a result they're not prepared to give you the sound advice you deserve. I will tell you what's most important right now – the rapidly deteriorating humanitarian crisis. We need to start addressing it urgently or we are going to fail.'

It was a heated exchange but, with the air cleared, and given the big-hearted man he is, we talked constructively for about half an hour and agreed to sleep on our differences. I still went to my bed wondering whether this was the end for me and I would be on a plane back to London before the day was out – a case of promising career over.

Early in the morning there was a knock on my door. It was the aide-de-camp to Cosgrove.

'What time are you going to put me on a plane?' I asked.

'Don't worry, Brigadier,' he said, 'I think you're fine but the General would like to see you in one hour.'

I drove down to see Cosgrove.

'David, I'll accept your offer for the Gurkhas to do it. It's a shitty task but if you want to do it, I'm happy to authorise a convoy.'

Knowing I was stepping on thin ice, I couldn't help but respond, with a grateful smile, 'General, you still haven't really got it. This is in good part what we are here to do.'

'Don't test me, David, don't test me,' he replied.

In the background, the UN had also had a go at him over the need to relieve the suffering in the east and Ian Martin had helped advance my cause.

The next day a twenty-strong detachment of Gurkhas led by Major Tim Warrington escorted a humanitarian relief convoy over very poor roads all the way to the east end of the island. When they got to the regional capital of Los Palos, they discovered that the food they had taken with them was desperately needed. While there, Major Warrington was informed by a Catholic priest of an even more acute problem in the port of Com, just north of Los Palos. The priest said thousands more refugees, without proper food or water, were being held against their will in the town by armed militia men and were in desperate need of help.

Unable to raise the Australians on the radio for further orders, Warrington contacted me on our net, unsure what he should do next. I told him to rely on our doctrine of 'mission command'. The mission in this case was to relieve the humanitarian crisis in the east and that by definition, I said, should include the village on the coast. This was neatly summed up in the pithy instruction, 'F****** go up there and do your job.'

Warrington, who was awarded the MBE for his conduct on that mission, went up that night. His men were fired on a couple of times as they approached the village but the militia dispersed to the hills and the Gurkhas were able to liberate the people who had been held captive. The soldiers fired a couple of warning shots at one point and managed to capture four of the twelve or so men who had been terrorising more than two thousand people.

Although the mission was a big success, the Australian headquarters staff were still not entirely happy with it. They subsequently proscribed such 'freelancing' and indicated that mission command was not to be used in future. What particularly irked them was that unfortunately most of the media had chosen to cover the Gurkha operation in Com, ignoring the impressive move by the Australians out of Dili to the west on the same day.

The Australians initially had a difficult relationship with the media in East Timor. To start with, they tried to restrict access to the island to all but twenty-four nominated correspondents, but plenty of others managed to get in and it was clear that the policy was not working. In the meantime, a consequence of the Australians' generally hostile attitude to journalists was that the Gurkhas got more air time in Australia than they did. The mounting resentment and frustration among the rank and file of Australian soldiers was brilliantly summed up by a Major in a television interview. He was asked what it was like working with the Gurkhas, to which he replied with words to the effect that it was 'great to be one of two thousand Aussies here in support of two hundred f****** Gurkhas!'

After my work with the media in Darwin, I did quite a bit more from East Timor, including a couple of live appearances on BBC's *Newsnight* when I was interviewed in the early hours of the East Timorese morning by Jeremy Paxman. I was grateful for the opportunity to get across to the public back home what we were trying to achieve. Of course, I was expecting a grilling but I never seemed to get one. After one interview, we were still talking and I said, 'Jeremy, you didn't give me nearly as hard a time as I was expecting.'

'Brigadier,' he replied, 'you're not a politician and you were telling the truth, so I had no need.'

Attending to the media was time-consuming but I learnt then, and benefited from doing so many times later on in my career, that it was essential to work with the press during a campaign. I regarded it as another vital arm of activity to go alongside the military, political and humanitarian work we were doing. My view on this was to influence what I did the following year in Sierra Leone, my conduct as NATO commander in Afghanistan in 2006–07 and my tenure as Chief of the Defence Staff. I always wanted to ensure that the media understood what we were trying to do and sought constructive relations with editors and journalists. Many senior military figures seek to avoid the press and I can understand why. I have been let down a number of times through misinterpretation by journalists, by an inflammatory or misleading headline or mistakes in reporting. But I still regard working with journalists as a risk a commander must take because of the opportunity it presents to communicate with the public and sometimes with your superiors. Too many times, though, my bosses, particularly politicians, have ignored the 90 per cent good reporting we achieved through this approach and chosen instead to concentrate their attention on the 10 per cent that can be less positive.

Early on in the East Timor deployment, a tragic event highlighted another aspect of media coverage of war zones and the importance of journalists not putting the lives of others in danger in the headlong pursuit of a story. Jon Swain of the *Sunday Times*, who had worked for that paper in Cambodia, where his life was saved by a translator in an episode portrayed in the film *The Killing Fields*, got into trouble when he decided to venture outside Dili. He and Chip Hires, an American photographer working for the Gamma agency, had persuaded their driver and translator to take them up into the hills at dusk to get a feel for the state of play outside the capital.

Not many miles outside Dili their car was stopped by militia gunmen. In a terrifying episode, the driver was hit on the side of the face with a rifle butt, blinding him in one eye, and the translator was led away never to be seen again. Swain and Hires managed to escape into the trees and Swain made a call on his dying satellite phone to his London office asking for help. The paper, in turn, called my headquarters. Having no armoured vehicles of our own, I asked the Australians to mount a rescue operation. This was successfully accomplished by troops in armoured vehicles, supported by a helicopter, and the three men were brought back to Dili.

The next morning as I was on my way to the semi-functioning hotel on the waterfront that was used for the regular morning media briefing, I saw Swain in a vehicle with his driver all bandaged up alongside him. He thanked me for organising his rescue and said he felt very guilty about the loss of his interpreter. He also informed me that the Australians had refused to treat his driver and did not want to fly him out, a decision I managed to get overturned. Jon Swain is a decent man and an intrepid journalist of considerable courage but it annoyed me then, and it still does now, that we had to send Australian soldiers out to rescue him when they had many other things to do.

A similar episode occurred in Sierra Leone the following year when an American journalist and a Spanish cameraman were killed after straying into an area we had expressly forbidden them from entering. When their colleagues started having a go at me for not protecting them, I really turned on them, emphasising that their friends' foolhardiness had led not only to their own deaths but to the deaths of a number of innocent locals as well. I was angry about it because I had seen this sort of thing happen too often.

A feature of the British deployment in East Timor was the excellent cooperation between the civil and military elements. Normally, where the Department for International Development (DFID) is established, their people are bureaucratic, quite slow to respond and restricted by tight rules. In the case of East Timor, they sent Dr Gilbert Greenhall, a man absolutely after my own heart. He is a seat of the pants reconstruction and development expert of whom Britain can be proud. Due to his flexibility, agility and preparedness to back his own judgement, Britain played a much bigger role on the development side than it could possibly have otherwise done. For example, Dr Greenhall was instrumental in finding vehicles and radios for the Gurkhas to use and when Major Warrington and his detachment set off on their relief mission to the east, he provided the money overnight to buy the stores to take with them. Normally, that would require a much longer process. Dr Greenhall, ably supported by retired Gurkha Colonel Bob Churcher, contracted by DFID for this operation, cut through the red tape, allowing dynamic civil/military cooperation to occur. Not for Gilbert the rather ponderous and often suspicious approach towards the military that DFID, sadly, sometimes exhibits, although things are better now. He and his team concentrated on restoring water and food supplies and helping people get back to their homes, all the time working closely with us. We provided the security for him and we were his intelligence arm. If we made a recommendation, the chances are he would follow it because he saw us as part of a bigger UK team.

Another key player was Lieutenant Colonel Lee Marler of the Army Legal Corps, who was my operational lawyer. Modern Generals need to have in their back pocket not the sapper and gunner of tradition, but a media man and a lawyer. If you haven't got those cards in your deck, you're lost. The Australians soon realised that they needed to put the new country of East Timor on a legal footing but they didn't have anyone within their military with that background. I had someone in Lee Marler. In the month or so that we were in East Timor, he worked all hours to draft a new constitution. He deserves huge credit for what he did. He based it on the international laws of war and it served as a transitional structure while a new long-term constitution was drafted, which the UN did the following year. The Australians did not much like the fact that my lawyer had done it but took it on the chin, generously giving Lee many plaudits when he left. Since leaving the Army, Marler has become a successful barrister with his own chambers.

I was in East Timor for a month and by the time I left in early October the Indonesians had gone. General Cosgrove and the Australians were well into their stride, at the head of a force that would eventually include twenty-two contributing countries, and they were doing a fine job. I handed over my command to Mark Lillington-Price, who became an acting Colonel and the Gurkhas stayed until Christmas.

From our point of view, it had been a successful operation and the first big test of the new Joint Rapid Reaction Force concept. Although I may appear critical of the Australians in those first few weeks, under General Cosgrove's inspirational leadership they learnt quickly and the operation should be viewed as a model of its kind. It was a privilege to work alongside some hugely capable and motivated people.

East Timor is still not as prosperous to this day as it might have been but it is a growing, free and democratic country, and it has discovered oil. If the Australians had not gone there with the commitment and speed that they did, it could have remained an Indonesian fiefdom in which people would have been oppressed for years to come.

Back in the UK, I was off to Egypt within days and made visits to the United States in between more training in the autumn. In February and March of 2000, Mozambique was affected by atrocious flooding that claimed hundreds of lives. My team was tasked with assessing what help Britain could give and I sent two officers to Maputo to report back. Naturally, as the commander of the JFHQ, I was ready to go, too, but I was contending with growing personal resentment about my role at one- and two-star level inside the Ministry of Defence.

There was a view among some senior officers that I had been on a bit of a roll, liaising directly with Robin Cook, running the high-profile British contribution to the East Timor deployment and working the channels with Charles Guthrie's office when I could not get what I wanted through the regular chain of command. My early exploits in Sierra Leone – of which more in the next two chapters – had earned me the nickname 'Richards of Africa' and there was a feeling that it was time I was put back in my box. It was professional envy and it materialised in an order countermanding my decision to head to Maputo myself. Despite my protestations that I was the commander and held responsibility for our assessment, I was not allowed to go.

I realised there was no point in disobeying such a clear order so I sent Lieutenant Colonel Andy Canning of the Royal Marines in my place, giving him my red tabs as he boarded the plane so he'd look the part. Then I got into a bit of a battle with the MoD. One Air Commodore, whom I considered particularly difficult, would go into meetings and say there was no need for me to deploy. This would, in his phrase 'up the ante' or, even worse, 'risk the UK getting its hands caught in the mangle'. In fact, I was trying to do things properly. It was an intolerable situation for any commander to find himself in. The people for whom I was responsible expected their commander to command them. I needed to see conditions for myself on the ground to satisfy myself that things were in order and I had a duty of care to my officers.

In the end, I went to Mozambique to visit my team but instead of staying for twenty-four hours as had been reluctantly agreed, I remained there for a week. We sent Puma helicopters that did an important job ferrying people and lifting food and our help was gratefully received – quite a contrast to the pathetic squabbling in London behind the scenes.

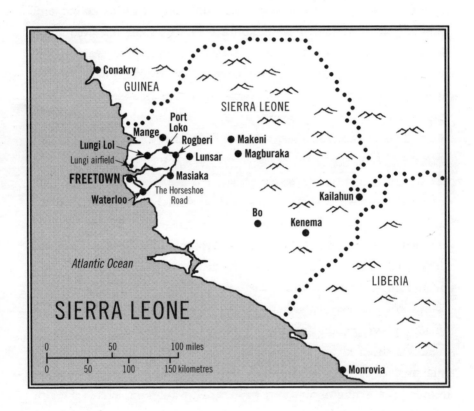

SEVEN

Freetown at War

As the former colonial power, Britain has a long-standing interest in Sierra Leone. The small West African state with a population of some five million people became independent in 1961. It was chronically poor, its tiny economy in decline, and its government was a ramshackle affair based on the writ of over two hundred tribal chiefs. The adult literacy rate stood at just 7.7 per cent.

The country achieved a measure of stability, and even prosperity, with the accession to power of its first president, Siaka Stevens, in 1971. But Stevens was a dictator, and a corrupt one at that, who retired in 1985 with a fortune of some $500 million, having turned the country's diamond industry into his personal preserve. He nominated his weak and equally corrupt army commander, Major General Joseph Momoh, as his successor.

Under Momoh, the institutions of Sierra Leone's society collapsed and the systematic looting of the country's diamond wealth continued to corrupt every aspect of the body politic. The education system stopped functioning when the government stopped paying teachers, unpaid civil servants ransacked their offices and much of the professional class emigrated to Europe and the United States. The endemic corruption, mismanagement and poverty was a toxic combination that was to give rise to a culture of lawlessness and eventually a civil war that reduced Sierra Leone to a state of anarchy by the 1990s.

That civil war shocked the world with its brutality – amputation of hands and feet, often of children, was a common feature plus random murder, rape and even cannibalism. It started in 1991 when a small group of about a hundred fighters entered Sierra Leone from Liberia. The Revolutionary United Front (RUF) led by Foday Sankoh, a 54-year-old former corporal in the Sierra Leone Army (SLA), was committed to the overthrow of Momoh's government. It also entertained ambitious plans for a pan-African revolution based on the ideas of the Libyan dictator Muammar Gaddafi.

The RUF had trained in Libya and Burkina Faso and was backed by Charles Taylor of Liberia, who wanted to get his hands on the Kono diamond fields in eastern Sierra Leone, close to the border with Liberia. He was also determined to prevent Sierra Leone from being used as a base by his opponents in Liberia. Taylor was eventually convicted by the International Criminal Court on eleven counts of war crimes and crimes against humanity in Sierra Leone.

The RUF rapidly developed from a collection of idealistic young men intent on ridding their country of Momoh, to a gang of drugged-up sadists ruling through brutality and terror, kidnapping young people, executing tribal chiefs and anyone associated with the government and living off the illicit profits of stolen diamonds. The RUF gained the support of gangs of unemployed youths and illicit diamond diggers and made a speciality out of the forcible recruitment of children. Indoctrinated and provided with drugs and weapons, they became a singular feature of the war. In addition to control of the country's diamond wealth, the RUF eventually overran Sierra Leone's bauxite and titanium mines as well.

The conflict ebbed and flowed throughout the 1990s with a constantly changing interaction of forces and alliances. The main players were the SLA and various splinters of it and the RUF. Among other irregulars were the Kamajor fighters – officially known as the Sierra Leone Civil Defence Forces – who were traditional hunters, and a group of opportunistic thugs who became known as the West Side Boys. There were also mercenaries from South Africa, Britain and elsewhere and a Nigerian-led, UN-mandated, intervention force – the Economic Community of West African States Monitoring Group, known by its acronym ECOMOG. There was a terrible unpredictability about the fighting and the fighters from the point of view of ordinary people. The war was characterised by shifting allegiances among irregulars and soldiers alike, the latter known as 'sobels' – soldiers by day, rebels by night.

The conflict had a devastating impact, claiming more than 50,000 lives, leaving thousands more mutilated and hundreds of thousands displaced at various times. It destroyed what was left of Sierra Leone's primitive basic services, leaving its government in chaos, its armed forces fractured, its towns and cities looted and its people traumatised and fearful. By the late 1990s, Sierra Leone was still at, or near, the bottom of world tables on poverty and development and had become a deeply failed state.

One beacon of light in an otherwise dismal landscape was the appointment of a new president after a democratic nationwide vote in March 1996, itself the result of huge international pressure. The election of Ahmad Tejan Kabbah, a former UN development worker, gave him a legitimacy that previous leaders had lacked. In their support for him, Britain and the international community had a focus for their efforts to stabilise the country. But Kabbah had, at best, a tenuous hold on power and the people paid a heavy price for his election. The RUF took revenge by cutting off the hands, arms or legs of villagers who had dared to vote for him.

After becoming president, Kabbah made a flimsy peace deal with the RUF leader Sankoh in late 1996 – something that was honoured in the breach. Mounting frustration within the Army, which was still hungry for power, led to a bloody coup by Major Johnny Paul Koroma. During the fighting with Kabbah's forces, large areas of Freetown were wrecked. Once in control, Koroma entered into a power-sharing arrangement of his own with the RUF. With Kabbah now in exile in Guinea, the new regime was condemned by the international community and the UN authorised ECOMOG to intervene. The Nigerian force launched a fierce attack on Freetown, which brought Koroma to the negotiating table. Military pressure eventually forced him out and Kabbah was restored to power in a ruined city in March 1998.

Tony Blair's government had become heavily involved in the battle for power in Freetown. It had faced allegations, in the so-called 'Arms to Africa' scandal, that it had flouted a UN arms embargo on Sierra Leone, which it had helped to draft, by supplying weapons to Kabbah. In the event, the weapons never reached the then deposed president. But the scandal, which involved the mercenary company Sandline International, was a major blow to the Blair government's doctrine of a foreign policy with an 'ethical' dimension. It also had a big impact on Robin Cook, the Foreign Secretary, the architect of that policy, who at one point offered to resign if any blame was attached to him over the affair.

I was sent to Sierra Leone for the first time in January 1999, nine months before the East Timor crisis described in the previous chapter. Kabbah was again in a perilous position. In alliance with Koroma's forces, the RUF had advanced across the country and into the capital, reversing the gains of the previous year by the Nigerian soldiers of ECOMOG and the rump of the SLA. True to form, I am afraid, the Nigerians were not bad at the tactical level, and knew how to fight, but some of their senior officers had started getting into businesses and making money, something that inevitably blunted their military edge.

The Blair government was concerned about Kabbah being deposed for a second time as the RUF rampaged towards and then into Freetown, killing and mutilating thousands of people as it did so. In my role as commander of the Joint Force Headquarters I was tasked to see if there was anything we could do to help.

I set off with a small team that a Special Forces officer and a protection party from the Royal Marines. Our first stop was Dakar in Senegal where the Type 23 frigate HMS *Norfolk* had been diverted from a trip to the West Indies to pick us up. I did an interview for CNN on the jetty explaining that we were going to Sierra Leone to try to assess what had been happening and what we could do. It was not possible for us to fly into Freetown because the airfield was considered too exposed to rebel fire.

Our next stop – for refuelling – was Conakry, the Guinean capital. When we had berthed, two black cars with shaded windows came down to meet the ship and two rather dodgy-looking men in suits and sunglasses emerged. 'Brigadier Richards is to come and see the president tomorrow morning at ten o'clock,' we were told. The next morning, on cue, they returned, ready to pick me up. I had with me Patrick O'Brien, the deputy ambassador to Senegal, who was also ambassador to Conakry. He had volunteered to travel down with us in case we needed his local knowledge. I discovered he had been trying to present his credentials in the Guinean capital for about eighteen months without success.

Much against the wishes of my close-protection team, who wisely pointed out that we had no idea who these people were and that at the very least we should travel in an approved vehicle, I decided we should accept the offer of the men in suits. As we embarked on a white-knuckle ride into the city, I found myself talking to a charming English-speaking chap who turned out to be the Guinean minister for mines. It dawned on me that this was going to be new territory for me; I had never met a president in my life.

Eventually, we reached the shell of a bullet-marked building. A completely ruined one stood just beyond it. Not long before there had been an attack on the president's palace, one of many attempts on his life. We were still chatting away as we walked under an arched gateway, and I saw what I thought was a janitor sitting in a chair by a pillar, waving the heat away with a fan made of palm frond. The minister suddenly stopped me, apologised for interrupting, and said, 'Brigadier Richards, let me introduce you to the president.' The 'janitor' turned out to be Lansana Conte, the feared second president of Guinea, who informed us that he would see us both 'in a minute'.

We were ushered into what was a typical official reception room in that part of the world. It featured a long line of expensive-looking black armchairs along the walls and two, even bigger, rather tasteless white leather ones at one end. We waited for some minutes. Then the president came in and indicated for me to sit beside him – a position of honour. I had no idea about diplomacy and made it all up as I went along. I started by saying that Her Majesty sent her good wishes and that our prime minister, Tony Blair, did too. 'Ah, very good,' said the chain-smoking president as all the ministers in the chairs along the walls nodded in agreement. Then he asked me about Sierra Leone. He was understandably most concerned that instability there could spread to his own country. He was keen to see Kabbah retain power, having hosted him in exile twice in the last four years. I got from him a good feel for what was going on in the region, especially the pernicious role played by Charles Taylor and by Sankoh, his henchman in Sierra Leone, whom I would go on to know well. Conte questioned me about world affairs. I gradually realised that he knew I had arrived in Conakry only because he had seen the interview on CNN that I had done in Dakar. I got the impression that he was almost totally cut off; alienated from France, Guinea's former colonial power, he was viewed with suspicion within the region and relied on television news to find out what was going on.

After about two hours of trying to sound knowledgeable on a range of subjects about which I knew little, I was running out of ideas. I thought, 'Sod it, what else can I say?'

What I did say was, 'Look, while I'm here, Mr President, could I ask you to accept the credentials of Mr Patrick O'Brien, who is our accredited ambassador to your country?'

Poor O'Brien's chin dropped on to his stomach. But it did the trick, something I have always teased my colleagues in the Foreign Office about.

Towards the end of what was a fairly gruelling session, the president said, to my astonishment, 'Brigadier, I see you are an economist.' It dawned on me that someone must have dredged up some sort of CV that said I had a BSc Econ from Cardiff. Actually, my subject was politics.

'I have studied it a little bit, Mr President,' I replied warily.

'We have a World Bank plan for our economy,' he said. 'My finance minister [to whom he pointed among the men in the chairs] sort of understands it, but no one else does. Can you talk to him and explain what we're meant to do?'

'Of course, Mr President,' I said.

Afterwards the finance minister took me aside and showed me the plan, which was pretty sophisticated from what I could see.

'I sort of understand this, and I have a degree from Harvard, but I have no one here who can help me implement it. It is actually hopeless,' he told me.

I remember thinking that we have got to do better by these countries in terms of helping them, a view that was reinforced by my subsequent experience in East Timor, Sierra Leone and elsewhere in the developing world. It struck me that too often the West and western institutions, such as the World Bank, would come up with highly sophisticated plans for unstable countries that salved their collective consciences but were too complex to be implemented. The absence of a strata of educated people in a country such as Guinea or Sierra Leone meant that often these plans were worth little more than the paper they were written on.

As a Major General, I came up with the concept of 'embedded support' whereby countries such as Britain would pay for real experts to spend five years – or whatever was needed – living in the country in need of aid to help implement a plan of this sort. I spoke on the concept widely, both in political and military circles, and made some headway, I believe, in drawing attention to this problem.

Before we set off for Freetown, I had a meeting over lunch with Peter Penfold, the brave and distinguished High Commissioner for Sierra Leone, whose career was unjustly brought to a premature end by the 'Arms to Africa' scandal. He was already a hero in Sierra Leone – he had been made a paramount chief – having helped evacuate hundreds of expatriates from Freetown as the RUF advanced in 1997. He had fled with Kabbah when Koroma took over and had then helped the deposed president plan his return from Guinea. He was now back in Conakry, after London ordered him out again amid fears that he might be captured by the RUF.

We met at the Hotel Camayenne where Penfold had set himself up as the High Commissioner in exile, and he gave me useful background and advice on who to make contact with in Freetown. He also made a special request. Would I be good enough to pop into one of his most cherished places in the capital, the Milton Margai School for the Blind? He was worried about the fate of the sixty or so children there, with the fighting ebbing and flowing throughout the city. I promised I would find the time to visit them. A serious, committed and conscientious man, Penfold saw the struggle for power in Sierra Leone in straightforward terms, and his analysis was essentially correct. It pitted the democratic forces for good of Kabbah against the anarchistic evil of the RUF. In my view, Peter was scapegoated over the 'Arms to Africa' affair – he was said to have got too close to the Kabbah government – which was grossly unfair, and he remains an individual to whom Britain is indebted.

Back on board HMS *Norfolk* we headed south for Freetown, enjoying a brief cruise in the sunshine, which turned out to be very much the calm before the storm. When we arrived in the bay off the city, we could see Alpha jets of the Nigerian Air Force bombing RUF columns advancing on the outskirts. Even in the deeper area of the bay, where *Norfolk* took up station, there were bodies in the water and they appeared to have been recently killed. Closer in, we came across more in the shallows; there could be no doubt that we were entering an active war zone.

To start with, the captain, Commander Bruce Williams, required me and my small team of five staff officers to wear white anti-flash kit in case of attack, and confined us to the lower decks. After a couple of hours, I decided I had had enough and headed up to the bridge where I discovered his officers were having great difficulty making contact with the Nigerians. They seemed overly cautious to me and in the end, in true yachtsman fashion, I resorted to getting on the ship's VHF radio myself and hailing two Nigerian Navy patrol vessels. We could see them elsewhere in the bay and eventually they grudgingly acknowledged our presence.

My close-protection party, led by the highly competent Rory Copinger-Symes, went ashore first to get the lie of the land and organise a couple of 'technicals' – Toyota jeeps – that we could use to get around. Captain Copinger-Symes judged that it was safe for me to land, although he warned that we would have to be careful since the RUF had infiltrated the city.

I went ashore in a RIB and saw for the first time the reality of civil war in Sierra Leone. The capital, a pretty scruffy environment at the best of times, was a dangerous place to be. Heavily armed soldiers and RUF fighters exchanged fire in ragged street battles that could be difficult to read. It was noisy and chaotic and terrifying for the local people caught in the crossfire. Captain Coppinger-Symes's warning proved right on the money as early on we blundered into a street fight, only to reverse smartly back out of it when we saw RUF gunmen approaching.

The fighting apart, you were immediately faced with the reality of life in one of the world's poorest cities, where unemployment was rampant, life expectancy low and incomes among the lowest in the world. The streets were rough, the buildings in varying states of disrepair and uncollected rubbish lay rotting and stinking in the tropical heat. In areas where there had been fighting, buildings were on fire and the place was almost deserted. Those brave souls who were left emerged nervously to stare at us.

I needed to get my bearings so I made it my business to try to meet as many of the key players as possible. Over the next few days I met Major General Timothy Shelpidi, who was head of ECOMOG forces, on two occasions. Clearly bright, he was nevertheless not the most decisive of officers and seemed suspicious of our motives for being there in the first place. Samuel Hinga Norman, the Sierra Leonian Deputy Defence Minister, was running his part of the battle from a garage in the bottom of Cockerill Barracks, the official military headquarters of the SLA. A short, bearded man with a ready smile and sincere eyes, who was always relaxed even while others around him were panicking, he was a lovely bloke. It was reassuring to find someone who quite clearly had such a good grasp of events.

I also met Maxwell Kobe, an articulate and self-confident Nigerian Brigadier General, who had been the successful commander of Nigerian forces in Sierra Leone eighteen months earlier. He had earned quite a reputation, so much so that he had been invited to stay on as Chief of Staff of the SLA. He was another impressive and brave soldier with whom I got on well.

We spent a few days looking at ECOMOG and Hinga Norman's battle plans and logistical requirements, trying to understand what they needed and where we could help. I spent one morning with Kobe, visiting the big Chinese-built sports stadium in the city. Named after Siaka Stevens, this had been turned into a giant refugee centre where 25,000 people who had fled from the advancing RUF were living in squalor. The stench and sheer misery of those people was shocking. I called Penfold in Conakry on a satellite phone from the stadium and he immediately got to work trying to requisition emergency food and medical supplies for them.

Afterwards, I went forward with my own team and watched Hinga Norman's SLA forces taking on the RUF over a dry riverbed that formed a key defensive line running through a northern suburb of Freetown. During that battle Norman – who did not know I was present and would later, and wrongly in my view, be prosecuted for war crimes – courageously stepped forward to prevent the summary execution by his Kamajor fighters of two RUF prisoners. He was brave enough to do this despite having seen the RUF gunmen brutally gun down some unarmed civilians only minutes before.

Then I went to the hospital where I met child victims of RUF amputations and visited an old people's home wherein lay two veterans of the West African Rifles, proudly wearing their Burma Star medals, who greeted me like a liberating hero, as described in the Introduction.

Early on in my visit I was driving near Cockerill Barracks when I noticed the sign for the blind school and remembered Peter's request. We stopped and turned into the compound. To start with I could not find anyone as I wandered around calling, 'Hello.' Then I realised that the entire school – sixty children aged from five to 20, all of whom were profoundly blind – were hiding at the back of the building along with their headmaster. They were clearly terrified that we were RUF fighters coming to kill them. Gradually, they emerged into the sunlight in their bright yellow shirts and I was able to talk to them, explain who I was, and reassure them that I felt that they were now safe. I encouraged Sam Campbell, the headmaster, who was blind himself, to start the school again and I told them I would come back in a few days' time, which I did. When I went back, the children sang their favourite anthem for me. It was called 'My West African Home' and had been composed by Peter. I included a recording of it, with Peter leading the verses and the children joining in on the chorus, in my selection for *Desert Island Discs* on BBC Radio 4, broadcast in early 2014. Here is the first verse:

No more guns, no more killing, no more crying and fear of living.
No more hunger, no more pain, no more hiding in the rain.
Peace and democracy that is what we want to see.
Here in Salone, Sierra Leone,
Wherever you roam
In this, my West African home.

Standing before these children and hearing them sing this for me was emotional and incredibly inspiring. Seeing the terror in their faces moments earlier, realising the hopelessness of their situation and knowing that no one was going to sort it out, was a great motivator. You could see how badly people needed our help. Even then, I could hear myself thinking, 'Come on, you have to bloody well do it and f*** the consequences.' At the same time, I was beginning to believe that a breakthrough against the RUF might not be as hard to achieve as some thought. My early sense then, which proved all too accurate a year later when I took them on, was that Sankoh's marauding bands of killers were little more than evil bullies who did not have the discipline or organisation to stand and fight if faced with properly coordinated and determined opposition. Today, they call me 'Uncle David' at the school and I am very proud to be one of their patrons.

I saw Kabbah at least three or four times during that week at his presidential lodge. Tall and handsome, he was a polite, gentle and

charming individual. You could see in his eyes and in his modest
demeanour that he was a good man, and I counted him a friend to the
day he died. He was worried during those days, with good cause, and
lived in a state of virtual siege on a ridge above the city, away from the
government buildings, which had been trashed. He kept a helicopter in
the grounds, ready to ferry him to safety at any moment if the RUF were
on their way to get him. He seemed terribly isolated – only the Nigerians
were standing by him – and uneasy. He sweated profusely, regularly
mopping his brow with a handkerchief while constantly clasping and
unclasping his hands, asking one question after another about what was
going on and what might happen. I felt pretty angry about it. The
international community, including the British government and the UN,
didn't seem to grasp the significance of the fact that he was a democratically
elected president, and they were prepared to give equivalent status to his
enemies, not least the RUF, who were in the pay of Liberia.

I remember the first time I went to see him. I introduced myself and
said, 'I've come to see how we can help.' The look of relief on his face
was palpable and he was close to tears. It was the fact that someone other
than the Nigerians had turned up – someone who clearly wanted to
understand his predicament. The fact that I was only a Brigadier was lost
on him. When I told him on my final visit what assistance for Sierra
Leone I would be recommending in my report to the British government,
he was effusive in his thanks and kept asking whether there was anything
more he could do to help. By that stage, the RUF had again been pushed
back outside the city by a combination of ECOMOG, loyal SLA units and
bands of irregulars, including the Kamajors. The situation had stabilised
to some extent, but Kabbah was not out of the woods quite yet and we
both knew that.

Back in England my recommendations were that Kabbah needed
money, logistical support and small-arms ammunition. I proposed that
this could all be done for no more than £20 million. I was clear in my
report that our duty lay in helping the democratically elected government.
I argued that with this support in hand, Hinga Norman could re-form the

rump of the SLA into an effective fighting force that could assist ECOMOG in pushing the RUF back and restoring order. It went to Cabinet where it was decided that Britain would give £10 million and that this should be matched by an equivalent sum from other international donors, which the Foreign Office would set to work obtaining.

The British portion of the funding came out of Clare Short's new and ambitious Department for International Development. She was understandably reluctant. I went to see her with Charles Guthrie, the Chief of the Defence Staff. We were a persuasive double act; I had the facts and Guthrie was very smooth. We argued that without this help Kabbah would go under and none of us could predict what might happen if the RUF succeeded in gaining control of Freetown. There is no doubt that the shadow of the genocide in Rwanda hung over these discussions and Short's humanitarian instincts overrode any theoretical ethical objections to the deal. It is interesting that this deal, which was not widely publicised at the time, was allowed to go ahead whereas the attempt to supply arms to Kabbah through Sandline two years earlier had caused such a storm. In this case, the supply of ammunition was not regarded as in contravention of the UN arms embargo on Sierra Leone because the aid was being delivered to, or through, ECOMOG. To my mind this still seems a bit of a muddle and unfair on Peter Penfold.

In late February I went back to Freetown to give Kabbah the good news and to see how things were going. This time our ship was the Type 23 frigate HMS *Westminster*, and with me came Penfold. We went to see Kabbah and I told him about the money and he was absolutely over the moon. Even then I was being seen as something of a hero in Freetown. Twenty million pounds was a lot of money for them. They also viewed me and my team as people who had helped them militarily, and in some little ways we had. We had helped instil confidence in their ability to resist the RUF and we had helped them optimise their campaign plan for pushing the rebels back into the interior.

That summer a war-weary Kabbah signed an unsatisfactory peace deal with the RUF in the Togan capital Lome. The Lome Agreement implemented an immediate ceasefire and granted the RUF four key government posts, including control over Sierra Leone's mineral wealth. In return, the RUF dropped its demand for the removal of ECOMOG forces. The agreement implemented a total amnesty for the RUF and lifted a death sentence imposed on Sankoh. Unsurprisingly, this deal was heavily criticised internationally and was regarded as a major victory for the RUF. I was among its critics, privately believing that it gave exactly the sort of equivalence of status to the RUF that I considered unjustified and that resulted from a misunderstanding of what was going on in Sierra Leone.

Robin Cook was heavily involved in the deal and supported it, but he'd got it wrong. Like the rest of the international community, the RUF had conned Cook into believing they would put their past behind them and start to play a constructive role in the new Sierra Leone government. I could understand Cook's reasons for backing the agreement. The alternative was that the war would start again and Britain and other countries would have to deal militarily with the RUF. Britain was not prepared to do that. An agreement with Sankoh was a risk worth taking in Cook's mind, but it was doomed to failure.

Under the peace deal, the RUF, along with the rump of the SLA, were meant to enter a process of disarmament, demobilisation and rehabilitation. This was supposed to be supervised not by the Nigerians but by a new UN peacekeeping force – the United Nations Mission in Sierra Leone (UNAMSIL). Initially 6,000-strong, this was increased to 11,000 and was led by India. In the event, the RUF did not go along with the demobilisation process while the SLA did. The result was that by the spring of 2000, the SLA was mainly back in its camps, its soldiers being prepared for life after the Army, while the RUF was on the front foot. To make matters worse, the new UN commander, despite having been given a UN Chapter VII mandate – the right to mount offensive operations to secure the UN's objectives – interpreted his role as a traditional peacekeeping one, remaining neutral between the warring parties. This seriously impeded the development of close relations with the Kabbah government and the SLA that the UN had gone there to support.

In mid-September of 1999, while I was deployed to Australia and making preparations for the UN-mandated intervention in East Timor, I had what, for me at least, would turn out to be a very important discussion about events in Sierra Leone with Robin Cook. He was passing through Sydney airport on his way to a conference in New Zealand and summoned me to the VIP lounge, anxious to use the opportunity to discuss the East Timor crisis but also to hear my thoughts on Sierra Leone. What he said then was absolutely fundamental to giving me the confidence to go against my orders in May 2000 because I remembered, if nothing else from that conversation, how much importance he and Tony Blair attached to Sierra Leone. When I got orders in May the following year that I knew would do nothing to stop the inevitable collapse of the Kabbah government, I said to myself, 'I don't think that's what TB or RC want.'

It was clear to me that for both men Sierra Leone was a special case. Cook reminded me that Tony Blair's father had taught at Freetown's Fourah Bay College in the 1960s and that Blair retained a special affection for the country. In Cook's case, it seemed to be playing more on his conscience – it was troubling him. I have no idea whether this was the legacy of the 'Arms to Africa' debacle or his unease about the deal that Kabbah had been pressured to make with Sankoh. But Cook took the opportunity to let me run a rule over the key players. He wanted assessments of Kabbah, of the RUF and ECOMOG and so on. At all points – and again I got the feeling that he was talking on behalf of the prime minster – his interest was in a peaceful solution and the welfare of the people. Of course, there was a lot at stake for him. Having backed the Lome deal, about which I knew little at the time, it would not look good for him if Kabbah was swept away. I remember telling him that poor armies can easily be made to look good, and I included in this the RUF. But they would be no match for the British Army, if ever we became involved. Little did I know what would happen eight months later.

In April 2000 I returned to Sierra Leone to find that things were not going well. The new UNAMSIL deployment was being hampered by the RUF, which would go on to launch attacks on Kenyan troops and by May would be holding over 500 Kenyans and Zambians hostage. Kabbah was friendly – I hadn't seen him since the previous February – but he was naturally worried about his future. Sankoh, meanwhile, the Minister for Mines, no less, was living the life of Riley in a house below the British High Commission. He was quite clearly doing his own thing and ignoring any obligation to conform with the Lome peace treaty. His rebels were running rings round the UN and coming much closer to Freetown than they should have been.

I went to see Maxwell Kobe, who, by this stage I knew well. He confirmed that the outlook was bleak. It was a brief meeting and I remember him asking me to come back in two days' time and he would tell me more. But that was the last time I saw him. I was staying with Peter Penfold, who was about to leave at the end of his posting. Peter got a call to say that Kobe had fallen seriously ill. I got involved because we thought we might need to medevac (medical evacuation) him to London for emergency treatment. In the event, he returned to Nigeria where he died – I always think rather mysteriously – a few weeks later.

Both Kabbah and Penfold asked me to stay in Freetown to take charge of the Army for a few days to help calm nerves in the wake of Kobe's sudden departure. The RUF were yet again on the advance and ECOMOG was losing interest as it prepared to hand over to the soldiers of UNAMSIL. Kabbah made a formal request to the Foreign Office and Penfold reinforced it with a request to the Head of the Africa Department. I sent my own message back to the Ministry of Defence, saying that they wanted to keep me there and what was the view. Very clearly and quickly I was told to get back to Britain and stop creating more wars and opportunities for glory and so on. I told Penfold I would have to go and that I did not believe the government was about to collapse. I also went to see Keith Biddle, an unflappable former deputy assistant commissioner of the Metropolitan Police, who was running – and reforming – the Sierra Leone police, along with one or two other former British officers. I had got to know Keith well and I will never forget him telling me he did not like the lie of the land ahead.

'David,' he said, 'my copper's bones tell me this is not going well.'

'Keith,' I reassured him, 'don't worry. If it goes tits up, I'll come back and rescue you.'

'You'd better make sure you do.'

EIGHT

Operation PALLISER

By May 2000, the security situation in Sierra Leone had reached a critical point. The RUF were back on the attack and threatening key towns and villages on the Horseshoe Road, which linked Freetown to its airfield. Retention of control over the road was regarded as essential to the security of the capital.

UNAMSIL, which was supposed to be overseeing the implementation of the Lome peace agreement, had got into big trouble. Made up of soldiers from nearly thirty nations, including Indians, Kenyans, Nigerians, Zambians, Jordanians and Guineans, and under the command of an Indian General, its troops were being attacked by the RUF and in some instances taken hostage.

In the days before I arrived on what was my fourth visit to Sierra Leone in seventeen months, the RUF had attacked Kenyan soldiers at Makeni in the centre of the country, and then taken hostage some 208 Zambian soldiers who had been sent to release them. Three British officers, who were part of a contingent of military observers attached to UNAMSIL, were also been held. By Saturday, 6 May – the day I flew into Freetown – the RUF were holding more than 500 UN soldiers hostage and were advancing on the capital, using captured UN armoured personnel carriers. The very real fear among a population still traumatised by the fighting of twelve months earlier was that the RUF would enter the capital again and this time gain control, wreaking terrible vengeance on people living in government-controlled areas. Rape, murder, traumatic amputation and the destruction of property were all on the cards again.

Earlier that week I had been preparing to leave for a routine exercise in Ghana in my role as *de facto* Commander Joint Rapid Reaction Force. I was in the West Country on a training day with 22 SAS, and I remarked to the commanding officer that things weren't looking too good in Sierra Leone. 'You never know,' I said, as I was leaving, 'the next time I see you might be in Freetown.' Three days later, the crisis in Sierra Leone had reached the top category of conflict at PJHQ. That meant it had progressed from 'quiescent' to 'stirring' to 'quickening' and finally to 'surfaced'.

Tony Blair's Cabinet met to consider the implications of President Kabbah being overthrown for a third time and of Freetown being overrun by the murderous RUF. They were also assessing a request from Kofi Anan, the UN Secretary General, to help shore up UNAMSIL. It took more than a week for London to work out a formal response. In the meantime, I was tasked under the codename Operation PALLISER to go to Sierra Leone with orders to prepare to conduct a Non-Combatant Evacuation Operation (NEO) of British and other expatriates who might be in danger.

I left late on a Friday afternoon from RAF Northholt, on the western outskirts of London, leading an enlarged sixty-strong reconnaissance team on board a Hercules C130 transport aircraft. Along with twelve members of my JRRF headquarters staff was a Special Forces team. As was our wont, we slung hammocks in the back of the Hercules and tried to get some sleep in the din of the noisy fuselage as we headed south.

Even then, I was formulating ways that I could make a real impact in Kabbah's favour. My previous visits to Sierra Leone had given me the opportunity to get to know the key players on the government side and to assess the RUF and how they might be beaten. I knew what was going wrong. Brave people, who were prepared to fight to stop the bullies from doing what bullies do, were not organised or properly trained to do so. If you give a bully a rap on the knuckles, he tends to back off. It needed some troops, but not a lot. What it badly required was organisation, a sense of purpose and commanders with a decent staff.

My headquarters and I could meet this need and we were well drilled by then. We'd done Albania, East Timor, Mozambique and Sierra Leone the year before, and we had worked hard to improve our performance. So I knew we could make a difference by just getting a grip on the situation. I also reminded myself of what Robin Cook had told me at our meeting in Sydney airport – Sierra Leone mattered to the government in an exceptional way.

It has been said that my decision to ignore my orders from London and intervene militarily in the civil war – which is what happened over the next days and weeks – was cavalier. It wasn't. It was the result of hard-nosed analysis. I knew what the first requirement was, even as I touched down without my troops, and that was to get the UN to fight. At the very least they had to be prepared to hold their positions and stop the RUF. Until then, the RUF were just going round and past UN positions or taking soldiers hostage, usually by surrounding them. It was vital that the confusion over the UN mandate was cleared up. UNAMSIL was entitled to intervene and its troops should do that to defend the government and protect the people. The UN apart, I needed to reassure my old friend President Kabbah and try to cobble together what we went on to call my 'Unholy Alliance' of forces to fight on his behalf.

We flew to the Senegalese capital Dakar and then made the short flight to Sierra Leone. As the Hercules rumbled to a stop in the stifling midday heat of Saturday, 6 May at Sierra Leone's Lungi airport, I was itching to get stuck in. As soon as we hit the ground, we established communications with PJHQ and then my close-protection team and I climbed aboard a UN helicopter for the flight across the Sierra Leone River estuary to the sprawling cityscape of Freetown. The city was much as I had always known it, a confusion of decrepit buildings and shanty-town improvisation, ravaged by years of war and upheaval.

My first visit was to Kabbah at his lodge up on a ridge overlooking the city. Once again, I found an extremely worried Sierra Leone president, ready at any minute to jump into his waiting helicopter. I tried to reassure him. He would not need the helicopter, I said, we can stop this and put it right. Much to his evident relief, I explained that this time I would be staying for a while and it wasn't only me coming to his aid from Britain, either. I checked in with Hinga Norman at Cockerill Barracks, who warmly greeted me, formally addressing me as 'Brigadier Richards' as always. I popped into the blind school on the way and went to see Keith Biddle.

'I told you I'd come back if you had a problem, Keith,' I said.

'Cut it fine, lad. What bloody kept you?' he replied in a deadpan voice.

Then I went to the British High Commission and met Peter Penfold's successor, Alan Jones, who offered me one of the bungalows in the grounds as a headquarters. I took one and left Lieutenant Colonel Neil Salisbury, a highly capable Argyll and Sutherland Highlander whom I had grown to admire in East Timor and trusted implicitly, to sort it out and the Special Forces used another.

By mid-afternoon on the first day I already had the essentials of a plan of action and had bounced it off Neil. Once again, I appointed him my Chief of Staff. Major Mark Mangham became my Military Assistant – Neil and Mark both insisted that I would need one, and they were right. Mark played a key role in Freetown, as of course did Neil. I told them I was going to work on the UN to get them to start taking offensive action to stop the RUF moving forward. At the same time, I would pull together the SLA, the Kamajor fighters and even the West Side Boys – if I could persuade them – into a loose alliance that would fight for Kabbah. After I explained the broad outline, Salisbury had the temerity to remind me that we did not have orders for what I was proposing but both he and Mangham indicated they were fully behind me. While I would rightly have born the brunt of failure, their careers would also have been blighted. I was therefore especially grateful to them. Their loyalty to me was vital to the success of what we did, and stiffened my resolve.

My objectives were far more ambitious than simply organising an evacuation of British nationals and other 'entitled persons'. In fact, we were so quick in getting on with our planning to intervene in the war that my orders from London, which arrived three days later, were barely relevant to what we were doing. They were exclusively concerned with the conduct of an emergency evacuation. They had nothing in them about helping the UN and nothing about creating a military alliance to help Kabbah.

In the afternoon of that first day I went down to the UN headquarters at the Mammy Yoko Hotel on the waterfront of Freetown's Aberdeen peninsula, for what turned out to be a critical meeting. Named after a remarkable nineteenth-century female tribal chief, the so-called Queen of Senehun, the hotel was functional but had been heavily damaged in the fighting of 1997. The Queen of Senehun had brought fourteen chiefdoms together through coalition, warfare and her alliance with the British, and was presented with a medal for her loyalty by Queen Victoria. She might have been quite handy in modern-day Sierra Leone. In her place, I was dealing with Major General Vijay Jetley, an extremely cautious UN commander who was fixated about not losing a single Indian soldier on this operation.

When I got to the hotel, I asked for him, explained who I was and said I had come to help. I was told Jetley was on the next floor up from the main offices of the UN where civilian staff were already being evacuated. It was clear they believed the game was up and the RUF was closing in. There was an air of Saigon 1975 about the place – panic and mental paralysis all at once. Jetley, it turned out, was in a meeting and it was made clear by a couple of guards on the door that I would have to wait. I didn't have time for diplomatic courtesies. I knocked, went in and saw a man who was quite obviously an Indian General sitting there in uniform and looking rather anxious.

'I'm Brigadier Richards,' I said. 'I've come to see if I can help. The British government has sent me in line with the UN request.'

'Yes, yes,' he said. 'I'll come and see you. Please wait.'

'This can't wait, General. We've got a problem here and we need to get on with it and get your guys to start fighting.'

As he tried to dismiss me, I repeated that we needed his men to commit themselves to the fight, we needed to work together and together we could stop the RUF. Still he batted me aside.

'I will come and see you, I will come and see you,' he said wearily.

A civilian who was sitting opposite the General then spoke up.

'General Jetley, let's hear what the Brigadier has to say.'

This turned out to be Bernard Miyet, the UN's Head of Peacekeeping Operations, who was visiting UNAMSIL from New York to see for himself what problems the force was facing. I couldn't believe my luck. I had stumbled upon a senior figure in the UN hierarchy, who was clearly not panicking and had all his wits about him. I set out my ideas and explained how critical I believed the situation around the Horseshoe Road was becoming, with the RUF advancing in the south around Masiaka and in the north at Mange. I was particularly concerned that UN forces might withdraw that night, surrendering more vital territory. I explained how Jetley must get his men actively to defend their positions to give me time to get the SLA and the Kamajors organised alongside them. I made it clear I would use my British forces when they arrived to reinforce their efforts.

'I like that idea, Brigadier,' said Miyet confidently. 'Can you come back tomorrow and give us your detailed plan?'

I thought to myself, 'Well now I've done it. I've just outlined a strategy that could turn this round and I'd better bloody well deliver it. I've just volunteered Britain for a war.'

It was all seat of the pants stuff, born of instinct but firmly based on a growing understanding of what made African wars tick. They are often about showmanship, bullying and terror, not proper military strategy. I was convinced that a bit of elan, fighting power and cohesion would have a huge impact on the RUF, because, like most African rebel groups, they were disorganised and ill-disciplined.

I had a sense that even though there were people in the Ministry of Defence chain of command who didn't want me to get involved, people at the very top political level probably did. But I had no links to them. I couldn't exactly pick up the phone and talk to Tony Blair or Robin Cook, although I had my conversation at Sydney airport with Cook to go on. So what was driving me was pure instinct reinforced by some analysis, combined with my own determination not to let Sierra Leone revert to the horrors that I'd witnessed the year before. Taken together, that's why I decided to chance my arm.

The following morning the first two RAF Chinook helicopters arrived in Freetown just thirty hours after being tasked and having flown 3,500 miles from the UK in an astonishing feat of airmanship. Two more were on their way. Also arriving were the first elements of the 1st Battalion the Parachute Regiment – the designated Spearhead Battalion – the bulk of whom I deployed to secure Lungi airfield. I then sent one company to strengthen the UN contingent on the Aberdeen Peninsula, an area that would be vital for the conduct of a NEO.

The way 1 Para came together and got themselves out to Sierra Leone in short order was itself quite remarkable. They had been given the green light on a Friday, when many of them were off base, on their way home for the weekend. But in a classic example of the army grapevine working at its best, involving e-mails, text messages, phone calls, messages left and so on, almost all of them made it to the mounting centre at South Cerney near Cirencester in time for the first flights. Many of them did not have their proper kit but the quartermasters anticipated that and arrived with uniforms and weapons and dished them out before they got on the plane. In the end, virtually the whole battalion – 600 men – were in Sierra Leone by Monday. They were short of weapons, ammunition, maps and other vital equipment, which was rushed out in the following days. They also hadn't had time to take malaria prevention pills and over the next few weeks a number of them went down with the illness, but their condition was quickly spotted and treated, because we knew what to look out for. The commander of 1 Para, Lieutenant Colonel Paul Gibson, had won a DSO in Kosovo the year before. Like me, he was considered something of a maverick. Gibson's self-reliance and confidence in his ability to interpret and execute my orders was to prove critical to the success of what we did in Sierra Leone.

The Paras and the SAS became my instructors and morale raisers. They went forward to UN or SLA positions, assessed their dispositions, stiffened resolve and made sure that the soldiers were doing what they were supposed to be doing. The SAS in particular, whose reputation preceded them to Sierra Leone, had a big impact on morale among troops who had been poorly led and, in the case of the UN soldiers, were confused about whether they should fight or not. Within a few hours of deploying, elements of the SAS were in Hastings and Waterloo to the south and east of Freetown and Port Loko to the north, ascertaining where the RUF had got to in their advance along the Horseshoe Road. They were instructed to defend themselves if necessary and did so.

It was when London discovered that I had sent the SAS, and indeed some elements of the Parachute battalion, that far forward that I started to be questioned about my motives. 'Why have you deployed your people so far outside Freetown?' I was asked. 'There is absolutely no need for it.' I fobbed them off with half-truths and explanations that were difficult to test from a distance of three thousand miles.

'Well, you don't defend an airfield by sitting on it. You obviously have to push people forward so you can tell from which way the enemy is approaching,' I said.

'Yes but not *thirty miles* forward and, anyway, what's wrong with your aircraft?'

'You have got to trust me,' I responded. 'It's a very confused situation on the ground out here and I need "eyes on". Trust me.'

There was little push-back from my own soldiers. To be frank, most of them did not know what I was doing. Having Paul Gibson in particular and Jacko Page onside, though, was vital. If they had questioned me and said, 'I'm not doing this,' I would have been in a difficult position. I took them totally into my confidence. But the rank and file soldiers, even most of the officers, just accepted the idea that we were using interesting tactics and were a bit further forward than perhaps we might have been. At least for the first week, as far as they were concerned, it was all about a NEO in a febrile situation. I made it clear to them that they had to fight, they had to get involved. If someone had been killed, I would have had to say we were protecting the NEO perimeter. I was lucky that I never had to do that.

I realised quite quickly that even a simple evacuation operation would be difficult to sustain by air alone and that we would need an amphibious element, too. We did not know how many civilians we might have to get out. In addition to the Britons, there were other Europeans, Americans, Canadians, Australians and New Zealanders who were entitled to be evacuated. This was a threatening situation. The RUF were capable of breaching our perimeter. We could not rely on the security of the airfield at Lungi, which was surrounded by dense forest. We needed artillery, lorries, Land Rovers and some landing craft to help us get around the estuary. Although I kept my ultimate goals to myself, it was easy to convince London that we should deploy a significant naval and amphibious component. In my mind, this was a classic test of the Joint Rapid Reaction Force concept that I had been developing, and I wanted the Royal Navy involved, partly to prove our capability in this respect.

I got on the satellite phone to Commodore Neil 'Chuckles' Kilgour, who commanded the Amphibious Ready Group (ARG), and Captain Scott Lidbetter in the amphibious assault ship HMS *Ocean*, who were on exercise in the Mediterranean. They are both excellent naval officers in the Nelsonian tradition. I explained what I needed and suggested they might like to start steaming towards the Straits of Gibralter. They took the hint and were well on their way before their formal orders caught up with them. In addition to HMS *Ocean* with 42 Commando embarked, the Royal Fleet Auxiliary *Fort George*, the logistics ships *Sir Tristram* and *Sir Bedivere*, the Type 23 frigates HMS *Argyll* and HMS *Iron Duke* and the Type 22 frigate HMS *Chatham* were soon on their way. Eventually, the whole amphibious warfare group would deploy, together with the aircraft carrier HMS *Illustrious*, equipped with thirteen Harrier jump jets, commanded by the future head of the Navy, Mark Stanhope.

After a sleepless night working up my plan with my team, I went back to the Mammy Yoko the following day and presented it to Miyet and Jetley. When I had finished, Miyet's direction was clear: 'Gentlemen, we have our orders, let's set to. General Jetley, please work closely with Brigadier Richards.' Despite his understandable discomfort, Jetley generously shook my hand. He was an earnest, well-meaning and risk-averse commander, who took his role extremely seriously. We saw each other virtually every day thereafter, although he never fully came to terms with the requirement to work with the SLA or with other elements of my Unholy Alliance, whom he viewed with as much suspicion as the RUF.

The following day I got a first-hand flavour of the fear and anger of a people despairing in the face of the renewed RUF threat. Outraged that the RUF leader, Foday Sankoh, was still living openly in Freetown as the nominal vice president, about 10,000 people marched on his house. Sankoh's bodyguards responded to the increasingly agitated crowd by firing AK47 rounds and even RPG 7 rockets at close range, killing twenty-one people. Sankoh escaped and fled the city. The people were angry not just with Sankoh and their own government but with the UN, whom they blamed for standing by while the RUF committed atrocities. At one point, Neil Salisbury rightly tasked our Chinooks to fly at low level over the crowd in a show of strength.

I knew nothing of this as I was driving back from the Mammy Yoko to my headquarters at the British High Commission. Not far from the hotel I got trapped in a large column of people chanting slogans as they marched from the sports stadium towards Sankoh's house. At this stage, the rioting had not begun but we knew immediately that we were in a dangerously combustible situation. My borrowed white Toyota Landcruiser looked just like a UN vehicle and, as the crowd turned on us, I felt genuinely worried for our lives. These were people at the end of their tether – many of them internal refugees who had seen family members mutilated, murdered or raped – and they were looking for someone to blame. For a minute or two they believed we were part of the UN deployment that had let them down. With me were two members of my close-protection team and Mark Mangham. I was forced to shout from the top of the bonnet to explain that we were British, not UN, and we were there to help the people of Sierra Leone. Eventually, the mood eased and we were able to drive slowly on to the High Commission, where shortly afterwards we found ourselves ducking to avoid the bullets and RPG 7 rounds being fired in our general direction by Sankoh's panic-stricken thugs.

The rioting was a worrying development and it prompted me to recommend to Alan Jones that we should start the NEO as soon as possible. That evening the Chinooks began ferrying people from 1 Para's evacuation centre at the Mammy Yoko across the water to Lungi where Hercules transports were waiting to fly them to Dakar. Of the total of 442 people evacuated, 300 left during the first 48 hours, leaving another 600 'entitled people' still in the city. After the initial deployment of our forces, the demand to leave quickly diminished as many expats, reassured by our presence, decided to stay.

As the first week progressed, the security situation improved. SLA units pushed the RUF back, or at the very least halted their advance. At the same time, more and more British assets were arriving, strengthening the impression that we meant business. I was asked by a local radio journalist towards the end of the week whether my force's mandate was now changing.

'There is discussion of that,' I replied, 'but because I have personally great affection for Sierra Leone and the people – as has my government – and am aware of all that you have been through, that mandate is being liberally interpreted.'

The hostage crisis was also abating. The three British officers, who had been working as observers with UNAMSIL and been captured by the RUF at Makeni, managed to escape. Major Phil Ashby, Major Andrew Samsonoff, Lieutenant Commander Paul Rowland plus Major David Lingard from New Zealand trekked forty miles through the jungle, travelling at night and hiding during the day, and were picked up by a Chinook from the town of Magburaka. Another British officer in the same deployment, Major Andy Harrison, remained in captivity in the eastern town of Kailahun but was rescued a month later. Most of the other UN troops were allowed to go free at various stages by the RUF, who were too disorganised to keep them in captivity. The brief advantage the rebels enjoyed with the use of the captured UN armoured personnel carriers evaporated when the vehicles either broke down or ran out of fuel.

My main task was to unify the disparate groups of fighters and armies – former and serving SLA soldiers, Kamajors and West Side Boys – and mould them into an adequate manoeuvre or strike force. My troops could encourage and coach, even serve as an example, but they were insufficient to push the RUF back on their own. And I needed to preserve them to secure key terrain and to act, in one case, as a lure to force the RUF into a decisive battle that would shatter their morale and set the psychological conditions for their eventual defeat.

A key component in making the alliance work was a young Lieutenant Colonel who was on secondment to the Staff College in Ghana and happened to be visiting Freetown on a liaison visit to the SLA. Simon Diggins of the Royal Regiment of Fusiliers found out where I was and came to see me. 'Right,' I said. 'I've got a job for you.' At that stage, my headquarters staff amounted to twelve people and I needed all the help I could get. Diggins turned out to be a godsend. A colourful character, who went on to serve as defence attaché in Kabul, he completely understood what I was trying to do and delivered my orders to the various components of the Unholy Alliance remarkably effectively. He was the glue that held that motley crew together. His initiative and organisation were an example to all of us and I cannot underline enough what a key role he played.

As his responsibilities expanded, Diggins needed his own staff. I had run out of people but I found an excellent Warrant Officer in Mark Snell, who could be spared from his normal duties. Rank mattered in Africa. He needed to be a figure of some standing, so I took it upon myself to give him a temporary field commission and promoted him to Major, using some spare rank badges from another officer. This way, when he told our Sierra Leonian friends what to do, they listened. I was similarly fortunate in the services of a visiting officer based in Lagos, who also volunteered to help. He kept me up to date with Liberia's intentions in the war and how the RUF was likely to reflect them. After about three weeks, Simon Diggins' place was taken by Jerry Thomas, who had generously agreed to stay behind in Northwood until everyone had successfully deployed. I then let Simon go back to Ghana, a little later than he had planned. Both these officers played a vital role in our success.

Tasking the SLA and the Kamajors through Hinga Norman was relatively straightforward. Less so was trying to get the West Side Boys on my side. In the past, this powerful private army, numbering several thousand heavily armed thugs, had fought against the government, but they could be bought off. I needed to make sure they came in on Kabbah's side this time, and decided to find their *de facto* leader, the former head of state of Sierra Leone and ex-Major in the SLA, Johnny Paul Koroma. 'Where the hell is he?' I asked Hinga Norman. Word came back that he might be holed up in a ruined building in a rough part of the city near the docks. I said to Mark Mangham and my close-protection team that we were going to go and find him. 'What?' was the simultaneous and incredulous reply. 'Yes, there's only one way to do this. We have to find him, and speak to him. There's some risk involved but nothing else will do the trick.'

We set off in two Land Rovers and headed towards the area by the docks, which was a picture of desolation and destruction – real heart of urban darkness stuff. As we approached their compound, we started to see heavily armed RUF-types, who were actually West Side Boys. Some of them had fought for the RUF in the past, some had been enlisted in the SLA or were ordinary civilians who had been recruited as child soldiers. They were notorious for using drugs, wearing women's wigs and flip-flops, and they were especially dangerous when drunk.

When we arrived, I climbed out and greeted the heavies surrounding the shattered building in traditional Sierra Leone style.

'Hi guys, how de body? I've come to see Johnny Paul. Can you show me to him?' I offered cheerfully. I was met with silence by gunmen in dark glasses and cheap suits. 'Is he in there? Can I go in?'

Eventually, someone with authority came down to meet me. To start with he would not allow anyone else in except me and I was not allowed to carry my sidearm. After some haggling, I managed to get permission for Mangham to accompany me. I said I needed him for note taking. Unarmed, we walked up the concrete stairs. On every landing we passed a grim-faced hood with a gun. At the top we entered a room with a big sofa in it on which sat the mustachioed, chubby-featured Johnny Paul Koroma.

'Yeah?' he said by way of a greeting. I went into overdrive. It was all or nothing.

'Johnny Paul,' I said, 'I've been wanting to meet you for many, many years. It's such a privilege.' He smiled. 'Look Johnny, I need you, Britain needs you, your country needs you; you've got to do the right thing. And if you do, I can't guarantee it, but I think I can help you if you face charges.'

After ousting Kabbah in May 1997, Koroma's regime, then in cahoots with the RUF, was involved in atrocities, including murder, rape and torture. He knew he might face war-crimes charges (as indeed he did in 2003). I had touched a nerve.

'Do the right thing; get your people to join my alliance and we're going to push the RUF back. You will be a national hero and we will rehabilitate you, and I'll do everything I can to help you get out of the hole you're in.'

I pointed out to him that in reality he had little choice but to throw in his lot with the government.

'What's the alternative? You're going to die one way or another, so why don't you do this with me and you'll have some prospects.' I could see that Mangham was trying to keep a straight face and couldn't quite believe what he was hearing.

Looking back – a Brigadier from the British Army doing a deal with a Third World warlord in his lair – I know many would question the moral basis of my actions. But at the time I had no qualms. I saw it as a matter of dealing with the lesser of two evils. I could try to save Sierra Leone from another RUF rampage, which the West Side Boys would probably join at some point, or I could swallow my principled objections about dealing with a man like Koroma, get him onside and deal with any consequences of that downstream.

I was street fighting. I have an idea that Tony Blair might have gone along with my gambit with Koroma but the more morally driven Robin Cook would not. It is important to remember that my offer was attractive to Koroma because he thought we had food and money – two commodities in short supply in Freetown at that time.

Koroma said he would think about it. I told him where I was and that he needed to get a message to me by the end of the day. Later that afternoon, two of his men turned up at Cockerill Barracks where Diggins was based.

'We have a message for Brigadier Richards,' they said. 'Johnny Paul says he'll do it.'

The next day Diggins went down to the docks and coordinated plans with Koroma's men. We had about 500 new fighters on our side, armed and with ammunition. They fought hard and they understood the RUF's tactics and the routes they used, so they were invaluable.

I made the effort to visit the Kamajor headquarters as well. These men were fierce fighters who, like Koroma's crew, knew the country and were a critical part of my alliance. By our standards, they probably did commit some atrocities of their own but nothing on the scale or frequency of the RUF. Crucially they were fighting to defend democracy and their way of life against a brutal enemy that had terrorised their communities. Hinga Norman did his best to control them and set the right example. The Kamajors were guardians of some rather eccentric tribal superstitions, not least the notion that the woolly coats they affected would protect them from gunfire.

I went to their base opposite the Pertemba Road Prison in Freetown, where you could smell the stench of the cells from across the road. The first thing they did was present me with a coat of my own. Then they indicated for me to go and stand in the firing range so they could shoot at me and demonstrate my invincibility.

'Hang on, Hinga,' I said. 'I'm not sure about this.'

'If you wear the coat, they will fire at you and you will be fine,' he said, with a straight face. I thought about his offer for a second and decided it might be one to turn down.

'Look, Hinga,' I said, 'I have absolute faith in their coats but I think I'm going to give it a miss.' He looked at me sympathetically and told me not to worry. They would have given it a miss, too.

I watched as others demonstrated the magic of their coats. It was really all about fighting prowess and morale. Another of their bizarre beliefs was that a mirror – any old mirror – held up in the direction of an incoming RPG 7 rocket would somehow deviate the missile. Luckily, they didn't demonstrate that one.

The key to making the Unholy Alliance work was to deploy the various elements in common cause but allow them to operate separately in the field. This helped avoid clashes between rival groups. Hinga Norman was an important cog because in addition to organising the Kamajors, he helped run the SLA and also knew Koroma. My initial orders to Simon Diggins were that while the UN held their ground and re-grouped, the Unholy Alliance were to advance on the axis between Hastings and Masiaka and then be prepared to take the key strategic town of Rogberi Junction, about fifty miles north-east of Freetown. In the northern sector, far fewer Unholy Alliance men were available. A Nigerian battalion was based at Lungi airfield, along with some SLA and the bulk of 1 Para. So I went on the defensive in the north and the offensive in the south, but I didn't want to lose Port Loko, where an SAS detachment was located along with some Nigerian troops. There was a lot of fighting there and it ebbed and flowed between the two sides.

None of this could have happened without Behrooz Sadry, the UN Deputy Head of Mission for Sierra Leone, who solved one of my biggest problems – how to feed the local forces I was bringing together. British troops had their rations, but the Sierra Leonian irregulars, and even the SLA, certainly did not. With the country in the grip of fear and no ships coming into Freetown, there was little food available. In the past, one of the main causes of fighting units breaking up was men wandering off to forage for food, often extorting it at the point of a gun. It was imperative that we overcame this problem and kept these people focused on the campaign.

In one of my many meetings with General Jetley, I pointed out that the only organisation that had stocks of rice was the UN. But Jetley was sticking to his rules and they were long-winded ones at that. There was no way that the UN was going to feed my army he said. It was out of the question. I expected he was going to say that. My next port of call was Sadry, an Iranian-born UN logician, who had been assisting the visiting Bernard Miyet and had stayed on after Miyet had left. I explained what I wanted and what Jetley had said.

'The General is right,' he said. 'Using our food is absolutely out of the question – it's against all the UN's rules and we are not here to take sides.'

I told him that he was absolutely wrong about that; the UN *was* there to take sides. Again he quoted what his superiors were saying. I pointed out to him that the whole project of trying to save the Kabbah regime was in danger of collapse if we did not have food.

'Can I ask you to think again?' I ventured.

Without another word, Sadry picked up a requisition book, filled in the top sheet, tore it off and gave it me.

'Take your lorries to the depot tonight at nine and you will be able to fill them,' he said.

Without his willingness to break the rules, I would have been defeated in those early days. The whole thing hinged on Behrooz Sadry and the rice he let us have.

One of the most important military assets at my disposal was a Russian-built Hind Mi-24 helicopter gunship flown by a South African mercenary. Neall Ellis, originally from Rhodesia and a veteran of conflicts in Angola, Zaire and Bosnia, was devoted to Sierra Leone and flew for many months without pay in support of Kabbah. When we got involved we underwrote his operations, including the nine-man team who kept his helicopter in working order. The gunship had a huge psychological impact on the RUF, who were terrified of its rockets and machine guns. They had sworn to capture Ellis, tear his heart out and eat it. In my mind, the Hind was worth the equivalent of a battalion of soldiers on its own. Ellis and his crew, which included larger than life Fijian ex-SAS gunner Fred Marafono, flew it bravely and with devastating effect. His team became fully integrated into my daily planning and Simon Diggins would often task them to fly ahead of SLA or Kamajor units.

The helicopter was also a useful reconnaissance tool – we could not risk our Chinooks in that role – and I was determined to use it myself to get a better idea of the lie of the land and the disposition of the RUF. I told Neil Salisbury that I wanted to go up with Ellis. Neil informed London of my plans in a routine briefing. The response was emphatic. No British personnel were to fly in the Hind under any circumstances. That was an edict I was prepared to acknowledge in the breach. Ellis took me up one morning and we flew inland just above the jungle canopy across the beautiful interior of Sierra Leone, over forests, rivers and savannah, as far as Makeni in the centre of the country, the stronghold of the RUF. The trip was worth every minute. I got a good sense of the geography and the key strategic points that we would need to hold and defend. Ellis took a pot shot or two at some RUF as we flew eastwards – I was getting a first-hand impression of the extraordinary operational impact that he and his team were having.

Once we started to get on top of the RUF, we used every weapon at our disposal to back up our early gains. The information war, even in a country of Sierra Leone's backwardness, was an element we could not afford to ignore. Although few people had a television and there was no internet in most areas, almost everyone had access to a radio, and that's how they found out about the progress of the war and the whereabouts of the RUF. The radio was the perfect way to influence opinion in remote corners of the country. Many people in rural areas were naturally suspicious of foreigners and of the UN. Somehow we needed to get the message across that we were different, and we needed to do it quickly. Major David Rose from my Joint Force Headquarters took charge of our Information Operations. He noticed that a key moment each day was the 5.00 p.m. news when you would see almost everyone with a little black transistor clamped to their ears, getting the latest information on the war. Rose persuaded the local radio station to let him have a brief 'Archers'-style slot just after 5.00 p.m. that he could use to disseminate positive messages about the British and the Unholy Alliance. He wrote scripts and hired two local actors to discuss the situation on air. Gradually, the local people's understanding and appreciation of the role that the 'Brits' were playing became more positive. Rose had them going from sceptical but curious to enthusiastically applauding what we were doing. He did a brilliant job and the programme certainly had an impact in helping to dispel suspicion and hostility. Rose was rightly recognised for his innovative work with an MBE.

My immediate goal was to try to get across to the RUF, and to the population at large, that we were there to fight. Orchestrated by my enterprising media officer, Lieutenant Commander Tony Cramp RN, I decided to go on the radio myself on a regular basis. At the end of the first week, I made it clear that we had stabilised the situation and I said that we were now going to take the fight to the interior. Little did I know that this would be picked up by the Reuters monitoring service and rebroadcast that evening in London where it caused mayhem. Charles Guthrie was called by No. 10. 'What's your man doing now?' they wanted to know. Guthrie got in touch with Vice Admiral Sir Ian Garnet, the three-star at PJHQ in charge of Joint Operations, who told him that I had overstepped the mark. The row triggered Guthrie's subsequent visit to Freetown to see for himself what we were up to.

On the second Sunday, I appeared live on *Breakfast with Frost*. The production team were rather proudly trying out a new video link for the first time.

'Now, Brigadier, what about Foday Sankoh, the man behind these atrocities? Where is he do you think?' said David Frost in his distinctive sing-song delivery. I said I didn't know. He might be hiding in the bush or he could be dead.

'You think he could be dead, Brigadier? What do you think about that?' Not normally good at soundbites, this time I hit the sweet spot.

'I normally wish no one dead,' I replied, 'but in the case of Foday Sankoh I am prepared to make an exception.' Frost chuckled at that.

'Well, Brigadier, you have made your view very clear there ...' And he concluded the programme by quoting me again.

About six months later I got an e-mail from someone alerting me to a website about 'Diamond Geezers'. There were three examples. The first was a picture of a diamond, the second was the gangster Reggie Kray – he was a '16-carat diamond geezer' – and the third was me, 'a 24 carat diamond geezer', with my quote about Sankoh. I've no idea who put me up there but it did my street cred no harm. More seriously, my comments on *Frost* placed Robin Cook in a difficult position. He found himself being asked in the House of Commons who was running British foreign policy in West Africa. Was it the Foreign Secretary or Brigadier Richards?

I used the media whenever I could to help the chain of command in London, and more importantly my political masters, understand that things were going better than they realised. I wanted to insinuate into minds in London the idea that we should not lose this opportunity to make a decisive impact, that we could do much more than simply evacuate people and get out. I was ahead of them, I was ahead of my orders, and I knew that a well-placed interview on the BBC could help bring them up to speed. In that regard, I made use of the presence of the outstanding BBC television news correspondent Allan Little and later his equally perceptive colleague from *Newsnight*, Robin Denselow. Mark Austin from ITN was also on hand.

I saw Little regularly and briefed him on an off-the-record basis on what we were doing. Before I spoke to him, his reporting had been sharply critical of what appeared to be a plan by Britain to get its people out and leave Sierra Leone to its own devices. Little had made the point that this would have been nothing short of a betrayal, given that Britain had persuaded Kabbah to sign at Lome and assured him that the UN would come to his aid if it started to unravel. I was thus pushing on an open door with him. At the end of the first week, Little did a piece for the main news in which he said that everyone in Sierra Leone now recognised that the only thing stopping the country from sliding into the chaos of civil war was the British military intervention.

'Britain is running this war now,' he said. 'British officers have taken command, not only of the UN troops but of Sierra Leone's own army and its pro-government militia groups.'

On the same programme James Robbins, the BBC's Diplomatic Correspondent, reporting from outside the Foreign Office, perfectly summed up what had been going on. He was asked by the news anchor, Peter Sissons, whether Little was right to have talked of Britain now running the war and whether I was right to say, in a short clip in Little's report, that my mandate was 'open to liberal interpretation'. Was this what Whitehall wanted, asked Sissons.

Robbins said: 'The fact is that the government is tolerating the liberal interpretation of the mandate that the Brigadier has taken. As one official in Whitehall put it to me, when soldiers get out in the field, they often find they can do more, they can do a bigger job than they were originally sent to do and they can persuade the politicians that it is worth doing. That seems to be what has happened in this case. But it is not incompatible with the government's aims,' he continued. 'What they want to do is to transform a disorganised Sierra Leone Army to make it into a fighting force. They want to turn the UN from humiliation into a really effective fighting force, put the two together, stop the rebel advance and turn it into a rebel retreat. Then they will have created the conditions for Britain to go home, job well done.'

Robbins also noted that sources in Whitehall had said at the outset that PALLISER might last a week to ten days. They had then steadily expanded its time frame from a few weeks to at least a month. Hearing about Robbins' report from friends in PJHQ, I quietly chuckled to myself. My intentions were filtering through remarkably effectively.

I never spoke to Robbins but I know Little had no idea I was using my briefings and interviews with him to try to drive policy in London. In 2010 in a BBC interview on *Newsnight* to mark the tenth anniversary of PALLISER, Little confronted me about it.

'Are you telling me, General, that you used people like me in order to persuade the British government that you could do what you wanted to do?' As he was framing the question, I was thinking, 'What on earth can I say except the truth?'

'Well, I suppose that's how it might be interpreted,' I replied.

NINE

The Battle of Lungi Lol
Turns the Tide

Ten hectic days after arriving in Sierra Leone, I got my second lot of orders from the Ministry of Defence. The first version said in terms 'Do a NEO and that is all you are there to do.' The updated ones were still very cautious, but by then the chain of command had been persuaded that we could do more than had originally been planned. They talked about giving support to the UN and helping them in any way possible but still completely ignored the critical role of the Unholy Alliance, where actually we were putting most of our effort. I did not much care about the discrepancy. By then I was committed to what we were doing and we were on a roll.

At about that time the Amphibious Ready Group arrived with 42 Commando embarked and shortly afterwards HMS *Illustrious* took up station just over the horizon from Freetown. She had the Harriers on board. We never used the aircraft to fire a shot in anger, deploying them principally on photographic reconnaissance missions. But we saw immediately that they could have a big impact in demonstrating our presence and our potential firepower. As soon as they were ready I wanted to send them on a noisy, low-level sortie over Freetown. London was having none of it. While they were content for us to conduct 'presence flights' over rural areas, it was made clear that we could not fly them over the city. I think the Ministry of Defence thought we were over-egging it. You could tell they were thinking, 'Why on earth does he want to fly

Harriers? He's getting too big for his boots.' They didn't seem to understand the psychological dimension of war and the big morale boost those planes could deliver over one of the poorest cities in the world. We took London at their word and dutifully instructed the pilots to fly right down the city's seafront with not a wing-tip over the land. One way or another we had the impact we wanted.

Back on day three, in concert with Paul Gibson, I had deployed the twenty-seven-strong Pathfinder platoon of 1 Para – the Pathfinders are specialist soldiers trained for insertion behind enemy lines – to dig in at a small settlement about thirty-five miles east north-east of Lungi airport. Lungi Lol is a collection of about fifty mud huts at a T-junction, deep in the jungle not far from Port Loko. It was chosen initially as a good advanced post from where the Pathfinders could warn us of impending attacks by the RUF in the northern sector of our perimeter. Our intelligence reports were suggesting that the rebels were massing east of Lungi Lol, rightly viewing the airport, due west of it, as a key objective. As PALLISER developed, they were determined to capture some British soldiers. Indeed, they called their activity in that area Operation Kill British. The RUF wanted to humiliate British dead, much as had happened to American soldiers after their disastrous foray into Mogadishu in 1993. They had seen how Bill Clinton had decided to withdraw his troops from Somalia as a result and they knew the impact that images of dead soldiers being dragged through the streets could have on public opinion in Britain.

The Pathfinders were isolated from the start. They had machine guns, mortars and two Pinzgauer six-wheeled, all-terrain vehicles. After being flown in by helicopter, they got themselves well-established around the edge of the village. They dug a series of slit trenches, protected by sharpened bamboo pikes, or *punji sticks*, a technique learned in jungle operations in Borneo. Like everyone else on PALLISER, they were short of ammunition and improvised anti-personnel mines to bolster their defences. The Quick Reaction Force of 1 Para was on standby at Lungi airport to fly in if the Pathfinders found themselves in danger of being overrun. Otherwise their only recourse would be to use the Pinzgauers to get back to government lines.

After a few days it struck me that what I needed from a strategic point of view was to find somewhere where we could tempt the RUF into a battle and then inflict a spectacular reverse on them. We needed to hit them hard so they realised in no uncertain terms that we meant business, something that might act as a deterrent to them continuing their campaign. Lungi Lol was the perfect setting. The Pathfinders were already there and they were élite troops but small in number. The RUF may well come to the conclusion that they were easy pickings and decide to take them on. I discussed it with Paul Gibson and we decided to take the risk of leaving the platoon in a relatively exposed setting as a lure.

As the days ticked by and our intelligence reports indicated a large RUF force was gathering in the jungle to the east of Lungi Lol, I became concerned that we had no heavy weaponry that we could bring to bear on the village to help the Pathfinders. I spoke to Chuckles Kilgour and suggested we should try to move a frigate up the estuary so that it could bring its 4.5mm gun in range. Kilgour chose HMS *Chatham*, captained by George Zambellas, who was awarded a Distinguished Service Cross for what he did next. He is now First Sea Lord.

The Sierra Leone River estuary is a very tricky area for shipping, full of shoals and uncharted mud banks and with a tidal rip that runs at eight knots in places. It is not a place to deploy a valuable and deep draft warship. But not only did Zambellas come into the upper reaches of the estuary, he took *Chatham* right up one of the smaller creeks, coming perilously close to grounding his ship, to get his gun in range. Despite his and his crews' efforts, however, he could not hold *Chatham* on station because of the tidal conditions and he had to retreat. On his way out, an accompanying landing craft ran into a small fishing canoe, two fisherman from which were unaccounted for, presumed drowned. The next morning at the start of my routine briefing with Kabbah, I said how profoundly sorry we were about what had happened.

'Please don't worry about that,' said Kabbah. 'The families will understand. We are so grateful for what you are doing for our country.'

Plan B on indirect fire support for Lungi Lol was to disembark the 105mm guns of 8 Commando Battery, from my first regiment, 29 Commando, that were sitting offshore on board HMS *Ocean*. These weapons, which needed Land Rovers to pull them, had a range of around ten miles, and we knew that we would be able to get them close enough to help. I ordered the guns to be brought ashore and then immediately ran into yet more objections from London. Almost without thinking, Neil Salisbury had mentioned in passing, during a briefing to our superiors at the Ministry of Defence, that we were about to bring the guns to the airfield. He was explicitly told not to do so. It was made clear that I had no authority to move them. After Neil told me what had happened, I said to him, 'We have *got* to get them ashore. We need them ashore; they are no bloody good sitting in *Ocean*.'

'Yes,' said Neil, 'but we have strict orders not to do this.'

'Bugger the orders,' I said and instructed everyone to go ahead with the lift operation that night under cover of darkness.

As before, most people had no idea we were going it alone, and that night three guns were hoisted off *Ocean* by the Chinooks. This was a highly risky operation, which had never been tried in peacetime before, let alone in a war. The Chinooks could not land on *Ocean* and they had a very small margin for error when hovering. Once again, their pilots demonstrated their exceptional ability. I went to bed and arrived in the morning to be told that three guns were now ashore, stored under tarpaulins at the back of a hanger. I was also told that two Chinooks had nearly crashed during the operation. That gave me a big fright. If we had lost a Chinook and its crew, I would have been cut off at the knees. The guns were now within fifteen minutes of being deployed. I felt hugely relieved that we had them, not only to assist in the defence of Lungi Lol but also to help defend the airfield.

In Lungi Lol the Pathfinders were still waiting in a jungle alive with strange sounds after dark. They knew from local people that RUF fighters were getting closer. Then, on their tenth mosquito-infested night, the attack that they had been preparing for suddenly erupted in the early hours of the morning. The Pathfinders had dubbed their deployment Operation Alamo, because they knew they were going to be outnumbered, but even they were surprised by the ferocity and scale of what happened next. Across the entire 600-yard length of their front line, the RUF had massed hundreds of fighters who simultaneously opened up with a withering barrage of machine gun, rifle and RPG 7 fire. It is a tribute to the Pathfinders' skills at preparing their defences that none of them were killed or seriously injured in what developed into a protracted battle as they fought off attempts by the RUF to overrun them from the front and then the side. All of those soldiers performed heroically that night, not least Sergeant Steve Heaney. Along with Captain Richard Cantrill of the Royal Marines – who just happened to be visiting the position when the attack was launched – Heaney crawled forward to no man's land between the opposing lines, dragging a mortar. Cantrill was dragging a bag of shells. Once there, Heaney fired a series of illumination mortar rounds that had the effect of backlighting the RUF gunmen, enabling the Pathfinders to direct their fire accurately. Heaney controlled the battle from that exposed position and did his best to try to prevent his soldiers from wasting precious ammunition. For his heroism he was awarded the Military Cross, becoming the first non-commissioned officer to receive one. Cantrill later won the MC, too, for leading a three-day assault against a Taliban position in Afghanistan.

The Pathfinders had inflicted just the sort of defeat I had wanted. No one knows how many RUF were killed. Five bodies were seen the following day but heavy blood trails in the jungle indicated there were many more casualties and local villagers spoke of being forced to bury at least twenty-four more bodies. Others drowned as the fleeing survivors attempted to cross the Little Scarcies River to the north of Lungi Lol. The victory sent a powerful message to the RUF, just as intended. We could tell that was the case because from then on they did not want to fight us. We followed up that huge psychological blow in the south by continuing to push east and north using the Unholy Alliance of SLA,

Kamajor militias and West Side Boys. The combination of that battle and our determination to keep the pressure on turned the war in our favour.

I decided to fly down to Lungi Lol to thank the Pathfinders in person. They were in ebullient form, even if they were somewhat surprised to learn that we had left them there as a lure for the RUF. There is nothing more enjoyable or rewarding for a commander than to get out of the headquarters, and all the entanglements that the working day there involves, to say thank you to soldiers in the field, who had put their lives on the line for what we were doing.

The morning of the battle proved a dramatic one in Freetown. Foday Sankoh, who had been on the run since fleeing his house ten days earlier, was captured by some brave local people and taken to the guardroom at Cockerill Barracks. While being apprehended, he had been shot in the leg. We were just beginning our regular morning staff meeting, known to one and all as 'morning prayers', when I noticed Neil Salisbury was on the phone.

'Gentlemen, it looks like Sankoh has been caught,' he said. Salisbury explained that he was being held at the barracks where an angry crowd had gathered outside the gates, scenting blood. Keith Biddle and his police had just arrived on the scene to try to control the situation and then phoned Salisbury to tell him he was going to need help in what was a very tense situation.

I had orders from London that if Sankoh was ever caught, we were to have nothing to do with it. He was regarded as a problem for Sierra Leone and the UN, not us. Then we got another call from Biddle. By that stage, he was worried that the crowd would break through the gates and go on the rampage in the barracks. In the meantime, Salisbury got on to London and informed them that Sankoh was in custody and asked what we should do. It turned out that the Chiefs of Staff were meeting at the time and we were told to wait while they deliberated. But we couldn't wait. I gave orders to lift Sankoh, using two Chinooks. They landed on a pad on the opposite side of the base to the gates. In the event, as the helicopter with Sankoh on board lifted off, the crowd burst through the gates and started ripping into the barracks. London then got back to us. The Chiefs had decided that under no circumstances were we to get involved.

'Too late,' replied Neil. 'The Brigadier has given the order and we have got him.' His opposite number in London had to swallow it.

'Ah,' he said. 'I'll go back to the Chiefs with that one.'

The question was what to do with this man whose forces had caused such appalling suffering in his country. I decided to fly him to Lungi airfield while we weighed up our options. We debated about putting him on one of our ships. In the end, that evening, we flew him back to the Aberdeen Peninsula area of the city and installed him in a safe house, the whereabouts of which were known to four people only. Eventually, Sankoh was transferred to prison and was indicted on seventeen counts of war-crimes charges. His arrest sparked huge celebrations around Sierra Leone as people began to believe that the menace of the RUF really was starting to recede. Sankoh lost his mind in captivity and died three years later before he could be tried. He had inflicted a nine-year reign of terror on his country, notable for its sadistic brutality. As the *Economist* put it on his death: 'He was not Africa's most prolific murderer, but he was one of the cruellest.'

With a sizeable fleet of warships in Freetown bay underlining the scale of our presence, the Unholy Alliance and the UN working increasingly well together and Sankoh permanently out of action, we were making progress. We took Rogberi after about three weeks but I couldn't guarantee holding it. I needed the UN to do that and eventually I persuaded General Jetley to release a well-drilled Indian battalion, equipped with armoured personnel carriers, who very impressively pushed their way up to Rogberi from Freetown, clashing with the RUF several times on the way. Once they were established at Rogberi, we knew the Horseshoe Road was safe. During this period, the special forces played an important role in telling me where the main bulk of the RUF forces were.

By this stage, 1 Para had handed over to 42 Commando, who had been held on HMS *Ocean*. The Paras had done an excellent job on very light kit from a standing start. I cannot praise their commander, Paul

Gibson, his company commanders and the whole battalion enough. The handover was executed seamlessly and with 42 Commando we got a more sustained presence with full back-up – more vehicles and heavier weapons. Their commander, Lieutenant Colonel Andy Salmon, was in the same mould as Gibson. Although a more politically canny operator than Paul, he was none the less effective for that. He went on to become a Major General in a NATO appointment and was the last British commander in Basra.

The pressure on me in Freetown was matched on the home front for Caroline, who was following events in Sierra Leone in any way she could. She even went out and bought a Sky box so she could keep an eye on rolling coverage. Caroline knew I was taking risks and she sent me regular messages that were encouraging and reassuring. Always robust, her view was that I must do what I had to do and not worry about the consequences. While I battled with my superiors at the Ministry of Defence – the exception being Charles Guthrie and his immediate staff – my commander at PJHQ was supportive. Admiral Ian Garnett had no experience of land operations but he had good instincts and was prepared to trust them despite having the odd wobble. His Chief of Staff, Major General Andrew Pringle, had the job of giving me direction on a day-to-day basis. A highly intelligent Green Jacket with a maverick side to his character, he sensed what I was really up to from quite an early stage. But he and another key figure at PJHQ, my old friend Brigadier Andrew Stewart, who was the senior operations officer, conspired to give me enough rope to do what was needed while privately making it quite clear that they could not protect me for long should London's orders not change.

Stewart was another independent-minded man and he was very helpful as my eyes and ears in London. He would take my messages and send me back useful tips. 'You've overdone it this time,' he would say, or 'watch your back on this', or 'there's talk about replacing you.' He would also bump into Caroline in Northwood and tell her how things were going and offer advice that she would pass on to me. Usually, it was along the lines of 'David needs to be bloody careful – he's really pushing his luck.' It did worry her a bit I have to admit.

A turning point in my struggle with London was when Charles Guthrie came out. He had been under pressure to sack me but he was pleased with what he found and his advice influenced key people in London in my favour. But I knew I had been lucky and realised that I had better not push my luck, especially after the close shave with the helicopters during the transfer of the guns. Otherwise, I felt confident all along that we could do what I planned, and I knew I had excellent people under my command who could make it happen.

Once the UN started to move – with the advance to Rogberi – I knew we had cracked it. By then, London was very happy and basking in reflected glory. Tony Blair never claimed to have made the key decisions but he took some of the credit and I didn't begrudge him that. I sensed that while he might question some of the risks I was taking at the tactical level, he would have entirely endorsed my aims in defence of a democratic government. As in almost all the most effective military actions, we had – to coin a phrase – clouted not dribbled. We had gone in hard like we meant it and it had paid dividends.

In many ways, it had been the perfect operation. No UK losses, a democratic government back on its feet and a people saved from more butchery. More than anything we had played a psychological game and won. Although we did accumulate significant assets in theatre, we did not have expansive ground-fighting capability at any stage. We relied on convincing the RUF that they would lose in any confrontation with us and that the UN and the Unholy Alliance would offer similarly robust resistance. I remember saying to David Rose, when discussing his radio programme, that we had to impress upon the RUF 'the inevitability of their defeat', and that is how I summarised my orders in my Commander's Intent. It was the best Intent I ever issued because everyone thought, 'We've got to play on the psychological dimension, we've got to do a Lungi Lol and, when we do it, we have to hit them hard.' The RUF needed to feel that the whole world was against them and that I walked on water with a whole panoply of weapons at my disposal. And they did. They became disillusioned and disorganised. They split into factions and many of their leaders were killed. In the long run, they were broken.

As things quietened down, Robin Cook came out for an official visit and didn't put a foot wrong. He spent twenty-four hours with us. I briefed him the night before in *Ocean*, and then spent all day with him. We toured the troops, visited a camp for amputees and went to see Kabbah and the government. He told them that Britain was 'ready to go the distance'. He said, 'Britain wants to be a long-term partner in securing a stable, successful, enterprising Sierra Leone.'

Four weeks in we had cracked it and it was becoming clear by then that London did not want me to stay. The view was 'Let's get out while the going is good and let's get a lot of the very expensive kit we had out there home.' The goal was to make the transition to a supporting role. As we prepared to leave, a 200-strong British Military Training Team came in and I handed over to Brigadier Gordon Hughes, a Royal Corps of Signals officer. I flew home on 15 June, getting back just in time for speech day at the girls' school.

That summer, the goal was to work hard training the SLA and to keep our foot on the throats of the RUF. Things were going well until a blunder by soldiers of the Royal Irish Regiment, who were attached to the training mission, resulted in some being taken hostage in late August by a group of West Side Boys. They were held in a village in the hills outside Freetown. Six were released after negotiations between the British Army and Foday Kally, the WSB leader, but five other soldiers together with an SLA liaison officer remained in captivity for a number of weeks. A decision was taken to mount a rescue operation. Operation BARRAS involved an assault by SBS, SAS and elements of 1 Para on two villages simultaneously with plenty of potential for things to go wrong. Twelve soldiers were injured. All five hostages were saved together with the SLA officer and twenty-five civilians who were being held. BARRAS had the effect of breaking the WSB. Twenty-five of them were killed in the assault and eighteen, including Kallay, were taken prisoner. Over the following two weeks 300 others surrendered to UNAMSIL.

I monitored BARRAS and advised on it from PJHQ at Northwood. I was annoyed that the Royal Irish had erred so unprofessionally, causing a rescue to be necessary and the death of a special forces soldier whom I knew. BARRAS marred what up until then had been a textbook operation. There was a silver lining of sorts, in that when I went back to Sierra Leone in the autumn, I was able to exploit the propaganda and psychological impact of BARRAS on the RUF – on top of Lungi Lol before it – to help force them to sign a formal ceasefire.

My deployment in the autumn, on what would be my last operational tour in Sierra Leone, came about because there was a resurgence of violence and worrying signs that the RUF were again on the warpath. The government decided that we needed to shore up the gains of PALLISER. So my Joint Force Headquarters and I were sent back to replace Brigadier Hughes. This time we had some assets of the Amphibious Ready Group offshore, including, once again, Andy Salmon and much of 42 Commando on board HMS *Ocean*, but my instructions were explicitly clear from the outset – we were not to get involved in any fighting. This time we sensed no need to do so but it was understood that I may want to *play* on our ability to do that if needed.

I deployed not only as the Joint Task Force Commander but took over as commander of the training mission as well as military adviser to Kabbah. I could see immediately that we had most of the right elements in place – the SLA was increasingly independent and capable, the Kamajor militias were still bravely doing their bit, the West Side Boys were not a threat and the UN was getting more robust. But there was a lack of leadership and organisation. I toured positions and instilled a greater sense of purpose and order. And we launched a concerted psychological warfare campaign against the RUF to force them to a ceasefire. We intimidated them on the radio net, telling them we knew where they were and we were going to get them, and then followed up with the Hind gunship blasting the hell out of them. And we played up my return in the local press. One paper led with 'RUF beware! British give thirty-day notice!' Another declared 'Britain shows big stick!' We conducted big demonstrations of our firepower and a large amphibious exercise to impress upon the RUF that we had the forces necessary to take the war back to them. We even allowed talk of a permanent RAF base for fast jets in the country.

The result was a ceasefire agreement with the RUF that our army lawyer – Lieutenant Colonel Darren Stewart, another in the Lee Marler mould – drafted for the government. It was signed in the Nigerian capital, Abuja, on 10 November 2000. At that point the UN writ ran right across the whole country and the UNAMSIL force was increased to over 25,000 troops. With my role in Sierra Leone finally complete, I handed over to Brigadier Jonathon Riley, Commander 1st Mechanised Brigade, and headed home for the last time. The ceasefire held and by the end of the following year the RUF had completely disarmed. President Kabbah was able to announce the formal end of all hostilities in January 2002.

My contentment at what had been professionally a satisfying year, was marred by my mother's death shortly before I deployed to Freetown for the final time. Recalling my father's rather free-spirited approach to life, I realized once again what a safe, reassuring and loving influence my mother had been. The proverbial rock around which we all revolved. As with my father, I realised how tremendously fortunate I was. They had given me the confidence to be myself, to trust my judgement. I determined to try and provide the same legacy for Joanna and Pippa, and can only hope I live up to Jim and Pam's example.

TEN

A Missed Opportunity
in Baghdad

After the drama of Sierra Leone, I found myself back in Germany and, two years later, involved, if only tangentially, in the other major conflict of the time: Iraq. I went to Baghdad just a few weeks after the fall of Saddam Hussein and made recommendations that would have involved British soldiers in the post-conflict stabilisation of the city. For reasons that will become clear, my plan was dismissed in London in one of the most frustrating episodes of my career.

On promotion to Major General in April 2001, I was appointed Chief of Staff of the Allied Rapid Reaction Corps (ARRC) based at Rheindahlen in Germany. This is a British-led NATO operational headquarters, standing ready for rapid deployment worldwide within five to thirty days.

By the time I joined, it had been in existence in various forms for nearly ten years and had already been successfully deployed to Bosnia in 1995–96 and more recently to Kosovo in 1999. The ARRC was a stroke of genius by the British Army hierarchy in the early 1990s. Its creation enabled Britain to preserve the all-important Corps level of capability, which it could not afford without the support of participating allies. By bringing in other nationalities and getting NATO to fund some of it, an essentially British headquarters was formed.

While 60 per cent of the staff at Rheindahlen were British, the other 40 per cent came from seventeen other NATO countries. There were Americans, who had about thirty officers, Italians, Germans, Dutch and

even Greeks, who had two. In total, we had about 350 staff plus our own
signals brigade. That apart, we did not have any troops based with us. We
did have forces permanently earmarked to us, however – two British
divisions, one division each from America, Germany and Italy and an
air-defence brigade from Poland. Most of the officers were pretty good.
Among the outstanding performers were the Italian Deputy Commander,
Major General Fabrizio Castagnetti, who gave the lie to any notion that
Italians do not make good soldiers, and Brigadier Matthew Sykes,
who had succeeded me as CO 3 RHA and was the ARRC's Chief
Coordinator of Joint Firepower.

At the ARRC, I learnt to play to people's strengths and mitigate
their weaknesses on a much bigger, multinational scale than hitherto.
Collectively, we tried to ensure a British officer was in a key post, not
necessarily the most senior, to make sure the machine as a whole
functioned efficiently. This preserved Britain's status as the so-called
'framework nation'. I don't think the foreigners minded this, many
admitting freely that for them being in the ARRC was a prized learning
appointment that would stand them in good stead in their future careers.
Without doubt, being the Chief of Staff enabled me to hit the ground
running when I took over as Commander ARRC a few years later and
deployed to Afghanistan.

The ARRC was not mainstream Army in many people's minds and I
know one or two of my more ambitious colleagues were not keen on a
posting to Rheindahlen, fearing they would be marginalised. That never
concerned me. I was grateful to be out of the UK rat race and in an
operational role once again. In that regard this was my third cracking job
on the trot – 4th Armoured Brigade, the Joint Rapid Reaction Force and
now the ARRC. At my rank this was almost unprecedented.

While I was at Rheindahlen, we were put through our paces on a new
NATO high-readiness certification process and we passed with flying
colours, which made us all very chuffed. We were being tested as the first
NATO High-Readiness Force (Land), or HRFL. This was part of the slow
switch by the Alliance away from the old certainties of Cold-War defence

to a new operating concept based on an 'out of area' role, something that led eventually to the deployment in Kabul. This was an interesting time and old ideas were dying hard. When I arrived, there was still some residue of the Cold War in evidence with plans to defend Greece and Turkey from the Soviets still knocking around. We took them seriously, as training vehicles if nothing else.

By then other nations in NATO had cottoned on to the considerable trick Britain had pulled off with the development of the ARRC and they wanted to create their own versions of it. So gradually we went from being the sole Corps headquarters at high readiness to becoming one of seven or eight HRFLs. The Italians developed one based in Milan, the Germans based theirs in Munster, the Spanish outside Madrid and so on. Each had multinational staffs. The concept was getting a bit diluted with all these lookalike ARRCs but to this day the original one remains the premier version.

Our commander was Lieutenant General Sir Christopher Drewry, a charming and intelligent Welsh Guards officer. We got on famously. He rarely did more than nudge the tiller, allowing me to lead the headquarters through the certification, and all the training that it involved. We were a happy team as a result and I learnt a lot. There wasn't anything that I would not do for Christopher. Caroline, and indeed I, felt the same about his hard-working and compassionate wife Miranda.

To my disappointment, I did just fifteen months in what was a very fulfilling job. The incoming Chief of the General Staff (CGS), General Sir Mike Jackson, had decided he wanted me to be his Assistant Chief (ACGS), a post some people refer to as the Army's chief executive to the CGS's chairman. That may not be entirely accurate but it's not a bad description. Mike was not due to start the job until the following January so, for the first four months, I had the pleasure of working for the unflappable and talented, but sometimes hard to energise, Sir Mike Walker. He was to take over from Admiral Sir Mike Boyce as CDS in April the following year, although, at the time I pitched-up to work for him, I am not certain Mike knew that. Either way, he had done his three years as CGS and was going to be CDS or retire.

I arrived in London in late September 2002 as the Ministry of Defence and the armed forces began to realise that there was a serious chance that we would be going to war in Iraq at some point in the next year. Two weeks before I started, President Bush had told world leaders at the UN General Assembly to confront the 'grave and gathering danger' of Saddam Hussein's Iraq or become 'irrelevant'. Days later the Blair government had published a controversial dossier outlining the apparent threat posed by Iraq. It included the claim that Saddam had weapons of mass destruction (WMD), some of which could be used within forty-five minutes of him giving an order. There were also claims that Iraq had sought significant quantities of uranium from Africa.

Although I was not in the operational chain of command, I regularly deputised for Mike Walker on the Chiefs of Staff Committee and generally helped to ensure that the Army would be ready if it was deployed against Iraq. I mention this because when I arrived at the Ministry of Defence, there was a consensus that the Army would not play a role. The view was that this would be an exclusively Royal Navy and Royal Air Force operation. I was baffled by this. If the UK wanted to wield influence politically and militarily with the Americans, it was my judgement and, more importantly by then, that of the CDS, Mike Boyce, that strategically the Army had to be involved. I was also concerned that the Army could end up being marginalised. I remember making the case for the Army forcefully with Mike Boyce and the reluctant Permanent Under Secretary of State at the Ministry of Defence, Sir Kevin Tebbit, as I stood-in for the CGS while he took some well-deserved leave.

This was still being debated as late as October – the invasion was to take place on 20 March. As a result, the Army was informed very late in the build-up that it would be involved. The official explanation was that Britain did not want to make a decision, the exposure of which could up the ante in negotiations with Saddam Hussein. Many of us felt that was exactly what we should have done – shown intent. But the upshot was that the Army, despite Herculean efforts by Mike Walker, Mike

Jackson and many others, did not have as much time to prepare as they would have liked.

I also recall being present at a Chiefs meeting when we pressed on Mike Boyce the importance of knowing that the operation on which the armed forces were about to embark – an invasion of Iraq and the removal of Saddam's apparent WMD capability – was legal. He needed no persuading, and courageously insisted that the government confirmed it *would* be legal, an act that I suspect reinforced the decision that he would do two years only in post.

Mike was a serious-minded and not very clubbable officer. He was possessed of great integrity and an excellent instinct for joint operations, even though he had spent much of his distinguished career as a submariner. When we heard that his tenure as CDS had been cut short, we were shocked and sad. I well remember summoning up the courage to go to say farewell to him just before he left. This provoked something approaching emotion in a man who rarely showed any.

Mike Jackson took over as CGS at the end of January and, in the colourful way that is his stock-in-trade, he soon made his presence felt in Whitehall and more widely. The Army knew it had a dynamic new personality at the helm and he set about ensuring that the large force that had deployed to Kuwait was as ready as could be for what was about to happen. Jackson made a difficult job fun at a difficult time. He was irreverent, prone to going off at a tangent if it amused him and always keen for a gossip. I thoroughly enjoyed working for him, even if it brought new meaning to the old 'work hard, play hard' mantra. He was a man of extraordinary stamina who thrived on partying until all hours and yet would still be able to function in the morning.

As Jackson rightly focused on Iraq, it was left to me to concentrate on the three-quarters of the Army that was not going to war. This was frustrating, especially as at one stage about two years before, I had been confidently tipped off by a number of well-placed officers that I was going to command 1st (UK) Armoured Division. This was the formation that was now deployed in Kuwait as the UK's principal land contribution to the Coalition effort. For various reasons, some good, some less good, that job never materialised. Professionally, while wishing my good friend Major General Robin Brims the very best of good fortune, I will concede a certain frustration. In the event, the Division and Robin did a magnificent job in Iraq and it did me no harm to experience a disappointment in my career. I knew what that felt like and I think it made me a more compassionate commander downstream.

I was hoping that at some stage I would get a chance to visit Iraq, but more important people than me were queuing up to get out there after the ground war had finished. So I resigned myself, rather impatiently, to a long wait. In the event, I found myself there much sooner than I had anticipated.

Just over a month after the fall of Baghdad, Walt Slocombe, a former Under Secretary of Defence in the Clinton administration, came through London to brief America's principal ally on his plans for security-sector reform in Iraq. Slocombe had been given responsibility for this critical area by the Bush administration. He would report to the new Administrator of the Coalition Provisional Authority, Paul Bremer, who had just taken over in Baghdad from the hapless retired US General Jay Garner. Bremer went on to take the fateful decision to disband the Iraqi Army and pursue a policy of removing anybody from public service who was associated with the old Ba'ath party, Saddam Hussein's powerbase. These decisions are regarded as having sowed the seeds for the bloody insurgency against American and British forces that started to take hold in the next few months.

Slocombe briefed Geoff Hoon, the Defence Secretary, and the Chiefs but their verdict was not positive. The consensus was that he was a good guy, and a capable one, but they were unimpressed with what they saw as his narrow focus on the Iraqi Army. He didn't seem to grasp the importance of other major security-sector areas, such as the police, prisons, the judiciary, customs and so on, all of which would be subject to so-called 'de-Ba'athification' by Bremer. Alarm bells were ringing and I was the person tasked to do something about it.

This came about after Jackson hosted a dinner party at his home in Kensington Palace the day after Slocombe flew on to Baghdad. Present, among others, were Hoon as principal guest, John Scarlett, Chairman of the Joint Intelligence Committee, and Richard Dearlove, head of the Secret Intelligence Service (MI6). The subject of Slocombe's limited grasp of priorities in Baghdad inevitably came up and Hoon surprised me by suggesting that this was my area of expertise and why didn't I jump on a plane and see if I could get in front of Slocombe before it was too late? Could I not help the Americans get on the front foot in Baghdad by bringing some of Britain's post-conflict experience to bear? I immediately saw a great opportunity to help and even come up with some concrete ideas that we could put to the Americans. Across the table Jackson was enthusiastic and so, after dinner, it was agreed that I would head out to Iraq. I had a visit to Freetown already arranged but this clearly took precedence. 'Sierra Leone cancelled; Baghdad instead!' I noted in my diary.

Heading out to Iraq on a whim of the Secretary of State was a mixed blessing for me. Indeed, an exciting and potentially important trip would turn into something of a poisoned chalice as people above me failed to prevent their resentment about the fact that I was going – and the unorthodox way I had been selected for the job – getting in the way of their professional judgement about what I would recommend.

The next morning, Hoon briefed Mike Walker, who was understandably upset that, as CDS, he had not been consulted. He reluctantly agreed to me deploying but I sensed that, despite our close relationship, he was not happy about it; nor were people happy in the joint operational chain of command in the Ministry of Defence or at the Permanent Joint Head-quarters at Northwood. I got the distinct impression that they all felt their role had been usurped, and to a degree this was the case. The Assistant Chief of the General Staff was not meant to deploy on operations and some resented the good run I had enjoyed in my previous job at the Joint Force Headquarters. I was coming up against the same strand of thinking that had got in the way of my deployment to Mozambique to coordinate

Britain's response to the flooding crisis there three years earlier. On this occasion, sentiment was not helped by the fact that Mike Jackson had publicly pressed for the Army to deploy to Baghdad and take charge of a sector of the city, in a show of solidarity with the clearly hard-pressed Americans. This had been firmly, and I think with the benefit of hindsight sensibly, rejected by the government. But what was now being considered was quite different and made a lot of sense. The US Army had no experience of operating in the situation they found themselves in, whereas we had quite a lot.

I did not think much more about this at the time. I was just excited to be going out to Iraq and to have a real operational purpose for doing so. Back in 2002 I was uneasy about the war and, with the benefit of hindsight, I now side with those who view it as a grand strategic error. In defeating Saddam Hussein, we removed the secular bulwark to Iranian ambition and fueled the flames of sectarian hatred. Only history will tell how big an error this has been.

I cobbled together some of my old team that evening: Lieutenant Colonel Neil Salisbury, who had been so important to the success of Operation PALLISER in Sierra Leone, was in the PJHQ and was allowed to come with me; Major Andrew Hughes, my Military Assistant, was available and ready to go, as was my ever-faithful 'Mr T' aka Sergeant Major Tranter – my house sergeant. His job was to take care of the admin on the trip. He started by losing his wallet at Heathrow. I had known Mr T since he was 19. He had come into the Army as a lanky, big-eared fellow from Hull. He was a great character and as loyal a person as you could possibly find. He could say anything he wanted to me, and often exercised that right. I would go as far as to say he was the son I never had and a great friend. On that trip his presence at my side turned out to be more important than ever.

We flew to Kuwait and then flew by Hercules C130 transport to Basra where the main British headquarters for 1 Division was based. At that time, the city was peaceful and there was no sign of the enormous difficulties that lay ahead. Yet I sensed almost immediately that things were not as they should be. I had noticed a certain slackness of attitude among the Americans in Kuwait and I saw the same thing in our soldiers in Basra. The view was 'we have just fought a major war, it went spectacularly well and for us, it's a case of job done.' I detected a general lack of enthusiasm among them for the next vital stage in the Coalition effort in Iraq – the post-conflict stabilisation phase that required creative and energetic thinking from officers and lots of routine patrolling by the men. At theatre level, US General Tommy Franks, who ran the war, was about to leave and retire, and Lieutenant General Ricardo Sanchez was coming in at short notice to take command of a rather cobbled-together Coalition Joint Task Force. There were other three-star officers around at the American headquarters in Kuwait but no one quite knew who was responsible to whom, or for what. At HQ 1 Division, Robin Brims, who ran the war, had gone and Major General Peter Wall had just taken over and had yet to get into his stride. There was a similar lack of oomph among people there and a singular reluctance to change plans. In military parlance, the HQ was a bit 'soggy'.

We flew on to Baghdad and found ourselves in Saddam's capital just a few short weeks after the city had fallen to the Americans in a stunning example of modern-day Blitzkrieg. The great statue of Saddam Hussein had been torn down and President George W. Bush had infamously declared that major combat operations in Iraq were over. He did that while standing on the deck of the aircraft carrier USS *Abraham Lincoln* off the Californian coast and in front of a banner declaring 'Mission Accomplished'. If only it had been that simple.

A semblance of normality had descended on Baghdad by the time I got there as people got used to the fact that the war had ended and decades of dictatorship had come to an end. We stayed with 22 SAS and spent some hours driving round the city with them in open-topped unarmoured Land Rovers. Whenever I could, I got out and talked to the locals. 'We're British and here to help,' was my opening offer to all and sundry. I got a lot of football and Man Utd-based chit-chat back. People were generally friendly but there had been one or two incidents against the Americans and lawlessness was in the air. Detectable resentment was building. To many ordinary Iraqis, life already seemed to be as bad, if not worse, than before. Were these Americans our friends or a new oppressor?

In areas such as Sadr City, the Shia suburb where the paramilitary Mahdi Army based itself, the atmosphere was malevolent. People were angry. There was no food or electricity and no one was talking to them. In my report to London I summed up as follows: 'Baghdad is the Coalition's centre of gravity and restoring a sense of law and order quickly is the highest priority. Not improving the current fragile situation quickly, seriously threatens success to date.' We had a wonderful opportunity in those precious weeks to get on top of this. I am not arguing that the insurgency could have been entirely prevented but there was certainly a chance to win over the hearts and minds of many, many more people to the Coalition's side.

I watched the Americans in the streets and you could see they had little understanding of how to handle the post-conflict challenges. Their idea of getting out and about was to drive around in their tanks and armoured personnel carriers with their guns at the ready and their dark glasses firmly clamped across their eyes. It is a detail but an important one – there was no eye contact, something we knew was critical in building trust. If they did get out of their noisy vehicles, the American idea of a patrol or even a checkpoint was to pick a spot, a so-called 'strong point', surround it with barbed wire and stand there doing very little.

We knew that getting out and about properly – on foot and on a regular basis – was critical for getting a feel for what was happening on the ground. The Americans had no preparation for this, as they candidly admitted at every level. Not only was there no plan for peace, there was no training in the tactics of how to operate in that environment. It was quite clear to me, and to many of their own officers whom I met, that they needed training and support in the disciplines of police and military cooperation in urban areas. In short, I realised that I could do much more than advise Slocombe for a few days – we could introduce practical British help on the ground.

I began an intensive series of meetings, talking to Slocombe, John Sawers, then the British representative at Bremer's headquarters, and senior US officers at their base in one of Saddam's palaces. Even Bremer himself was good enough to offer me – a lowly Major General from Britain – an hour of his time, on two occasions. My suggestion to the Americans was that Britain would deploy troops up to Baghdad from Basra for a limited period to work with Iraqi police and American troops, developing a programme of urban patrolling. My idea was to deploy the 3–4,000 soldiers of 16 Air Assault Brigade, who were in Basra at that stage but not doing a huge amount. They had taken part in the war but had not seen a great deal of action. I knew that at Battalion level, their commanders were up for something like this because they felt they still needed to make a contribution. I proposed that British and American troops would work with around 7,000 Iraqi policemen to begin with – at that stage only 400 had come forward but we were told this was largely for want of a purpose and organisation – and this could turn the tide against the lawlessness that was spreading through Baghdad.

My team and I worked continuously for thirty-six hours. Neil Salisbury was in charge of drafting. We even roped in a UK military police colonel, the excellent Eddie Forster-Knight, who had just arrived in Baghdad, as an ad hoc fourth member of our team. He gave us good ideas based on early British experience in Basra and some of the language we needed to get our proposal just right. With a supportive Walt Slocombe by my side, I then pitched the plan to six or seven senior US officers led by Lieutenant General Scott Wallace and Major General William 'Fuzzy' Webster, by then appointed the Deputy Commander of all allied ground forces in Iraq. When I had finished what was, I have to say, a rather well-swept-up presentation in the circumstances, Fuzzy turned round to the American one-star who was responsible for military policing and asked him for his comments.

'I don't much like this,' he said. And then he made reference to the *Sun* newspaper of all things. 'The *Sun* will make it look like the Brits have come to the rescue.' Fuzzy nodded sagely in agreement. 'But,' continued the one star, 'we need this plan – we need these guys.'

I thought, 'We're in business here.' Having given it the thumbs up, the Americans sent the outline of the proposal to their headquarters in Kuwait and they became very enthusiastic. I telephoned Mike Walker in London and updated him on what was developing. He was supportive.

'High stakes,' he said, 'but I like the idea. Don't commit but I think it sounds good.'

We flew down to Kuwait via Basra where the 'sogginess' I described earlier was all too evident in the cool reception for my plan. Although the battalion commanders of 16 Air Assault Brigade were keen, the brigade commander, Brigadier Jacko Page, was not – he had already sent some of his officers and soldiers home – and neither was Peter Wall. The latter, an old friend, was perfectly civil about it but he was not a supporter on this. It was put to us that US troops were better placed to support the police in Baghdad and it was unnecessary to send British soldiers up there. It became very obvious that the operational chain of command, driven by PJHQ in the UK, had made up its mind that 16 Air Assault Brigade was on its way out and they did not want that decision counter-manded for reasons they were struggling over, with all the work and upheaval that would entail.

Undeterred, we continued to Kuwait to follow up in person with the Americans and again the reception was positive. The Pentagon had the plan and, I was told, it had gone to the White House. I made it clear to the Americans that I was proposing a three-month British deployment. They were ready to sign up for that. I knew there were risks involved for our soldiers but the potential gains for the Coalition effort far outweighed them. In Kuwait, I came across a briefing team, sent out by Tony Blair, whose presence in the region I was unaware of – David Manning, Blair's No. 10-based foreign policy adviser, John Scarlett and Tony Pigott, a Deputy Chief of the Defence Staff. They were all enthusiastic about my plan, especially Manning.

Back in Baghdad on our fifth and final night of an eventful visit, I joined diplomats and other officers at a reception to mark the re-opening of the old British embassy on the banks of the Tigris. It was a beautiful setting but I mention it not for that reason but because I ate something there that was to turn my journey home into a hellish experience. Before the consequences of that fateful reception had fully taken hold, I turned up next morning at Baghdad airport for our final Hercules trip back to Kuwait and then our connection to London.

Without going into too much detail I knew I wasn't right before we boarded the Kuwait Airlines flight to London. We were all sitting in different areas of the plane and I was near the back in the aisle seat of a central block of four, next to a rather large Kuwaiti woman. Not long after we took off the food poisoning hit me with spectacular force. I became semi-conscious and rolled slowly out of my seat and on to the floor where I lay prostrate for some minutes while the cabin staff stepped over me as if nothing had happened. Eventually, the alarm was raised and a Kuwaiti doctor appeared. He gave me an injection and put me on a drip. Then he got me sitting up and suggested I try to get back in my seat. As I did so, I was sick all over the aisle. By that stage, I seriously thought I was dying and Mr T had come to sit next to me. All the way back to London this tough, no-nonsense squaddie from Hull held my hand to reassure me – I can tell you it meant a lot.

By the time we touched down at Heathrow I was starting to feel a little better. The doctor on the plane was adamant that I go to hospital immediately but I just wanted to get home to bed in our apartment in St James's Palace. In the taxi with Mr T, I decided I ought to make a call to Mike Jackson just to let him know that I was back. He came on the phone keen as mustard to get a brief on what I had seen. I told him I wasn't feeling too good. He said something like, 'Yeah, don't worry about that, just get over here, boy, and tell me what I need to know.' I looked at Mr T and thought, 'I've got no choice.'

I was determined I was not going to see the Chief of the General Staff with the contraption the doctor had used to insert the drip still attached to my arm. So I started to try to pull it out without success. Mr T decided he knew best.

'Give me your arm, Sir,' he instructed. Then he gave the thing a bloody great yank and out it came, spraying blood all over the taxi. We had to stop to clean it up and find something to bandage my arm with. The taxi driver was not impressed but he got a decent tip for his trouble.

When I arrived at Jackson's house, his wife, Sarah, took one look at me and said, 'You're not well.'

'I know,' I replied. 'I think I nearly died actually.'

Jackson wasn't having any of it.

'Get him some flat Coke,' he growled and ushered me into his study.

He was delighted with my plan and the way it had gone down with the Americans. He informed me that it would be up to me to present it to the Chiefs of Staff in the morning, at a meeting that he unfortunately would not be able to attend. It was a no-brainer, he said as he released me back in to Mr T's care.

The next morning I turned up at the Old War Office building in Whitehall and went up to the briefing room where the Chiefs met. The walls were adorned with pictures of previous Chiefs and the room was dominated by a large table around which were a series of expensive-looking leather swing armchairs. As Chief of the Defence Staff, Mike Walker sat at one end with the single-service chiefs down from him. Then there were other staff officers and various hangers-on sitting in chairs along the walls. It was quite an intimidating setting for someone with a task like mine that morning. Among others present were John Sawers, who had flown back to support my recommendations, and Tony Pigott, whom I knew backed my plan.

I made a short presentation, knowing the Chiefs had been sent a summary. Immediately, I could tell that Rob Fry, Chief of Staff at the Permanent Joint Headquarters at Northwood, and Mike Walker were agin it – the latter despite his initial reaction to me on the phone. In their camp was the Permanent Secretary Kevin Tebbit. They kept talking of there being only 'anecdotal' evidence of a growing law and order problem in Baghdad. I said angrily that it was not anecdotal. I had just been there and seen for myself what was going on. None of my interlocutors had been there; the only Chief who had – who had returned from Baghdad ten days earlier – was Mike Jackson and he was not present. John Sawers spoke eloquently in favour of my proposal, as did Tony Pigott. The Chiefs came up with all sorts of objections – how would 16 Air Assault Brigade get up there, how would it be supplied, what were the command and control arrangements? How long would it be for? I had answers to all those questions. They concentrated on the risks but completely missed the point of the potential gains.

The Chiefs, fed by the PJHQ who had most at stake, had assembled respectable arguments against my plan, but I sensed their real beef was with me and the mission I had been sent on. I had the impression that they were not prepared to be told what to do on Iraq by an officer in a non-operational appointment who had been sent out by the Defence Secretary outside the normal chain of command. I think no matter how sensible and well-thought-out my plans arguably were, they were not going to accept them on principle – although of course they would not say so in those terms. It had the appearance of a decision taken to assert the authority of those who were responsible for the conduct of the war, irrespective of the sense of the recommendations. I also think some non-Army people in that meeting saw the whole thing – quite wrongly – as an Army plot to keep the Royal Air Force and Royal Navy on the sidelines.

I don't get angry easily but I was livid. I knew what was at stake and I had given my word to the Americans. I was particularly annoyed with my fellow Assistant Chiefs – who were sitting in for their bosses – because they had clearly been told to say no and it seemed didn't have the balls to look at the proposal on its merits. As the meeting broke up, one of them came over to apologise. I wasn't having any of it.

'Don't f****** talk to me about it,' I thundered. 'How do you know what's right? You haven't been near Baghdad.' I walked off in a state of fury and I am sure Mike Walker got the message that I was not happy.

I marched myself back to my office and when I got there the phone rang. It was David Manning at No. 10.

'Is it true?' he wanted to know. I told him it was.

'I can't believe it,' he replied. He told me that he had just briefed Tony Blair on the plan and the Prime Minister, recognising how critical to the whole campaign establishing law and order in Baghdad was, had thought it was a great idea. Now he would have to tell him that Hoon's office would be writing to him on behalf of the Chiefs to say it had been scrapped. I suggested that the Prime Minister might like to tell them to get on with it, but I got the impression that was not going to happen. The government had just had a difficult time with Mike Boyce as CDS and, having got rid of him early, they did not want to get off on the wrong foot with Mike Walker.

A letter was duly drafted for Hoon, recommending that we did not go ahead, and forwarded to No. 10. The next day in a written response entitled 'Security in Baghdad' – which Manning told me included the biggest bollocking by the Prime Minister in writing that he had ever seen – Blair said he would accept the advice of the Chiefs. But he pointed out that it was 'at odds with what Paul Bremer had told John Sawers, David Manning and David Richards' a few days earlier. Blair reminded the Chiefs that Bremer had said that help from 16 Air Assault Brigade would be a valuable contribution to stabilising the precarious security situation in Baghdad. The skills of British troops would have been particularly welcome. The Prime Minister also reminded the MoD that the stakes in Iraq were very high, given the danger that we might be approaching a point of 'strategic failure'. He said he had no doubt that the Chiefs would now be encouraging their US counterparts to ensure that other remedial action was taken to deal with the security situation. The Prime Minister concluded by demanding a report within forty-eight hours, updating him on what steps the Americans were taking both to deal with security in Baghdad and police training.

I felt some vindication when I read it. Of course, regular British troops were never deployed outside the south of Iraq, except for one occasion when the Black Watch was posted to Camp Dogwood between Fallujah and Karbala. Some will say thank God my plan did fail and that British lives might have been lost by soldiers patrolling in Baghdad. But I still believe there was an opportunity there to arrest the slide into anarchy and for Britain to use its experience to help our most important ally in her hour of need. The debacle over my plan was scarring but I made a mental note that if ever I was in the sort of position that the Chiefs found themselves in that morning, I would do my best to judge the facts on their strategic merits.

Despite that setback, my tenure as ACGS was marked by a success that I am still proud of today – saving one battalion from the knife of the bean counters with the creation of the Special Forces Support Group. Under the latest mini defence review in 2004, the civil service, together with the other two services, wanted to cut the Army from 40 battalions to 26. This was a big step in the wrong direction from my point of view and Mike Jackson, with my help and the help of others, managed to talk this back up to 36. But I was still determined to see if I could save one more battalion of the four heading for the chop.

One day I had a eureka moment in the bath. The special forces were growing in importance but they did not have their own, in-house, Ranger Battalion to provide expert close support. This was a unit that could provide the SAS with specialised extra firepower when they needed it, or protective cordons, or even diversionary tactics. The SAS was borrowing this capability on an *ad hoc* basis, usually from the Royal Marines or, more often, the Parachute Regiment, but these units had their own jobs to do and it was quite hit or miss. It struck me that we could create a Ranger Battalion from the manpower in one of the four battalions listed for dissolution. From a special forces perspective, the case for doing so was growing all the time. But I knew the system would be hostile to any proposal like this. As far as the suits were concerned, this was a decision taken and it was too late to change it. I went to Mike Jackson.

'I think we could save another one,' I told him.

'Well good on you, go for it. I have done my bit but if you can do it, I will be delighted.'

I needed to get in front of Geoff Hoon. Apart from anything else, I could see there was political capital in it for him. Keeping another battalion

Above: On exercise with 19 Mechanised Brigade in 1992 are Brigadier Evelyn Webb-Carter (centre right) and his 'Gunner', Lieutenant Colonel Richards (right), plus close-protection team.

Right: As CO of 3rd Regiment Royal Horse Artillery, briefing the new Secretary of State for Defence, Malcolm Rifkind, Salisbury Plain 1992.

Below: Commander 4 Armoured Brigade – on exercise with the Kings Royal Hussars, Poland 1996.

Above: Dili, East Timor,
September 1999 –
presiding over my
daily Orders Group.
Lieutenant Colonel Neil
Salisbury is to my left
and Lieutenant Colonel
Mark Lillington-Price,
Royal Gurkha Rifles, is
to his left.

Right: East Timorese
freedom fighters, the
Falantil.

Left: Talking to
locals outside Dili,
September 1999.

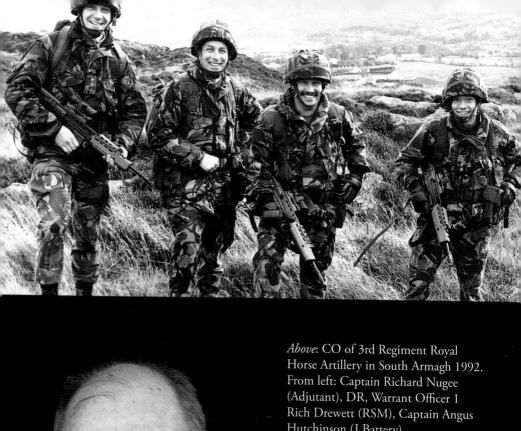

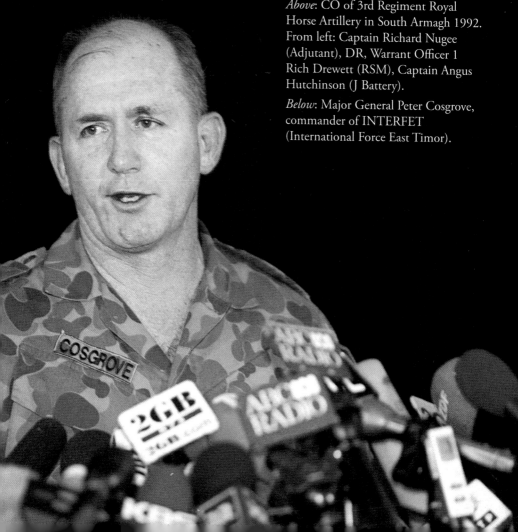

Above: CO of 3rd Regiment Royal Horse Artillery in South Armagh 1992. From left: Captain Richard Nugee (Adjutant), DR, Warrant Officer 1 Rich Drewett (RSM), Captain Angus Hutchinson (J Battery).

Below: Major General Peter Cosgrove, commander of INTERFET (International Force East Timor).

Above: Freetown Blind School. The selfless Deputy Head Barbara Davidson MBE is in the foreground.

Right: Keith Biddle.

Below: Charles Guthrie visits Sierra Leone, May 2000. From left: DR, Guthrie, Colonel Tommy Carew (acting chief, Sierra Leone Army).

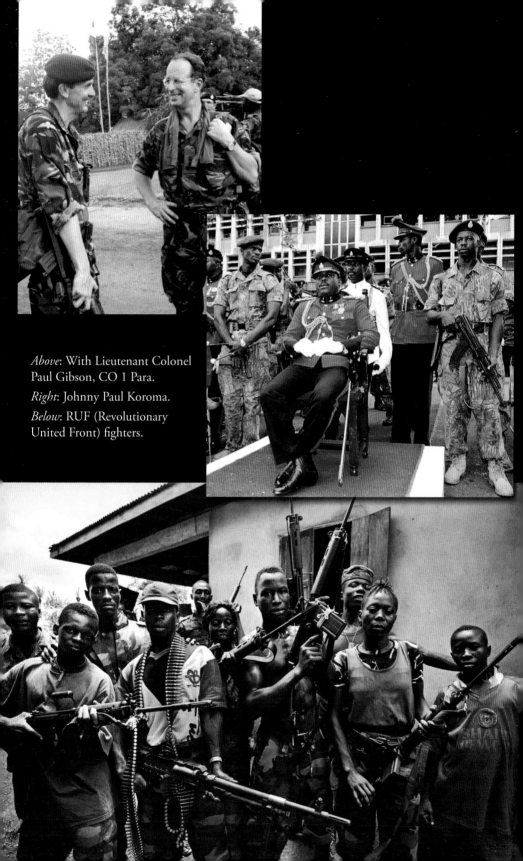

Above: With Lieutenant Colonel Paul Gibson, CO 1 Para.

Right: Johnny Paul Koroma.

Below: RUF (Revolutionary United Front) fighters.

Above: A Kamajor militiaman.

Left: Royal Navy helicopters put marines from 42 Commando ashore in a show of strength, Sierra Leone.

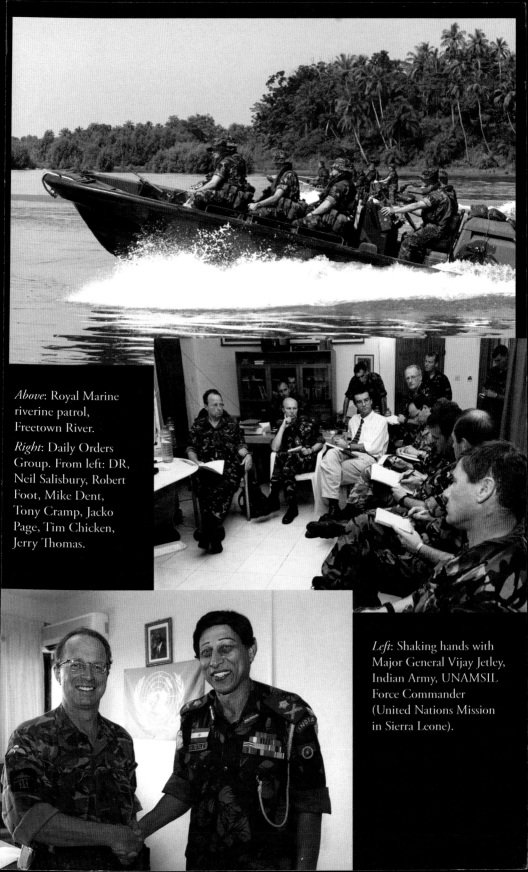

Above: Royal Marine riverine patrol, Freetown River.

Right: Daily Orders Group. From left: DR, Neil Salisbury, Robert Foot, Mike Dent, Tony Cramp, Jacko Page, Tim Chicken, Jerry Thomas.

Left: Shaking hands with Major General Vijay Jetley, Indian Army, UNAMSIL Force Commander (United Nations Mission in Sierra Leone).

Above: Baghdad, 21 May 2003. From left: DR, Walt Slocombe, John Scarlet
Tony Piggott, David Manning
Below: A British soldier watches Iraqi oilfields burn early in the wa

would save hundreds of jobs that would otherwise go on the scrapheap and so protect livelihoods. His civil servants would never let me see him if they knew the real reason I was there, so I came up with a pretext. I e-mailed Hoon's private secretary, a senior civil servant, saying I had been asked to contribute to a book on Sierra Leone and I wanted to check that my interpretation of events and those of the Secretary of State were the same. He took the bait and a date was agreed, one that fell before a final decision on infantry battalions was due to be made.

Somebody must have spotted my ruse, because the meeting was abruptly put back until after the battalion decision. In the meantime, I had been invited to a reception at the Royal Hospital, Chelsea, which I had declined. But when I discovered that Hoon was attending, I saw the perfect opportunity and changed my mind. He and I had quite a good relationship. I had done one or two things for his government – in East Timor and Sierra Leone – so I felt confident I could make some headway.

I got there early and placed myself conspicuously close to the entrance. When Hoon arrived, he immediately saw me and came over. I explained how he could save a battalion and provide a vital new capability for our special forces to boot. He was intrigued and asked me to come and see him at his office in the morning. I did note, however, that one of his junior civil servants was listening to our conversation – not a good thing.

The next morning I arrived at Hoon's office at ten, accompanied by the Director Special Forces. Through the glass wall, we could see Hoon being lectured by Tebbit and we were left waiting for twenty minutes while this went on. I had a sinking feeling.

'The civil service have got to him,' I said.

Eventually, we were ushered in and the four of us sat round a small table. I was opposite Tebbit, and Hoon was to one side, in a kind of umpiring role. He opened the discussion by asking me to amplify my argument of the previous evening and explain why I thought he was on the wrong track. I started to explain but was interrupted by Tebbit, who launched into an exposition of his own that contained some errors of fact. I could not allow these to go unchallenged and interrupted him to say that he had clearly been misinformed. At this Tebbit turned on me and accused me of having conducted a ruthless lobbying campaign for months. Now it was *his* time to speak, he said. It is fair to say that he was annoyed with me.

While Tebbit rattled on, I caught Hoon's eye and I knew in an instant that I had won the argument. He was going to approve my plan. He didn't want to cut the Army anyway. He wanted to bolster our special forces and was keen to avoid a row in Yorkshire. (The unit that was going to be cut was the Green Howards, a Yorkshire battalion.) The Special Forces Support Group would be created. I was over the moon. It came into service in April 2006 and is based at St Athan, near Cardiff. It now supports the SAS, the Special Reconnaissance Regiment and the Special Boat Service.

ELEVEN

Fighting Battles on My Way to Kabul

It was near the end of my tour as Assistant Chief of the General Staff that I was told that my next appointment, on promotion to Lieutenant General, would be as Commander of the Allied Rapid Reaction Corps (ARRC). This was the British Army's senior operational command.

Not many days before that, the Prime Minister, Tony Blair, had agreed at the Istanbul NATO summit that Britain would lead NATO's adoption of responsibility for Afghanistan in the south and the east, thereby completing its authority over the whole country. So I knew, as I left London and reported for duty in January 2005, that this huge operation was going to be mine.

I arrived in Rheindahlen in Germany, where the ARRC was based, to find that Richard Dannatt, my predecessor, had agreed on advice from his own and NATO's staffs that the headquarters would do conventional war-fighting training until October that year. No commander wants to change his predecessor's design for the immediate months ahead; I felt obliged to do just that.

I had done a lot of studying in preparation for Afghanistan before I arrived in Germany, something that Richard and the ARRC staff had not had time to do because of other pressures. I knew that what we were going to be asked to do needed a team that was well trained and well honed, and that understood the country and the people as well as possible. Leaving just a few months to prepare for such a complex task risked failure.

When I raised the issue on my arrival in Rheindahlen the atmosphere became 'interesting' because the senior staff – the Major Generals and the Brigadier Generals – had all contributed to Richard's decision. I asked Chris Brown, a Major General and my Chief of Staff.

'Why have you left less than six months to prepare?'

Chris explained that the NATO training system designed to prepare headquarters for operations had decreed that the ARRC would not be placed on their training roster until October at the earliest. The ARRC staff had not been very happy with the decision but had gone along with it, deciding that the headquarters would make virtue of necessity by concentrating on conventional warfighting until then.

'Right,' I said. 'I'm going to think about this.'

When I got him and a couple of others back in, I told them I was not happy with the existing plans. Not for the first or last time, I found myself ignoring my superior headquarter's intentions. I directed that we were going to turn our attention to Afghanistan immediately. I could feel resentment. I could sense my staff thinking, 'Who the hell is this new guy? He doesn't know anything.'

Six weeks later, Brigadier General Steve Layfield, my outstanding American one-star operations officer on my Afghan tour, came to see me. 'General, I wouldn't normally say this, because it might seem like sycophancy,' he said, 'but that was the best decision any General of mine ever took.' This was because, by then, they had got stuck into the preparation work and had realised the immensity of the task that we faced, running a war involving thirty-seven nations across a huge land area and against a proven and tough adversary in the Taliban.

As our in-depth understanding of what we were about to face grew, this powerful headquarters came into its own. The key players were all Brigadiers and Colonels, not relatively inexperienced Majors and Captains, coordinated by Major General Brown, a highly capable and experienced officer. This was big stuff, a big unit with over 350 personnel in peacetime structured and ready to go to war at short notice. Once we got over the problem of my change of tack, we really began to understand what was required of us in Afghanistan. We had no other responsibility. We did not have troops to command on a day-to-day basis, so we did nothing else except prepare for operations. It was a wonderful job.

During the summer it became clear to me that London in particular was still underestimating the task I had been set. I was a British General about to command a major NATO campaign but my own country was not prepared to give me a helicopter or an aircraft to fly around a country that was half the size of Europe so I could properly exercise command. More important than that, I had no proper reserve force of any kind. No military commander, even at platoon or company level, will go on operations without a reserve. I had none and NATO and my own country appeared content with this. I argued and argued about it, including two stand-up rows with a fellow three-star General in London – literally shouting matches. While undoubtedly he was a competent officer, in this context he was wrong and, I thought, not doing his job properly.

The mood was one of increasing animosity and tension. I remember, for example, one senior female civil servant's reaction during a planning meeting when I referred to the 'NATO plan for Afghanistan', reminding her that my staff and I were deploying as part of a NATO operation. She looked straight at me and said, 'What NATO plan?' I reminded her that there was a NATO campaign plan, to which the UK was a signatory, but she didn't know about it and didn't appear interested.

Mike Walker, the Chief of the Defence Staff, assured me I would have what was required and I know he meant it. But, for whatever reason, I never got my own means of transport for Afghanistan, nor did Britain ever provide a reserve, as I had requested. In the event, the only reserve unit I had was provided by NATO in the form of a light infantry company from Portugal. They were to become firm favourites of mine. They performed heroically, but I could not use them in the toughest areas.

It was John Reid, the Defence Secretary, who came, in part at least, to my aid. He had come to see our big final exercise in Germany before we packed up to go and I explained what had been happening and not happening. 'Tell me more,' he said, and I told him more. His problem was that he didn't want Mike Walker or Lieutenant General Rob Fry, who by then was the MoD's three-star operations officer, to know he was talking directly to me without going through them. So when Reid's special adviser, Matt Cavanagh, asked for another meeting, we had to do it secretly, which seemed a bit absurd then as well as in retrospect. We ended up having a clandestine breakfast meeting in Berlin when Reid was there for a NATO summit. I was summoned by his office and got to Berlin the night before. The next morning I had an hour and a half with him. At the end, he told me, 'I've got this. I will make sure that you get Apache helicopters and artillery and more troops.'

Notwithstanding Reid's promise, shortly before Christmas my sense of being let down by my own country reached its lowest point. We were visited in Rheindahlen by one of the Chiefs of Staff Committee, one of the five most senior officers in the armed forces. He stayed in our house and we held a dinner party for him. After the other guests had left, the two of us sat down in our drawing room to talk about the forthcoming deployment to Afghanistan. It became clear that he felt I was exaggerating the need for more troops and better equipment. Things became fractious. Our raised voices woke Caroline in our bedroom above. Worried, she came down to listen at the door and heard, to her horror, the senior officer say to me, 'If you don't stop making such a fuss about what you think you need in Afghanistan, I cannot guarantee you a fourth star.' Effectively, he was saying to me, if you don't shut-up your career's over. We parted company in ill-humour. I felt very let down but resolved not to stop saying whatever I felt was right to get the operation properly resourced.

If I had a difficult relationship with the UK, it wasn't much better with NATO. My superior in the chain of command was the German General, Gerhard Back. He was a somewhat prickly air-force officer based in Brunssum in the Netherlands. Above him, was US General Jim Jones, the Supreme Allied Commander Europe (SACEUR). Jones was very much the classic, square-jawed, imposing US Marine tough guy. In terms of my relationship with Britain, I wasn't actually in the British chain of command.

I would command British forces in Helmand down a NATO chain, through a subordinate Canadian-led headquarters in Kandahar.

There was a strange episode with General Back at the very end of our preparatory period. Like any senior commander, he was supposed to come to observe my final exercise, but he kept prevaricating, failing to firm up arrangements. On the last day, I was suddenly summoned to breakfast with him but I arrived at his office in Brunssum to find this was clearly going to be a breakfast without food. It was a ticking off. He told me in terms: 'If you don't start conforming, you won't necessarily keep this command.' He was irritated; I was freelancing; I was having too many ideas; I was making a lot of noise about inadequate resourcing and implying that he and others in NATO didn't understand what was needed.

I wasn't going to take this, particularly on an empty stomach on the eve of departure. I turned on him and gave him both barrels.

'*You* don't understand,' I said. 'We've done all this work and I'm telling you, General, you will bear responsibility if we screw this up because I have told you what we need and you're not faithfully repeating that up the chain of command.' To do him credit, Back took the point and I even got some breakfast in the end.

At one point, I was also in hot water with Jim Jones for agreeing to discuss the region and Afghanistan with the Iranian ambassador to the UN whom I met in New York. This seemed a touch unfair given that the meeting with Ambassador Zarif had been organised by the British ambassador to the UN. Sir Emyr Jones-Parry knew NATO and its sensitivities well from his time as the UK's permanent representative at the alliance's headquarters in Brussels. But Jones gave me a really hard time for 'straying out of my lane'. It was to prove a foretaste of what was to come.

My job I discovered – by default – was much more than military, because while there were some perfectly capable people working in Kabul at that time, there were few diplomatic big-hitters. All the civilian activity that was supposed to accompany our activity just wasn't happening, or certainly not on the scale promised to the Afghans. There was no effective process of coordination between the civilian and the military aspects of the Afghan and international effort. It was all rather random and every nation involved had its own agenda and own ideas.

When I got to Kabul, my major military objective was to unify the operation into a single coherent campaign and to improve cohesion among the disparate nations contributing to my force. Cultural, linguistic and operational differences needed to be synthesised. This military activity had to be combined with the political realities of Kabul and the interests of the complex international coalition that I both represented and answered to.

In a technical sense, I never found the military aspects a major challenge. We were well honed and properly prepared. We knew it wouldn't go as per the plan – no plan survives first contact – but that part of our task worked a treat. When I arrived, the Americans were running the two more difficult regions, south and east. On 31 July, I took over the south from the Americans and on 4 October I took over the east from them. So for the last four months I ran the whole show. At that point I had 40,000 troops under me and a large multinational air force. My command was split into five regional headquarters, one in Kabul led by the French, one in the north in Mazar-i-Sharif under the Germans, one in the east in Herat under the Italians, one in the south in Kandahar under the Canadians and one at the huge airbase at Bagram under the Americans.

The first months were dominated by laying the groundwork for achieving those goals and then working on trying to marry the civilian effort with what we were doing and with the inputs from the Afghan government. So how did I solve that? My answer was to devise the Policy Action Group (PAG). This was a high-level Afghan government/international committee that would meet regularly to agree and execute all military and civilian policy in Afghanistan. My diary, some of which follows this chapter, doesn't really cover the key moment – what I call my 'wet towel moment' – when I realised something had to be done. It was after a day of violence in Kabul when an American convoy accidentally ploughed into a street market after the brakes failed on one of the lead vehicles. This quickly led to serious rioting in which several people were killed and NATO soldiers alongside their Afghan counterparts had to use live rounds to restore order.

Such an alarming episode underlined the fact that the security situation was beginning to deteriorate even in Kabul. More importantly, the response to it demonstrated that while the NATO coalition was working well on the ground militarily, there was poor coordination between it and the Afghan government and between the many nations with a stake in Afghanistan, some of which were not under the NATO umbrella. I told my staff, 'We cannot go on like this.' Using Chris Brown and my ever-faithful Military Assistant Lieutenant Colonel Felix Gedney as my sounding boards, I came up with the PAG concept. Critically, it gave the lead in decision-making and implementation to the Afghans.

I went with the proposal to Hanif Atmar, the influential and talented Afghan Minister for Education. He was enthusiastic but doubtful the President would accept what he might view as a dilution of his authority.

'We need this,' he told me. 'But Karzai will never agree to it because he likes to control the country like an old Afghan warlord.'

I took the hint and put an enormous amount of effort into Karzai and building a relationship with him. I would even say to him during our long meetings, 'Mr President, I am *your* General.' It paid off in the end with the successful establishment of the PAG.

The idea was to give him a proper tool for decision-making and coordination, one that had real teeth and could get things done. The committee was chaired by either Karzai himself or his national security adviser Dr Zalmai Rassoul. Tom Koenigs, the UN boss, or sometimes his outstanding Canadian deputy Chris Alexander, was always there, plus myself, Lieutenant General Karl Eikenberry, my US counterpart for the first few months, and the ambassadors from Britain, the Netherlands, Canada and the US. We all sat on one side of a very long table while opposite us were the key Afghan ministers. Occasionally, we would be joined by the visiting boss of the World Bank or other big-hitters.

The PAG was pulled together by a small secretariat led by Arabella

Phillimore from the UK and one of my own officers, initially Group Captain Ray Goodall of the RAF followed by the equally efficient Colonel Ronnie Bradford of the Army. We usually met in the Presidential Palace in a large cabinet room and were invariably treated, as is the Afghan way, to green tea or pomegranate juice, two things the Afghans do better than anyone.

The PAG survived for a while after I left until Sherard Cowper-Coles, British ambassador to Afghanistan and a man of considerable self-conviction, apparently decided there was a better solution. I know that there were people who tried to keep it alive, but without active support from Sherard and his American counterpart it fell into disrepair from the summer of 2007.

My other innovation was the Afghan Development Zone (ADZ). This was a way of ensuring that the civilian and military efforts of NATO and the Afghan government were brought together in ways that would rapidly result in tangible improvements to people's lives. I started working up the idea back in Rheindahlen before I deployed. The aim was to focus our effort in carefully defined areas. They were to be no larger than could be properly secured by our limited number of troops. Over time our beneficial impact could spread out, psychologically as well as geographically, rather like an ink spot on a blotter.

Over Christmas of 2005 I agreed with Colonel Stuart Tootal, commander of 3 Para and a pivotal figure in British operations in Helmand in 2006, that we would pioneer the ADZ concept in Helmand. We agreed at that stage that the British would stay very narrowly focused on Lashkar Gar, the provincial capital, and its environs rather than be distributed thinly all over the place. Even then it was clear to Stuart and me that we just would not have the troops to do more. The thinking behind the concept was that you couldn't be everywhere at once in such a large country. You had to concentrate your military force and your economic and other efforts so that people within the zones would genuinely feel the fruits of Western help. Those outside it would see this and think, 'Actually, I want that, not the hopeless future the Taliban is offering us.' It was, as is so much else in country-insurgency campaigns, a psychological operation in the true sense.

Of course, in Helmand things didn't quite work out like that. Under the national command of Brigadier Ed Butler, who came under pressure from the local Afghan governor, British troops ended up being spread out in fixed positions in a number of small towns – in so-called 'platoon houses' – where they attracted intense enemy activity and suffered significant losses. Trying to sort out a better way forward for the British was one of the main tasks I inherited during the late summer of my deployment.

Like the PAG initiative, the ADZ plan took a great deal of time and energy to get established and accepted. Some people, especially in national capitals, didn't like it because it was not the product of international agreement. It was also seen as something outside the remit of a military commander. That's how inflexible people were. The Germans, for example, objected to their part of northern Afghanistan being considered as an Afghan Development Zone. They didn't want to be part of a structure they regarded as casting aspersions on their efforts. They also feared that creating ADZs would result in too much emphasis on the south and east of the country at their expense in the north. They missed the psychological element of the plan completely and the fact that its real virtue was bringing military and civilian effort together within a single unifying concept.

As far as the prosecution of the war was concerned, things were deteriorating when I arrived but the violence was on a scale that felt manageable. I believed it could be recovered through the proper application of the ADZs, the coordinating power of the PAG, the clinical use of military power and, if necessary, its decisive use. We demonstrated this in my main set-piece battle in Kandahar in the late summer when we inflicted heavy casualties on the Taliban during NATO's Operation MEDUSA. Even then, I also talked about reconciliation. There had to be some political process, too. I saw it as a triad of civilian effort, very focused military effort and political effort.

I used the military in a way that reflected their capability. I would use the Afghan Army and Police, who were often very brave but pretty poor at that time, for unsophisticated tasks, such as guarding checkpoints. Their main task would be to grow in size and capability over the next few years. The next level up was for units that could manoeuvre and confidently take on the Taliban. These would be principally supplied by regular army forces from contributing coalition countries. The targeted, clinical stuff was largely the province of special forces.

I had to work hard – of that there was no doubt – but I was hugely motivated. I was commander of the first 'hot war' in NATO's history and I had no doubt that the campaign could succeed, as long as it was properly resourced and conducted. Although I was keenly aware that my every move was being scrutinised in a number of capitals, I enjoyed tremendous support from my talented and resourceful headquarters team and my subordinate commanders. The combination of that and my affection for the Afghans – who generally offered me strong support as well – gave me the confidence to push on and do what I felt was needed.

I've always enjoyed the non-military aspects of high command and I would spend hours with the tribal leaders and with politicians, trying to integrate all our efforts into a proper strategy. On the military side, I had to get my subordinates, from whatever country, to become accustomed to working to Commander's Intent, a formal written summary of my objectives, what was required of them, and why. I had to accept that every country would probably interpret their orders differently and do things in ways that I had not anticipated. I quickly began to see that. So I put a lot of effort into my Intent. I then told my commanders: 'You do it as you wish, but that's what you've got to achieve.'

My experiences in Afghanistan have convinced me that these big coalitions of disparate forces can work but they need a sophisticated touch at the top. On more conventional tactical operations it wasn't too much of a problem, through an unambiguous Intent and clear coordinating orders and structures. But overall, at the highest level, where politics and the military meet, it is very difficult. Hence the need for a cohering mechanism, along the lines of the PAG. Indeed, in 2008 the Rand Corporation, in a major work on counter-insurgency, concluded that a mechanism 'such as the PAG is a *sine qua non* of success' in such operations.

It is important to remember that I did not have ultimate authority over the nation. That was President Karzai's job. He was the President, so he had to be involved in the PAG. When he chaired our meetings, he was usually very impressive. People have looked at what I was doing in Afghanistan and compared me with Field Marshal Templer, who played a decisive role in defeating the insurgency in Malaya in the 1950s. The point I would make is that, in Malaya, Templer had all the organs of the state under his command – police, military, intelligence, civil agencies, economists, the banks, everything. As a result, he could devise and implement a coherent strategy. If he said 'turn right', the whole machine would turn right and go in that direction. When I said 'turn right' in Kabul, they would all say, 'Well, who are you to tell us anything? We have got to consult our capitals. And secondly, we might not want to do it that way.' So I had to have my initiatives very clearly thought out and I had to have enormous drive to get them through.

I came up with an aphorism to describe how someone in my position had to operate at the civilian/military interface – the 'LIC Principle'. LIC stood for 'listen, influence, coordinate'. While applying this meant matters might take longer to sort out than one might have wanted, we were more likely to get there in the end. And, of course, it allowed for the considerable *integrating* power of a well-honed military headquarters to be applied to the implementation of whatever was agreed.

As soon as capitals did get in the way, it was paralysis, even in the case of London on occasion. I used to say to everyone – and it became a bit of a joke but I meant it – 'Don't ask, don't tell, just do it.' I didn't ask permission for MEDUSA because I knew there would be a two-month period when all the nations and NATO would agonise over whether they could attempt such a big thing. So I just did it. I didn't ask if I could implement the ADZs or the PAG, either. When countries found out about them and said, 'This isn't anything to do with the military,' I replied, 'It's too late.'

Looking ahead at the long-term prospects for Afghanistan and back at the legacy of the war we fought there, I remain largely positive. I believe the West can succeed in its main aim, which was to make sure that the country does not slip back into what it was – a sanctuary for terrorism. We have got to remember that not a single terrorist attack has been planned or executed from Afghanistan since the autumn of 2001 and that a lot of people have given their lives to keep us free of that curse. We owe them and the Afghan people a certainty that we won't betray their sacrifice. And this is by no means just about military effort. Succeeding in the non-military sphere over time is vital if we are to keep a desperately poor nation from giving up on the West, the hopes we raised in their hearts having been dashed. If we fail, at least parts of the country could so easily once again become a haven for people who cold-bloodedly delight in the thought of bringing death and destruction to those who do not share their extreme convictions, be they Christian or Muslim. Memories of 9/11 seem very short, and naivety over the threat we still face is remarkably widespread in political and liberal circles. While we struggle over what to do with ISIS in Iraq and Syria, we can at least help ensure that Afghanistan does not become another part of the so-called caliphate. An accommodation with the Taliban must be a part of the solution in Afghanistan, but only if they explicitly reject their links with Al-Qaeda and it can be adequately policed.

The following three chapters consist of edited versions of the diary that I kept during my deployment as commander of NATO forces in Afghanistan. Every night before I turned in at our heavily fortified compound in Kabul, I sat down at my computer and summarised the key events of the day and my own thoughts on the conduct of the campaign and my role in it.

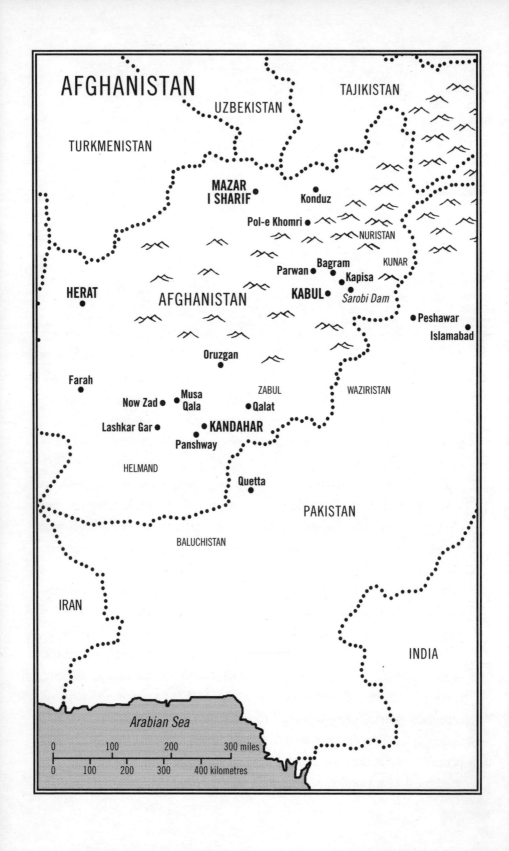

TWELVE

Afghanistan I – NATO
is Here to Fight

My Afghan diary starts in this abridged version on the day I assumed command of NATO forces in Afghanistan, 4 May 2006, taking over from Italian General Mauro del Vecchio. In this first section, I get to grips with the varied elements under my command – soldiers from as far afield as Canada, Germany, Australia and, of course, the USA – and put much effort into building my relationship with President Karzai, often referred to as 'K'. My intention in quoting this contemporaneous record is twofold – to underline the excellent job carried out by the International Security Assistance Force (ISAF) in difficult circumstances in Afghanistan, and to offer a glimpse into the life of a modern commander in time of war and the pressures he is under. I hope that both the military professional and lay reader will find my experience of interest and value.

In these opening months, my principal military focus was to prepare for the smooth takeover by NATO of the hitherto US-led operation in the south and east of Afghanistan, resulting in my command of a single, unified campaign across the whole country. This meant taking substantial numbers of American troops under my command and having to reconcile their instinctively muscular approach with NATO's greater emphasis on reconstruction and development. At the same time, I needed to persuade those NATO nations who were reluctant to acknowledge that this was a proper war that they would need to fight and fight hard. In this respect, I tried hard to introduce more pragmatic reporting, within NATO and in the international press, on the reality of the situation. I also worked on establishing my two key innovations in the running of Afghanistan, the Policy Action Group and Afghan Development Zones.

Among my other tasks was trying to sort out the predicament of British troops in Helmand, where the Brigadier in overall charge, Ed Butler, was coping with intense enemy activity around fixed garrisons, known as platoon houses. I also worked on building relationships with senior military and political figures in Pakistan. And I was getting to grips with the key personnel – diplomatic, political and military – who ran the war in Kabul. Last but not least, I tried to visit as many of my soldiers in the field as possible.

I would ask the reader to remember that I wrote these words late at night after an inevitably long and usually rather taxing day. Tired, my frustration and disappointment is sometimes evident, especially with my superiors in NATO and, sadly, my own country. I would ask those about whom I am sometimes less kind than they would wish or deserve to forgive me and to place my remarks in context.

Thursday, 4 May

The great day arrived. Went into a flurry of TV and radio interviews, including prime time on the *Today* programme. Interviewed by the lovely sounding Sarah Montague. Went down well with my masters in Whitehall and Brussels apparently, so a useful chance to get them to understand that they can trust me.

Then the parade; far too long and some of the flag guard flaked out. General Wardak, the Afghanistan Minister for Defence, made a good speech and said that his friend the 'legendary' General Richards would soon be known not as 'Richards of Africa' but rather 'Richards of Afghanistan'! Not certain General Back (Gerhard Back, a German Air Force officer based in the Netherlands and my immediate superior at NATO's Joint Force Command Brunssum) appreciated it, but most did.

My speech seemed to hit the mark, at least with the US ambassador, Ronald Neumann, who at the reception afterwards told everyone that it was just what they needed to hear and clearly I meant business.

Friday, 5 May

The honeymoon is over – two Italians KIA (Killed in Action) in an off-road IED (Improvised Explosive Device) and four WIA (Wounded in Action). The Bulgarian brigade commander and his team reacted well, as did the German IED team. Italians understandably emotional but Emilio Gay (Major General and my deputy commander) bucked up quickly and seems to be getting a grip. Very sad that one of those killed was a young officer on his last patrol before end of tour and his replacement, a Warrant Officer, was the other fatality.

Otherwise the day was dominated by a very good visit to the US CJTF 76 HQ (US Forces HQ at Bagram). Major General Ben Freakley is bright and a good leader and I know we can get it right together. They are clearly determined to make a good impression on me and I have to say they succeeded. In taking them under command I must be certain not to chuck out a hell of a lot of good baby with any necessary bathwater. They are a class act, make no mistake. Need to get them thinking long term and to seek non-kinetic alternatives (i.e. solutions that do not involve using offensive weaponry). But, broadly, they are trying to do that already and it's a much more joined-up operation, given their ability to chuck money and resources at it, than anything we could do. We have to take the softer approach in part because we have no alternative!

Big reshuffle today at home. John Reid goes to the Home Office as I anticipated and is replaced by the unknown Des Brown. While I understand he's a bit egocentric for some, I'll miss Reid. We had a rapport and I counted him an ally. I'll now have to work on Des Brown! Having just hit it off with Jack Straw, it's a shame he's gone, too; I genuinely liked him. He's been replaced as Foreign Secretary by Margaret Beckett. I hear she can be rather aloof and difficult to deal with.

Monday, 8 May

Pippa's birthday! I hope my card has reached her. Had a rotten night with a stomach bug and a bit of a lie-in as a result. Then had no option but to get into my stride. The antibiotics seemed to get to work halfway through the day, which was just as well. Meeting with Cetin [Hikmet Cetin, Turkish former Foreign Affairs Minister, serving as NATO's first Senior Civilian Representative in Afghanistan] in which he apologised for not being able to take me to Pakistan with him; blamed NATO HQ, which tallies. Either way, he seems a great bloke who understands the country well and I look forward to working closely with him. Then lunch with Ron Neumann, US ambassador; I think we'll get on fine and I can turn him into a supporter. Back to HQ. Took a welcome call from the Secretary General of NATO, Jaap de Hoop Scheffer, who expressed firm support and wished me well – good of him and I hope we can develop a relationship. Shortly after that on to my first session as COMISAF [Commander International Security Assistance Force] with President Karzai. I wait for feedback but Terence Jagger [my political adviser, a senior MoD civil servant] whom I took with me, was positive. Certainly the atmosphere seemed very good.

Thursday, 18 May

Dinner for a group of visiting British MPs. I had to make another speech. I sometimes wonder if I am a politician or a soldier. Nicest thing to happen to me all day, though, was when one of the MPs told me that my officers did not like me, they loved me and would follow me anywhere. It's the sort of feedback that does a chap good! I asked him how he knew this and he said he had been talking to a lot of people and it was a consistent theme. Pride before a fall . . .

Saturday, 20 May

Some horrendous reports of Coalition and ANA [Afghan National Army] reverses are coming in. Effective enemy attacks, lots of casualties and not much on the upside. We have a war on our hands, whatever our reluctant politicians like to think, and they'd better start giving us the tools, rules and resources required to win it. Good command group supper and should be in bed by 2330 hours. Luxury.

Thursday, 25 May

A very pleasant duty: some soldiers led by the redoubtable Transport NCO, Corporal Mummery, had organised a Virtual World Cup competition. Tonight was the final, Japan v. Ecuador. Most of the teams, including these two, were British. It was all done in great style with me 'meeting' the teams before the match with national anthems, acquired from the Internet. Good match won by Japan. Afterwards we had the prize-giving and some special prizes. Made a short speech thanking everyone; showed soldiers at their very best, especially as it was all in aid of Caroline's Rheindahlen Afghan Appeal (so far over 1,000 Euros raised, which is splendid). Then had one of those revolting buffet suppers of fat-soaked 'bits' but enjoyed having a great chat with the soldiers.

Saturday, 27 May

Straight to a German reception; some useful networking with Afghans and diplomats alike. Met the head of the Gailani family (hugely influential and like to compare themselves with the Hashemite family *et al*) and tickled him pink when I said that I had just been talking to his brother. In fact, it was his rather portly son. Also talked to General Wardak and the Speaker of the Upper House, whom I met the other day for the first time. I sense a consensus on need to get a grip on the international community and donors, and many compliments for the way I handled the PRT [Provincial Reconstruction Team] meeting two days ago.

Sunday, 28 May

A long but interesting and productive day. Started very early and flew by German C160 to Konduz. Short chat with an impressive German Colonel who runs the PRT there; look forward to visiting him properly in a few weeks' time. Then a white-knuckle and exhilarating flight by German CH53 helicopter at very low level to Pol-e Khomri. Took what I hope will be some good video from the open back of the aircraft. Some stunning terrain, from wild, craggy mountains and fast-flowing rivers to almost rolling pastureland. Good visit to the Dutch PRT there and, although one wonders if they really read anything one sends them, they are on the right tracks and doing a good job. My biggest concern is the thought of the well-intentioned but inexperienced and hopelessly ill-resourced Hungarian unit due to replace them in October.

Monday, 29 May

A US Army heavy lorry coming into Kabul had break failure and careered into a crowd of bystanders and some parked cars. A number of people were killed and injured. The crowd understandably made their dissatisfaction apparent. The young, inexperienced and no doubt alarmed US soldiers overreacted and either fired into the crowd or certainly into the air, including with large calibre machine guns. The upshot was that we had rioting crowds rampaging through central Kabul most of the day. A number of NGO/IC compounds and houses were targeted and some looted and burnt-out. The merry sound of gunfire could frequently be heard by us, some of it very close. At one stage, I had to order some Royal Marines to extricate the EU compound team and then go back into the centre of town to get a four-year-old child from a crèche. Not surprisingly, all concerned were emotionally grateful. I quipped to their boss that perhaps we might get some EU money now. The HQ played a key role in stabilising things. Steve Layfield [US Brigadier General, my Deputy Chief of Staff Operations, often referred to hereafter as Steve] was very impressive.

Saturday, 3 June

Back to an interesting intellectual jousting session with Simon Jenkins of the *Sunday Times* and *Guardian*. He has been a powerful critic of what the international community and NATO are attempting to do here. I hope I helped put him right – he was not seeing the strategic wood for the trees and overestimates the value of straight military power in a counter-insurgency operation – but, again, we must await events. It would be a real coup to turn him, even partially. Rory Stewart, an eccentric yet intrepid old Etonian and ex-FCO [Foreign and Commonwealth Office] diplomat, was with him. Had lunch with them both and got the grey cells working.

Monday, 5 June

Started early with a trip to have breakfast with Stephen Evans [British ambassador to Afghanistan] and Hilary Benn [Secretary of State for International Development], plus some hangers-on. Benn is an impressive man – listens and is more decisive than his rather earnest appearance suggests. Took my point about his department's spending needing to match the harsh realities of the security situation. His civil servants were more resistant, typically, but I sense headway being made.

Then to the very smart BAC 146 of the Queen's Flight we have for the trip to Islamabad. Karl Eikenberry (Lieutenant General and Commander of the US Combined Forces Command, my US counterpart) and two Afghan Lieutenant Generals were suitably impressed, which was the aim. Karl had his photo taken sitting in the seat HM normally occupies and confided that his ambition was for him and his wife to meet the Queen. Leverage to store away. On arrival, went straight to see Sir Mark Lyall-Grant, the British High Commissioner. Straightforward, natural man whom I liked intuitively. Gave me an excellent summary of the situation from the Pakistan perspective and we agreed a few ways in which together we might improve matters between the two countries.

Tuesday, 6 June

A fascinating day. Major General Pasha, the Pakistan Army's Director General of Military Operations, explained confidentially and reasonably why Pakistan did not deal with the Taliban in Quetta – it risked upsetting 2.5 million Afghan Pashtuns, turning them into violent enemies of President Musharraf, to join many in Baluchistan, Waziristan and, simmering away, many other places. He admitted it just was not in their national interest at this stage to try to crack down heavily. However, they did not support or incite trouble in Afghanistan, whatever the position might have been even five years ago. I accepted much of it, although he agreed that he could not account completely for some elements in the ISI [Inter-Services Intelligence – Pakistan's leading intelligence agency].

Pasha 'frankly' questioned whether we knew our enemy. We could kill hundreds but if we did not know even how many there were or what really motivated them, what was the point? This was clearly directed at the US approach but completely lost on the Americans with me, who persuaded themselves that he was talking about the need for better intelligence rather than making a much more fundamental point. I agreed and asked whether we should be looking at expanding the scope of the operation, taking a much more theatre-level approach that might eventually result in a proper joint campaign, involving Afghanistan and Pakistan. Pasha and Lieutenant General Karimi [Chief Operations Officer of the Afghan National Army] were in support, Eikenberry more muted. One reason may be that my press conference on Sunday has upset the US. They do not like the inference (theirs) that we need to do things differently because they have screwed up. I reassured him that, because of their hard work, we can now emphasise reconstruction and development. I refused to back down on the need for us all to drive much more carefully. He seemed mollified but I will write to him and Ben Freakley explaining what I said and why.

Back on the 146 with Steve – just my own team this time. A relaxing flight. Straight to a long dinner at the Kabul UK Battalion HQ with General Richard Dannatt [Commander in Chief, Land Forces] who is here on a visit. Long discussion with him over dinner and then a private chat. Supportive and in good form. Updated me on some Military Secretary stuff that I actually knew, but refused to confirm what lay in store for me next, although hinted that it would be his position, if I produced the goods here. Understandably perhaps, he will not wish to commit himself until the last moment.

Thursday, 8 June

A fascinating meeting with two tribal leaders from Helmand. Very keen to help but want their controversial ex-governor reinstated. I was tough on an implied threat to UK troops if this did not happen but supportive in principle if all concerned, especially the man in question, Sheer Mohammed Akinzada, were clear that he had to be squeaky clean – no corruption, no narcotics. They said he would agree to this and I said I would have him sacked at a hint of it. Agreed to meet again and that action may have to wait until 31 July. What faces they have – strength and wisdom combined with cunning. Straight out of the first Flashman book.

Friday, 9 June

A fascinating day. Started steadily but rapidly gathered pace. Got up late (Friday is our morning off) and headed for my first really long meeting with Karzai. I wait to hear corroboration but he seemed to be hanging on every word. As I spoke, I became conscious that I was influencing a crucially important man and I had better be right; the stakes are very high. We discussed Pakistan and I think I helped him keep things in perspective; talked up Major General Pasha and other moderate influences. Discussed the desirability of slowly developing a joint campaign with Pakistan and he seemed to see the logic. He was not nearly as vehement about them as others had warned me he would be, and I know he has been. On the 2.5 million Afghans that Musharraf is frightened of turning against him if he takes out the Taliban leadership in Quetta, K says he could keep them sweet for him and he should not worry about it. I think the next step, because this holds very exciting possibilities, will be to talk to the British High Commissioner in Islamabad to see if he thinks he could broach it with Musharraf.

On the riots in Kabul, I took a chance and told him that I didn't think there was a big conspiracy and that most of it was spontaneous looting, with little real political coordination. He, again, seemed to take it well. On the big issue of my new plan/approach, he seemed really excited by the opportunity it offers him to assert his leadership. We discussed the mechanics and, by the end of the meeting, which lasted well over my allotted forty-five minutes, he agreed to get together the key Afghan ministers, key ambassadors, me and Karl, and Tom Koenigs, the UN Special Representative of the Secretary General, to give us clear strategic direction. We would establish a new Afghan/international community joint committee (I recommended it be called the Policy Action Group) chaired by him and charged with translating his Intent into early action, focusing on the south initially (our pilot scheme) . . .

A few other meetings, most important of which was with Nick Kay of the FCO, who is the UK's Regional Coordinator in Kandahar. Terence reckoned I would not like him but he was fine and we can certainly do business together; we must. He had on a very crumply summer suit and has a beard, which suits him. He's like someone out of a Graham Greene novel.

Tomorrow's a very busy day: trip to the south and then back to a call with Karl and then a dinner with Francesc Vendrell [EU ambassador to Kabul] et al. So far so good but my goodness this is complex stuff. So much depends on instinct and whether one is prepared to take a risk. Interestingly, Steve said Karl is not a risk taker and very ambitious, which explains his caution. He said I was just the opposite; was this a compliment – not certain really, although it was meant to be.

Saturday, 10 June

Flew down to Kandahar and had a long but thoroughly worthwhile discussion with the Canadian Brigadier General David Fraser and his command team. David seems excellent and I look forward to taking him and his troops under command. Then on to Camp Bastion in the middle of Helmand Province and 3 Para. I know Lieutenant Colonel Stuart Tootal, the CO, well from when he was my Military Assistant in my stint as ACGS [Assistant Chief of the General Staff]. He is serious and ambitious but justifiably so and I rate him highly. Again, his instincts are spot on and he, too, is being over-commanded by virtually everyone above him, whether formally in his chain of command or not. The UK Colonel in Helmand is not proving up to the job and needs his span of command reduced. I will discuss with Ed Butler [Commander British Forces in

Afghanistan] who should be much more focused on Helmand than he is. Ed is very capable but, without meaning to, wears his talent on his sleeve. He is the sort of competent but slightly arrogant British officer that upset the US in the Second World War. David Fraser told me earlier that Ben Freakley has no time for him but, as he appears to have little for me at the moment, maybe David's reading too much into it. Also met Tom Tugendhat; highly intelligent, charming character straight out of the Great Game. [Nineteenth-century rivalry between British and Russian Empires for control in Central Asia]. He is Governor Daoud's UK adviser and very knowledgeable.

Tuesday, 13 June

A day entirely dominated by General James L. Jones's visit [NATO's Supreme Allied Commander Europe]. I warmed to him more as the day went on and he visibly relaxed. Very supportive but at the same time pragmatic. I could not ask for more from my superior. With him and General Back looking after us – and today at any rate I do feel that – I feel more confident still about having the courage to trust my instincts. On a video teleconference with the Secretary General, he apparently painted a rosy picture about a 'real change of atmosphere' and some 'innovative, fresh planning'. Karzai told him that I was 'very popular here in Afghanistan'; all helps. Most of the day spent in briefings and office calls.

Wednesday, 14 June

Another very busy day started with breakfast with the Secretary of State for Defence, my new friend and boss Des Brown. He was fine but tired and no doubt bemused by some of the military jargon. He took in the big points, though, and I sense an ally. Jock Stirrup, the CDS, was there, too. Told him his excuse on the lamentable state of R&R flights would not work on our soldiers and that he should buy some new planes, if that's what it takes. Des took notice when I asked if he wants to start seeing letters in the papers from wives and families who feel this vital moral contract is being ignored. Jock was in good enough form, although he is no tactician and sensibly wants to stay clear of it.

Went straight from breakfast to the airfield to fly south to Kandahar and then Lashkar Gar in Helmand. A good visit to Charlie Knaggs [Commander of Britain's Task Force Helmand] and his team. Knaggs brought home the complexity and difficulty well, and nicely echoed my prescription, which was good of him. Then back to Kandahar – fifty-five minutes by Blackhawk helicopter each way, which emphasised the immensity of this country (two provinces in the south are the size of the whole of Iraq) – and an overlong but useful enough series of presentations by US and Canadian officers. After the US talk on their concept, a very bright US two star whispered over my shoulder, 'What happens after that?' He was getting at a key point – the US appear to have no campaign plan, just a series of tactical objectives wrapped around 'kinetic' solutions, rather than seeking to cure the causes of the conflict. That's something I can help them address. General Jones and I then coxed and boxed at a press conference. I have genuinely started to like this big, talented man who is perfect at his job, other than perhaps, rumour has it, not standing up robustly to his political masters when needed. We shall see.

Friday, 16 June

A slightly worried phone call from Ed Butler in Helmand, who, between him and the MoD, has caused a thirty-six-hour delay to Operation MOUNTAIN THRUST, the US's big drive in the south. It has infuriated Ben Freakley, who is due to come under me shortly. He is already in poor humour because of us, but Ed may be right and, if so, good for him, in principle, for getting the US to do a rethink. I wish it had not been so late in the day, though; both he and the UK have known about this operation for a few weeks now. Soldiers living out in the hills will be waiting to start moving; that bit is not good and I told Ed so. That said, I certainly would not be conducting this sort of operation and will not do so when I take over that area from Karl in a few weeks. Big sweeping movements are more akin to conventional operations and how do you sustain the effect once the troops withdraw?

Saturday, 24 June

First big event was with K, his key ministers and international community members, a kind of PAG proof of concept. He did not grip it in the way I had wanted but I am pleased to report that, fundamentally, and thanks to some good footwork by Hamid Atmar [Minister for Education] and me, we have what I was after. He made it clear that he was not happy with the way things were going and gave us two weeks to come up with an alternative plan. This has given me the headroom I need, especially as he also used some other one-liners we had fed him on the need for a much more coherent and focused approach, starting in the south. This allows me to propose my security zones concept with some authority and I have strong support already from Atmar and most of the international community. I will need to see General Wardak and Moqdel (Interior) to ensure that they properly understand and support the way I propose to use their assets in a less demanding role, one that better suits their training state and equipment. In essence, they will primarily perform the largely static and more routine security tasks, my more capable ISAF troops will have a manoeuvre role linked closely to the protection at distance of the security zones, and I will use special forces in depth to retain the initiative and keep the enemy guessing.

Sunday, 25 June

I am not certain that Ben Freakley yet has his heart in it; everything about him suggests resentment and absolute focus on so-called 'kinetic' solutions. He does not seem to understand that we are not going to do things in the way the US has done them. Even if we could, which we can't, I would not want to. Herein lies the source of his resentment. It's combined with a belief that we don't appreciate the strength of the enemy, but even this is not that pertinent. He thinks we can defeat the Taliban principally through killing more of them. I don't share this view, seeing it as just one weapon in the armoury, along with much speedier reconstruction and development, a political outreach programme, and much else. As he will shortly be responsible for delivering much of my campaign, I am worried, although Steve keeps telling me that he will do as he is told. Is this good enough? The irony is I genuinely like him but he must have his heart in it . . .

After a good and harmonious lunch with Karl, had to move quickly to a two-hour meeting chaired by Tom Keonigs in response to yesterday's direction from Karzai. While continuing to try to keep my fingerprints off the ownership of this (I think the US certainly has wind of it but it does not appear to be upsetting them so far), I think I am persuading everyone to do as K wishes. At one stage, the Netherlands ambassador said, 'Why, after we have been trying to persuade Karzai to do things like this for three years, has he suddenly sparked?'

Thursday, 29 June

A day dominated by a very satisfying visit to a far-flung part of Afghanistan – Farah Province. Right down in the south-west corner it shares a border with both Iran (predominantly) and Pakistan. Very neglected and very poor as a result, with a largely agnostic Pashtun population. But, having spent well over two hours talking with everyone from the Deputy Governor (the Governor has done three years in a US prison for drugs offences and seems to have gone AWOL!) to some small boys and shopkeepers, I am certain that it is 'recoverable'. As ever, despite a nervous close-protection team, the high spot was talking to the shopkeepers and local population. They are a decent, straightforward bunch who deserve so much better. I asked the boys, all clad in rags really and patently unwashed, what they wanted to do when they grew up. One replied 'an investment banker'! Employment is key: jobs, jobs, jobs! Much too much development money goes on sandal-wearing initiatives that have no economic impact.

Sunday, 2 July

It is quite clear that people are increasingly aware of my influence over K and are intrigued by it. I need to keep a low profile or all the usual rivalries will kick in to undermine my aims.

Monday, 3 July

Every UK position except the main base came under fire last night, but because, mercifully, there were no casualties, it did not merit a mention in the press. The situation down there is serious and we need to bring it home to people. Then a short briefing from my GCHQ officer on atmospherics – useful before I see Karzai later today. My GCHQ guy is a great chap, full of initiative and very loyal – I hope he prospers.

Thursday, 6 July/Bahrain

A long day spent ensconced under the able and relaxed chairmanship of UK's Chief of Joint Operations Lieutenant General Nick Houghton. While I am concerned about the command and control arrangements he has agreed to in Helmand, Nick is very capable and a good friend, as is Peter Wall [Major General] who leads on Afghanistan at two-star level in the MoD. The conference took place in a typically smart US naval HQ about ten minutes from our hotel; all British, other than an hour when Brigadier General Mark Kimmit joined us. He is the Chief Planner at US Central Command based at Tampa, Florida. Mark is very intelligent but a rather cold and ambitious officer who apparently has few friends to go with the respect everyone holds him in. He put up a chart that was meant to list all US Central Command's achievements since 2001. It included a tick against 'Taliban Defeated'. I took issue with that and he mumbled something unconvincing. It may explain why I am having trouble persuading some in the US to proceed quickly to Stage 4 (takeover of Regional Command East by NATO). A more sinister thought also occurred to me. If they can persuade themselves, and others, that the US has defeated the Taliban, in due course and with a bit of creative accountancy, they might convince people that all was hunky-dory until NATO took over. Perish the thought!

Friday, 7 July

Back to discover some good news. The UK has agreed to send some 800 or so reinforcements to Afghanistan, including two companies of infantry and half a regiment of sappers, together with some odds and sods. Perhaps Ed Butler and I are being listened to after all? They will come under my command on 31 July, along with the rest of the UK forces. The Secretary of State and CDS both want to speak to me on Monday morning, the former certainly to discuss how to handle the media and any suggestion in the House that the UK is doing all this but the rest of NATO are not doing enough. I have a good story to tell and am confident that I can get him out of this potential trap. It tallies with Nick Houghton's report in Bahrain that, after his recent visit, Jock Stirrup, the new CDS, has told people in the MoD to raise their game and that we need to win this one before worrying about armed forces reconstitution etc. At last; I knew Jock had it in him, even if he can appear a bit of a cold fish.

Saturday, 8 July

A wearing day in which I found myself constantly having to bolster people's resolve and work hard to ensure the various initiatives I have set in train remain on track. At one point I found myself uncharacteristically despondent; I seemed, in my own mind, to be having personally to keep the entire show on the road, from the low tactical through to the strategic. By the time I knocked off, though, things had improved and my usual optimistic spirits had been reignited. Even Donald Rumsfeld [US Secretary of Defense] has changed his programme for next Tuesday in order to give me a forty-five-minute office call, after which he's asked me to join him on his visit to K, including lunch; amazing, someone's got to him! I also seemed to have got almost 100 per cent agreement from the Afghan government and the international community on my PAG proposals. If K agrees our recommendations, we will have transformed the political and military landscape in the last four weeks; it's been a hard slog and there's some way to go to deliver it all, but at least we have set the strategic and many of the military conditions for success. The US's sensitivities are my biggest problem. The only sadness was the death of a Spanish soldier in Farah Province; there will be doubts raised about whether the medevac [medical evacuation] capability in that area was sufficient and I directed that we must have the answers ready ...

Then a session with my GCHQ officer before a useful and necessarily over-long meeting with my two-star officers. From the sublime to the ridiculous, our discussion ranged from my turning down a proposal that we should have full-body massages delivered by Russian female masseuses in a room in the gym (an Italian idea) through to a review of our communications plans for Stage 3 expansion (my assumption of command for the south). This must somehow accommodate NATO's desire to make a big splash as well as the US's sensitivity to any suggestion that we will do things differently or any better. We'll find a way – somehow!

Sunday, 9 July

A red-letter day – how things can change in twenty-four hours. Then I felt war weary, fed up with battering sense into people. Today, I have gained almost everything I set out to do less than a month ago. Mixed with a feeling of elation, there is much relief. I do not know what I would have done without strong support from the Afghan government and the international community. I suppose I would have got on and implemented the security zones idea, now officially to be called Afghan Development Zones (ADZs), but without others it would not have been a great success, at least in the short term. Through adopting the Policy Action Group concept (Minister Atmar was gracious enough to acknowledge that he had misjudged K's appetite for it and congratulated me on pulling it off) and its probably even more important Implementation Team, as well as the ADZs, we may soon be able to achieve genuine unity of effort across military and non-military activity, all driving towards a commonly agreed aim.

Monday, 10 July

Rushed off for a bizarre sail in a clapped-out dinghy on a lake about thirty minutes from the HQ with Michael Semple, an eccentric but very brave Irishman. Michael works for the charming, highly experienced EU Ambassador Francesc Vendrell and has an encyclopaedic knowledge of the country. He speaks fluent Pashtu and his Dari is almost as good, and he is a huge supporter of the subtle approach I am seeking to institute, as well as innovations such as the PAG. On the way out to the lake, he gave me some very useful advice on ADZs and how to exploit Afghan culture.

Much of his job is spent trying to persuade the Taliban to enter the reconciliation programme under ex-President Mojaddedi. He travels in native clothes to the most dangerous areas and is altogether, with his long beard and boyish face, something out of the Great Game. We had a short but very wet sail on the lake; I was completely soaked but enjoyed my few minutes at the helm. An ex-Taliban commander is building up a minor tourist spot there – very tatty in a charming way with some distance to go, but a brilliant start. Back late for Command Group dinner.

Tuesday, 11 July

To the US HQ for my session with Donald Rumsfeld. We sat opposite each other with just Karl and the Assistant Secretary and Acting Ambassador in the room. Rumsfeld opened by saying that a lot of people had told him I was 'something special' and he should listen to me. He asked me for my summary of key issues. No time for use of notes or prompts and in for a penny, in for a pound. He listened intently, asking the right questions when a point needed some elaboration. Then we got to the key issue of Stage 3 to 4. I explained my position and stressed the need for a single, coherent operation, especially given the seriousness of the situation. He asked why things had got worse in the south and I explained that there had not been sufficient troops and civilian investment. Of course, this appeared a criticism of his policies and he retorted that there were enough troops. I pushed back gently, saying that, for good reason, they had been concentrated in the east and Zabul, a model operation (!). In Helmand, on any given day there were rarely more than 150; nor were there sufficient in Kandahar. He seemed reluctant to accept my point but nodded, and we moved on. At the end he thanked me cordially and said he was not certain whether I was the five star and he was the three star, with a genuine smile on his face.

While he was having a pee before we moved on to see K, the Deputy Ambassador said I had landed a 'killer blow'. I am not certain what he was referring to. It could have been my point about the need for more resources in the south, or the way I stressed that NATO nations were now fighting properly when needed and had already agreed to some limited deployment from the north to the south, a useful first step. I hoped he was referring to the need to synchronise Stage 3 and 4, but he could have meant I had killed off my career!

We walked together to the vehicles. I asked Rumsfeld how he kept so fit (he looks not much more than 60 to 65, certainly not his 74 years) and he explained it was by playing squash, which he did with 'cunning', which I believed. He was very convivial and I have a photograph of us together that confirms it. He spoke of me to the President as someone who 'had just given me my marching orders and is clearly the five star!' K seemed delighted, which was good.

Wednesday, 12 July

A dreary Group of Principals meeting chaired by the NATO Senior Civilian Representative. Good time for me to update and grip a bunch of largely second-order diplomats for their country's failure to provide helicopters for their troops. I had a particular dig at the French and Turks on this point. Both countries have got plenty of helicopters sitting idle at home. Described it as irresponsible, which hit home. Next major event was a meeting with Karzai, Karl and Chris Alexander (the superb Canadian Deputy Special Representative to the UN) to discuss allegations against the Uzbek leader Dostum. Whatever the rights and wrongs, we had to conclude that no action could be taken because GOA did not have sufficient authority or clout to act, nor did we have the means.

Thursday, 13 July

Routine stuff before a short meeting with the Belgian Vice Chief of Defence, who was full of sorrow over the fact that he had not been able to deliver on his honestly given pledge to deploy a company of Belgian infantry. His useless parliament had, contrary to his expectations, voted against it. He bought me a nice paperweight shaped like Belgium as a consolation. I do not know if I want a memento of this often rather uninspiring country but the people individually cannot be held to account for their collective failings. As I was returning to the office from a two-star group meeting, my Military Assistant said he had been telephoned on the quiet by his MoD counterpart to ask what my view would be on doing an eighteen-month tour. It would appear that I had gone down too well with Rummy. I am hugely flattered as the US Army has fought hard to put a US officer in my job next. It's a huge vote of confidence but has big implications for Caroline and the family, as well as for me.

Friday, 14 July

Off to the airport for a trip to Bagram, the largest US military base in Afghanistan, and a day spent with various types of US special forces; a very privileged few hours in which they told us things that few if any Brits know. The Delta Force types are impressive and the Army special forces not much less so. Very brave, very determined men who are genuinely at war. There is a place for such people, and if they have been tasked to do things that are sometimes counter-productive, I do not blame them.

Friday, 21 July/London

After dropping into the MoD to do some useful corridor walking – powerful elements in the Pentagon are definitely after me extending but no consensus yet – on to No. 10 for a useful session with Sir Nigel Sheinwald (foreign policy adviser to Tony Blair) to discuss some points Karzai made to Blair in a recent phone call. Apparently, K insisted that the PM must see me. Blair is out of London but Nigel is in many ways as good and was robustly helpful, although with a UK-centric view, especially on narcotics, which I hope I placed in context for him. We shall see.

From there back to the RAG (Army and Navy Club) and a fifteen-minute phone call with David Cameron, the new Tory party leader, who is visiting Afghanistan next week. He wanted to talk before his visit, and just in case we miss each other, which is a possibility. He seemed genuinely interested and spoke naturally, asking me what the key issues are and stressing that he was supportive yet wanted constructively to offer any criticism or advice to the government.

Saturday, 22 July/Wiltshire

Pretty quiet other than a call from General Sir Rupert Smith [retired senior army officer with extensive operational experience] enquiring how things were going. At some point, I may understand this business better than Rupert does but in the meantime I am grateful for his interest and advice. His firmest suggestion was to keep a lower media profile. As a commander, he was never comfortable with the media and many of his considerable admirers feel he failed to influence events as much as he could and should have done. There are risks attached to any media exposure but, in modern operations, there are big gains to be had, too. A balance has to be struck and, on this one anyway, I think Rupert's advice may be wrong; I need to drive opinion, especially when there is so much confusion in Afghanistan as well as in many national capitals.

That said, I received an email from Terry McNamee of RUSI (Royal United Services Institute) apologising for the Guardian misquoting my speech yesterday. The headline was that I had said there was 'near anarchy' in Afghanistan. What I actually said was that the way some international organisations, PSCs [private security companies] and NGOs [non-governmental organisations] operated was close to anarchy and that they needed to pull together and work to common aims. I then spoke of the way President Karzai was firmly gripping this tendency through the creation of his Policy Action Group etc. My concern is that the *Guardian* article will appear to Karzai as if I am saying that he has no grip and authority, the opposite of what I was attempting to portray. It could damage my relationship with him at a critical juncture in the operation.

Monday, 24 July

What a fuss over the *Guardian* misquotation. Nato's Supreme Allied Commander Europe rang me from Washington ostensibly on Stage 3 criteria but really because the Secretary General, Jaap de Hoop Scheffer, had returned to his office from his habitual weekend off to read the *Guardian* article and had been 'very angry' about it. The *Guardian* had twisted my words and I am angry about that but does it justify this petty response? Any thought for all the good we have done for a rather supine organisation that in most people's view had 'lost' the media battle before we arrived? Today, while we need to do much more, things are vastly better and we are being given the benefit of the doubt. This is partly because we have been honest instead of trying to spin our way out of problems and criticism.

Mark Laity [now NATO spokesman, Kabul] rang later warning me that things were bad in Brussels and that I was on 'a yellow card'. From the tone of his voice I sensed that he was enjoying this little drama, especially when he made the mistake of telling me that if he had seen the speech before I had given it, he would have removed the offending sentence. No doubt this is what he has told his mischief-making pals in Brussels instead of explaining I was misquoted and emphasising all we were achieving for them, as I told him in no uncertain terms he had better start doing. Anyway, I made it clear that I wa unrepentant, although I regret very much any damage caused to my relationship with Karzai.

Saturday, 29 July

An excellent medal ceremony for my favourite contingent – the Portuguese Commando company. They leave shortly and in my third speech of the day, I made the high regard in which I hold these excellent troops very clear. They deserve the highest praise for what they have done tactically but also because of the strategic example they have set at such a critical time. Back for some farewell office calls from loyal ARRC staff, sadly leaving, followed by a very necessary but all too brief session in the gym. Then a phone call from General Back but he brought up the f***ing just wish they would all tell the Dutchman that he should be grateful for what we are doing out here and not be obsessed by one bad headline. I know what it will lead to – a belief that I am a good operational soldier but not suitable for the political complexities of four-star rank. I would like to see them try to juggle all these pressures and egos and still actually achieve something worth having as opposed to being the unadventurous, cautious crew that most of them clearly are.

Sunday, 30 July

Well, in less than two hours I will be responsible for sorting out the turmoil in the south. It rather sticks in my gullet that, in order to appease a very few less than honest Americans (most are surprisingly frank), I have to portray their performance in the south as a success on which the International Security Assistance Force will now build. The troops are generally great. There just have not been enough of them. The reality is we are being bequeathed the proverbial dog's dinner – a resurgent

Taliban, a disillusioned population and corrupt, poppy-driven local administrations. In my heart of hearts, do I genuinely have the confidence I am forced to demonstrate on a daily basis to my staff, my commanders and indeed the whole force?

Monday, 31 July

A very hot plane to Kandahar; as I was leaving for the airfield, a dose of Delhi belly hit me, which did not make the rest of the day too easy but I fought through and survived. The US arrangements were pretty chaotic and the otherwise excellent Transfer of Authority parade was spoilt only by overlong speeches to which I also plead guilty. They would be fine if it was not for the time taken to translate them. In a very bad them pretty bad, but the overall aim was achieved and the atmospherics good. Karl and I took a joint press conference afterwards, which we survived and landed a few good points. The line I used in my speech and at the press conference, which has been picked up by the BBC and local leaders, is that thirty-seven of the most powerful and prosperous nations in the world have recommitted themselves to the people of Afghanistan. The millions who support their government should be reassured by this and know that we are here for the long haul. The few thousand who oppose us all should realise that they will not be allowed to succeed . . . A good chat with David Fraser, who has agreed to my proposal on future command arrangements in Helmand, putting Ed Butler in command but with David very much his commander. I reassured him that if there was a hint of Ed failing to do what David ordered I would have him sacked. David was reassured and I will tell Ed again that he is on trial. The enmity people towards Ed suggests most of the fault lies

Wednesday, 2 August

Well, a hell of a day. Overnight, three UK soldiers were killed, and one badly injured, in a well-coordinated attack on their vehicles travelling in the difficult area of Musa Qala in Helmand. I am not convinced that some basic tactical rules are being followed, and this was confirmed later in the day when I spoke to Stuart Tootal. In close terrain, armoured vehicles must be protected by dismounted infantry. I tasked Steve to ensure the whole force understood the importance of carrying out these operations in a canny manner – not for the first time.

I have not had time to muse on how best to withstand pressure but must try at some point. Certainly, if one needs to prepare carefully and have staff briefs etc etc, one could not do what I am doing today. It's instinct, experience and character that allows one to survive and, hopefully, succeed/prosper. Judgement on top of that, but that's something to do with experience, although some is definitely genetic. The moral courage to stand up to politicians and give them sound military advice as opposed to what they want to hear – sadly, all too often, the same quality is required in respect of senior military officers – where does that come from? Upbringing certainly. My parents were brilliant, unobtrusive examples, and they showed me on a daily basis how important it is to treat all people equally and with respect. The role of one's family is crucial. I could not be more fortunate. I love Caroline deeply and she could not be more strongly and sensibly supportive. Po [daughter Joanna] and Pips, both of whom I adore, would forgive me anything as I would them of course! All these things combine mysteriously to let someone in my position command, lead and inspire (at least I hope so).

Thursday, 3 August

I gave approval to proceed with an operation designed to lift a really nasty hood in the Kandahar area. If we pull it off, it will counter any doubts about our resolve in the face of casualties (there do not yet appear to be any but . . .). This became more relevant when shortly afterwards I was told that the Canadians had suffered their second fatality of the day (one soldier overnight) but this time far worse – four KIA and nine WIA. I rang David Fraser to commiserate and check if I could help in any way.

Friday, 4 August

Well, a welcome few hours to myself in the first half of the morning. Woke naturally at about 0830 hours and after a breakfast of fruit and yoghurt in my room, jogged off to the gym for a really excellent session on a ski machine. Back to read the morning update file, before the first of what could be a very useful weekly video teleconference with the Supreme Allied Commander Europe. He explained that he was doing this to ensure they understood my priorities, so that together they could all help us – their primary aim. At last, we might get to the key issues without the sometimes huge time lag and friction created by having to put everything through Brunssum [NATO's Allied Joint Force Command base in the Netherlands]. It is not that Gerhard Back himself is not a good commander; it's the simple fact that his staff are not up to the mark, and they are undermanned to boot. There is little operational experience in the HQ and it is, with one or two honourable exceptions, distinctly second or third eleven. Jones handled it excellently and took advantage of General Back's absence to establish a few important ground rules, including that intermediate HQs are not to amend operational commander's reports, only add comment or qualification. Back was away on leave, but this will seriously upset him.

Monday, 7 August

A snatched meal before climbing aboard a C130 to fly south for two days of visits and, this evening, to attend a dignified repatriation ceremony at Kandahar Airfield in honour of the three British soldiers killed a few days ago in Helmand: Captain Alex Eida, Lieutenant Ralph Johnson and Corporal Ross Nicholls. Afterwards, a quick discussion on the next day's programme with Ben Freakley and David Fraser. Then to bed, only to be woken within minutes by a rocket attack on the camp, but was able to turn over and go back to sleep.

Tuesday, 8 August

Off in a Blackhawk helicopter to Zabul province to meet the best governor in the south, Governor Armand. Full of energy, deeply intelligent and clearly able to connect with the local people, he has brought Zabul to a much more stable position, helped enormously by US dollars and sufficient US troops, well deployed and well disciplined. The day included a visit to the new US/Romanian camp outside Qalat, followed by a trip into town via some impressive new buildings. At the Governor's compound, we had an excellent discussion with Armand and his team, followed by a real feast in his house. At the end, he very kindly presented me with a fine Pashtun turban, cloak and a beautiful rug. I gave him a decent enough but rather modest clock in return. I had twenty minutes alone with him during which he agreed strongly to support the ADZ concept. Then he held my hand as we walked towards my helicopter before giving me a fine kiss and hug, as is their custom.

Thursday, 10 August

Apparently, London is upset because of an inaccurate BBC report that I had said I would be 'withdrawing' UK troops from some of their tactically useless but politically important (for K) outposts in Helmand in which they were essentially fixed with the soldiers in them pinned down (platoon houses). Without a reserve, I have to create some manoeuvre capability from within the force and will do so regardless of London worrying about being seen to have cocked up, which they and Ed Butler were drawn in to doing. It does show just how sensitive London is and how little they appreciate what we are up against here, especially as they never gave me the theatre reserve that would unlock so many of my and their, ironically, tactical problems. Then to an untroubled sleep.

Friday, 11 August

Did not go to work until 1400 hours when I had an interesting brief from my Counter Intelligence team, who do some pretty good work, predominantly here in Kabul. Then a farewell call from Colonel David Jones, the cerebral but quietly effective Deputy Chief of Communications. I am sorry to see him go; he's strong, honest and capable. Kindly, he said how much pleasure he'd derived from working within a genuine mission-command environment, and how rare it was in his experience.

Then I am told that the Vice Chief of the Defence Staff General Tim Granville-Chapman must speak to me. He is deputising for Jock, who is on leave. He gently chides me for causing some embarrassment to my (ex?) friend Des but overall, as ever, is supportive and understands that I must retain people's (including the media's) confidence in me. There is very little confidence in NATO's political leadership; if they lose it in me too, we are pretty well doomed. To suggest, as some bright spark in the MoD has, that I should respond to questions on what I am going do in the face of the parlous situation in the south with the words

'I am reviewing the options' completely misses what generalship is all about. I have to inspire confidence and optimism or this thing will go tits up.

Saturday, 12 August

More short meetings and a telephone call to the British ambassador. The latter agreed to support the creation of auxiliary police – two down and three to go. I said, though, that I was very annoyed about a diptel [diplomatic cable/telegram] sent by a junior official in the Embassy that had hopelessly misreported yesterday's PAG decision on the ADZs but worse had concluded by saying that the author hoped the initiative would not get in the way of the serious business of delivering security and development – its very purpose! Stephen Evans (UK ambassador in Kabul) apologised and said he would be signing off an authoritative diptel for next Monday that would correct this completely inaccurate and misleading message. I told Stephen I did not trust the judgement of one or two of his people and that he needed to get a grip.

Monday, 14 August

An hour with the Gailani brothers, who brought former Helmand governor and warlord Sheer Mohammad Akunzada with them. SMA, as he is known, wants to recommence his dealings in Helmand. He does have influence and needs to be utilised but, whether true or not, rumours are rife about his past, and it sticks in the gut. He wanted me to persuade Pres K that he should be allowed to raise his militia and within three months he would reduce the problems there by 60 per cent. I told him very clearly that he might be rehabilitated but only if he clearly gave the new governor his full support and ensured his troops were incorporated in the new auxiliary police. If he did this, then I said in six months I would tell

K that he had done his penance, proved he could behave constructively and should be rewarded. We shall see!

After a good command group supper back in Kabul, I was told the disturbing news that the Taliban/Al-Qaeda were starting to use a new higher tech IED initiation system that was hard to beat. Gave orders to key guys to work round the clock on this. UK has counter systems available but among other nations not even the US do – Northern Ireland has its uses still.

Tuesday, 15 August

Visit to the Pakistan ambassador. Good hour but I am not yet certain that I can trust much of what they have to say. I want to, and I want to help them and the Afghans, but they are endemically suspicious and have different agendas. He stressed that Afghans were naturally inclined towards, and needed, an Islamic state and the West should accept it. I did not demur but we agreed that our trick would be to allow this but for it to be tolerant and allow freedom of worship. I reminded him that this was what Jinnah believed. Back for briefings on the new set of top targets, which I endorsed, followed by a special forces update. Special forces are undermanned and under-resourced but at least I have a capability and it is under my command. The Colonel in charge has worked amazingly well to bring this about.

Wednesday, 16 August

Well, well – what a difference a day can make. I could not be more pleased. A poor dress rehearsal resulted in an excellent first night. We achieved everything I could have hoped for. Two months ago there was no mechanism for coherent, timely, prioritised government/international community decision making. Today the PAG functioned well, allowing people, and K in particular, to see what a powerful tool we have given him. Secondly, two months ago there was no agreed, coherent campaign plan that drew all the essential elements together in a focused manner, reflecting the seriousness of the situation and the need to regain the support – the consent – of the people. Today, we agreed the ADZ concept in its entirety and K directed its immediate implementation. One minister said, 'this is a fabulous idea; we have been waiting for this for three years.' The finance minister said we needed to redirect funds from existing projects into new ones in the ADZs to exploit this 'outstanding opportunity'. K said he now understood things he had not understood before. To add icing to the cake, the PAG agreed the need for Auxiliary Police, another key plank of the plan in order to free up troops for manoeuvre operations.

When not contributing to the debate – and I had to present the concept and then lead the discussion – I sat there almost pinching myself. Months of hard work had led to greater success than I had ever seriously imagined we would achieve in one step. My outstanding team, to whom I owe so much, and I have achieved the operational-level cohesion that is a key step in winning the war. Of course, we have to implement it all but I have the moral authority to knock heads together and I am reasonably confident that it will take off now that the Afghan government and key international community members appear to have grasped its essentials.

Thursday, 17 August

An excellent dinner with my best friend, General Wardak, at his home, in honour of Mr Cetin, who sadly soon departs Kabul. He was in great form and, along with many Afghans, asked me if I would consider staying on next year. I explained it was unlikely but I would do so if asked formally. Mrs Wardak was charming and played a major role in hosting her husband's guests – not traditional Afghan style at all. She was very outspoken and I offered her a job as my agent of influence, which she rightly declined! It became clear during the evening that there are some reservations about Karl. I talked him up and suggested that he might be my successor. That said, I must help him develop a warmer side.

Saturday, 19 August

A busy networking day and some useful 'influence' operations achieved. It effectively started with my attendance at the Afghan National Independence (from Great Britain) Day. A lot of sitting around to begin with but then a really excellent hour that revealed the breadth and depth of the ethnic, tribal and cultural diversity here. Group after group paraded past us, chaotically, though less so for the Army and police. Scouts, beautiful girls in exotic costumes, outrageous and precarious turbans on top of fierce bearded heads, skilled horseman on top of beautiful horses, whirling dervishes, raucous but somehow melodic music. Of course, all this diversity is one reason for the country's problems but watching it I became even more committed to what we are doing.

Sunday, 20 August

Normal early morning routine of update and a couple of quick office calls from senior staff. Then off to the Intercontinental Hotel to address a conference of all provincial governors and their police chiefs. Not certain how much I achieved but the process of restoring confidence is a gradual one and letting them see and hear that I understand their problems and trust in their solutions is an important start. Back for lunch but then had to grip some sloppy reporting of an incident in Helmand in which a British soldier died and three were wounded. Secretly I am concerned that our minor tactics are not that good and I need to know what this guy was doing; was his death unavoidable? I set the Chief of Staff on to it with a very clear warning that I was not convinced and things needed to be better. I will speak to Ed Butler, who returns from his R&R shortly. In a rather bad mood; off to the gym to let off steam – excellent therapy as always.

Later, secrets brief was not good news. Things are fragile in a number of areas and we need to start getting the upper hand soon – all part of the ADZ concept but we do not have the luxury of time. The Pakistan peace with militants in Waziristan is giving the Taliban, HIG and Al-Qaeda the freedom to come across the border from that direction in greater strength than before. (HIG is Gulbuddin Hekmatyr's group, Hezb-e Islami. Hekmatyr had originally made his name as a Mujahideen leader in the war against the Soviets. After the civil war, he briefly became prime minister before committing his men to the fight against ISAF.) We are faced by an insurgent force that is growing in strength and now has two sanctuaries that we cannot touch easily. The Pakistanis must tackle this with us, or Afghanistan could slip inexorably under the Taliban, with the north perhaps moving separately their own way.

Monday, 21 August

The good news is that the operation I authorised yesterday was 100 per cent successful. Nine Taliban killed in a field in Helmand, one of them a known IED maker and commander. This success, on top of the recent combined Canadian, Afghan National Army and police operation south-west of Kandahar in which between forty and seventy Taliban were killed, is allowing us to prove decisively that NATO is every bit as capable as the US at dealing with the Taliban robustly when it is needed.

Wednesday, 23 August

Got back for a short period in the office to take a call from the VCDS, still standing in for Jock S. This was one of the most difficult conversations I have had with one of the most senior officers in the Services, and that's saying something. In essence, it was a ticking off. I was asked not to put my major concerns in writing – explaining the severity of the situation, hinting at the risk of additional casualties and proposing the solution of an additional battalion – in case they were leaked to the press. I said that phone calls never aroused any interest. Tim GC, an officer of the highest integrity, said that he would convey my concerns to ministers but he had been instructed to tell me this and he had no option. I felt I was being criticised for telling the truth, for fear of it upsetting our political masters. To understand my concerns better he then asked me, what is it that I cannot do? Patiently I explained, emphasising what we could do with the right resources. I asked him to explain to ministers that it was my duty to be frank and honest, that I had a responsibility to fight for my soldiers. Anyway, there's no way they will put me in a job like VCDS. I would be a complete thorn in the politicians' flesh and they must know it.

Saturday, 26 August

Spent a very intimate hour and a half with Pres K; none of his advisers present except his Chief of Staff and much of it took place without even him. For the first time, he asked me to join him in one of the presidential guest houses and we sat out on the terrace enjoying tea and cake. I spoke very frankly about what he needed to do: get his weak ministers to exploit the PAG, sort out his media team, etc. We hatched a plot by which he would drop in to the next PAG (the plan is he will chair about one in three of the weekly meetings) and ask some searching questions that I would discuss with him in advance. We agreed that a visit by the PAG to the south would send all the right messages and force his ministers to confront reality.

THIRTEEN

Afghanistan II – Operation MEDUSA

It became clear during August that the Taliban intended to confront ISAF troops in the southern province of Kandahar by forcing us to deal with a strongly defended position that was key – psychologically as well as tactically – to control of the province. The battle I initiated south-west of Kandahar city in the Panshway district was NATO's first large-scale offensive operation in its history. I had no alternative but to take up the Taliban's challenge and my diary records the pressures that we all felt as we executed a difficult but necessary operation.

The tactical commander was Canadian Brigadier General David Fraser and the lead element were Canadian troops. They started well, inflicting heavy casualties on the Taliban, but they lost momentum and for a while some of their habitual confidence. I spent much of my time and energy during these days helping the Canadians reignite their natural will to fight. I was fortunate that American Colonel Steve Williams, whose primary task was protecting Kandahar airfield, agreed to take command of a rapidly cobbled-together group of Americans, Canadians and Afghan National Army. Seizing the initiative, he directed his ad hoc force towards our objective on one axis while the main Canadian force approached it from the north on another. Thanks to the courage and initiative of Steve Williams and his Canadian comrades in arms, NATO prevailed in what I, and many Afghans, saw as a critical test of our will to fight. We dealt a significant blow to the Taliban, wresting the initiative back from them for the rest of 2006 and in the process reassuring the population that we could protect them.

At the same time, the predicament of British forces in their so-called platoon houses in Helmand continued to underline the MoD's failure to understand the nature of the conflict in the south. They and Brigadier Ed Butler, the British tactical commander, wanted unilaterally to withdraw the British force from one of these bases in the key town of Musa Qala. I fiercely opposed what I knew would be seen throughout Afghanistan as an outright defeat for NATO and Britain and a big win for the Taliban. Instead, I worked on what I called a 'tribal solution' to the problem, persuading the provincial governor and the tribal elders in Musa Qala to act as go-betweens to allow Butler's troops to withdraw without the Taliban taking over. As my diary records, for a while there was little love lost between me and my MoD colleagues.

Monday, 28 August

The Taliban are digging in, confident that they can defeat us when, as they know we must, we attack in order to remove their psychological stranglehold on Kandahar and thus the whole region. As many as eight hundred fighters, perhaps more, are getting ready to take us on in prepared positions in perfect defensive country – orchards, irrigation ditches, high walls, small villages. When we attack, we must succeed: the credibility of NATO in the eyes of the government of Afghanistan and the people, especially those who will chuck in their lot with the side that looks like winning, is at stake. Succeed, and the positive communication spin-off will be fantastic; fail and we had better watch out. It is not too fanciful to say it could lead to the loss of Kandahar and thus the whole southern region. Once the consent of the population is lost, getting it back will be well nigh impossible.

Yet, as became clear in today's briefing, I do not have sufficient forces to mount the operation. We face at least a battalion in defence.

Conventional military logic requires at least a strong brigade to win, with a decent reserve to hand. I have half this and no reserve. I ordered Deputy Commander Security (now US Major General Ben Freakley) to come back to me with a plan that allowed for the correct correlation of forces and accepted risk elsewhere in the region if required. I declared Operation MEDUSA, as we now called the operation, to be my tactical main effort and I expected everyone, including other provincial task forces, to reflect it in their own plans.

Friday, 1 September

Early start and off to Kandahar to take the rock drill [rehearsal] for the brigade attack we are putting in against the strong Taliban position centred on Panshway. With some modifications to improve the correlation of forces and to ensure that it was not too methodical and 'tidy minded', the plan looked reasonably good and I was happy to give it my consent. I emphasised the critical importance of the operation to NATO, to the government of Afghanistan and to Pres K. The Canadian Lieutenant Colonel who will bear primary responsibility at the low tactical level came over well. The UK has been brought kicking and screaming to the party, in contrast to the Dutch who were very gung-ho and keen to do their bit. We will have to compensate for relative lack of troops with firepower but that plays to our strength and exploits the Taliban's biggest weakness. After the formal bit I spoke to all the tactical commanders and assured them of my 100 per cent support and confidence in them.

Saturday, 2 September

My first visitor of the day was General Sir Richard Dannatt, the newly appointed CGS [Chief of the General Staff]. Richard was my predecessor as Commander of the ARRC. I do not agree with him on everything but he is a good guy and I am pleased that he now heads the Army. Sadly, no suggestion from him that the UK realises the seriousness of their position in the south and might start looking to see how they can find some additional reinforcements. Max Hastings was with him. It was great to see him again although he seemed pretty downbeat which was a shame.

A situation report on MEDUSA indicated so far so good. The sensitive targets that I cleared two nights ago were hit during the night and it looks like we might have struck gold. Some key leaders were in the buildings in question and their absence from the battlefield seems to have led to a muddled response to the Canadian attack. Perfect start — a risk that might hopefully have paid off in spades.

Sunday, 3 September

Running through the whole day is the major brigade attack southwest of Kandahar. The Canadians lost four during the day, exposing their left flank before even getting across the river that was their start line. Between them and the US-supported Afghan 'kandaks' (battalion equivalent), they have killed something over 230, and 80-plus have been picked up by the Afghan National Police, but there are worrying signs that low-level tactics have not been good and some commanders are losing heart. The morale of the outwardly impressive Lieutenant Colonel commanding the Canadian battle group on the main axis was described to me by David Fraser as fragile. While still positive, David himself sounded very tired. The Canadians are finding it difficult to maintain momentum and are guilty of penny packeting, failing to concentrate force. About the last thing I said at the rock drill was do not be bound by the plan, especially their phases (too deliberate), and 'clout, don't dribble' i.e. use plenty of combat power up front. It appears that caution and an understandable lack of experience at certain levels has caused them to ignore both pieces of advice. Steve Layfield is in his element and very reassuring but he is worried about tomorrow. David plans to concentrate everything he's got, as he concedes should have happened today, and we have got him all the air and ISTAR [Intelligence, Surveillance, Target Acquisition and Reconnaissance] he needs. But, when all is said and done, it will be low-level fighting skills and raw courage that will win the day. So much hangs on this battle. There is nervousness in NATO and in Ottawa. Karl E. offered much moral support and said that if the Canadians wobbled at the political level, he would bring in Washington to stiffen their resolve – an offer I am sure I will not need to take up. Anyway, to top it all, I am feeling pretty lousy – a mild temperature and a tummy – and I have the nightmare of the North Atlantic Council visit tomorrow at what could not be a worse time.

Monday, 4 September

Since I've been in Afghanistan, I've had a few days to remember, but this probably beats any. Woken to be told that a US A10 (Thunderbolt II/ tank-buster) had mistakenly strafed a Canadian company preparing to conduct an assault river crossing (they were over the river yesterday but disappointingly withdrew to the home bank in the evening for 'resupply') on the southern edge of MEDUSA. The Canadian battle group commander has lost much of his confidence and this appears to have spread deeper into his command. David Fraser, himself clearly shaken, is pondering whether to sack him. Either way, the attack was eventually delayed, at least until tomorrow. The problem is inexperience. There is no shortage of guts. At the rock drill, Ben Freakley and I encouraged them in the strongest possible terms to concentrate force, yet they steadfastly opt for one company up at a time. And then David could not, in the event, concentrate his forces yesterday in the way he had planned. Yesterday's ambush by the Taliban was successful only because the company had no flank protection out. I am sure they will come through this but I will have to give them space to get a grip of themselves for another 24/36 hours. Ben F. very critical and understandably impatient – loss of momentum, surprise etc – but if the Canadians cannot relaunch their attack yet, we will have to take the risk delay entails. Good news is that we have got the French to agree to go south and the Dutch are already on route: new NATO?

The only nation that has not covered itself in glory – and this is not the fighting troops, who have, as always, done very well – is the UK, who are inward-looking and lacking in vision at both the strategic and tactical level. This came to a head when I was rung late this evening by Nick Houghton, who announced that the UK was thinking of unilaterally withdrawing from Musa Qala and Now Zad. I gave Nick the works, explaining what a balls-up the UK had made of things and that far from succeeding in setting the agenda in terms of security and development, they were in danger of becoming ISAF's laughing stock. Huge relative 'input' with much razzmatazz is followed by very little 'output'. DFID [Department for International Development] has already effectively withdrawn and no reconstruction and development is occurring. The locals are bitterly disappointed and increasingly critical. I detect increasing criticism in Kabul, too, from both the international community and Afghans, partly caused by a cleverer-than-thou attitude – too much talk of Helmand being an 'exemplar province' etc. To suggest that the MoD could contain the media fallout is a joke and shows how little London understands the true situation. Anything other than a carefully orchestrated operation that keeps the districts out of Taliban hands will be portrayed by the media as a British defeat, which it will most certainly be. The reason London wants to do this is because they have at last accepted that their forces are fixed in the platoon houses and unable to manoeuvre, thus ceding the tactical initiative to the Taliban. They are rightly worried that there will be mounting criticism of their lack of progress and they 'fear a catastrophic loss' in the shape of a downed helicopter. This is partly a knee-jerk response to the Nimrod crash a few weeks ago that, ironically, was nothing to do with enemy action but more likely due to the fact that it was an old aircraft. Their analysis is right but their solution quite wrong. I told Nick that Ed Butler needed to get properly stuck in to Helmand and find agreed solutions with the Governor, the Chief of Police and Afghan National Army commanders. He cannot simply order activity in the form of a unilateral withdrawal that completely ignores the strategic and political reality of the environment in which he is operating.

Wednesday, 6 September

Breakfast meeting with the NAC [North Atlantic Council] at the Serena Hotel (without food, which was rather disappointing!) I answered questions from a clearly tired and rather self-important group of NATO diplomats, who it is nevertheless important to keep onside. From there it was off to parliament for a symbolically important NAC visit, well co-chaired by Speaker Quanooni and the Secretary General. I took a lovely snap of the Supreme Allied Commander Europe, General Jim Jones, solidly and very obviously asleep, mouth open and eyes firmly shut!

From there, down to Kandahar with the NAC to find a very tired David Fraser. He painted a bleak picture, factually correct but oversold and likely to deter and frighten rather than encourage nations. General Jones agreed to my suggestion that I should say a few things at the end of David's briefing to provide some balance, clear on what was still needed by the way of troops but optimistic that we could succeed. I then said farewell to the Secretary General, Jim Jones, the Chairman of the Military Committee et al and went off to David Fraser's office.

To my great disappointment, it soon became clear that the Canadians were not prepared to renew the attack on Panshway. I encouraged, threatened and sought common ground, explaining how vital it was to press on, to exploit success and build confidence in us among a people who wanted us to beat the Taliban. It was clear that David's sombre assessment had been picked up in Ottawa and hugely magnified by concerns about further casualties. In the end, I agreed a compromise but David, whom I continue to rate highly, was not able to deliver on the deal. It became clear that I would have to persuade Ottawa myself. I arrived back in Kabul with my brain full of mega problems and the search for some quick, workable solutions.

Thursday, 7 September

Only three hours sleep but it seemed to do the trick. At a session with Adam Ingram, my old friend the Minister for Armed Forces, he joked that he would never have risen above Sergeant in the Army. He is a straightforward and honest man whom I respect and like. He got the message on the need for a coordinated solution to the Helmand problem and understood the huge risks to the UK of unilateral withdrawal. I reassured him that I thought I had sufficient influence with Pres K to swing some kind of deal.

Then it was on to a series of short meetings to thrash out the Canadian plan in more detail, building on late-night calls with Ottawa. As the morning wore on, it became clear that their attack had almost spontaneously restarted. Their fighting soldiers on the ground were taking advantage of opportunities as they appeared. David F. seemed to be back in his habitual good form and told me on the phone that the Taliban had been hit very hard, by air as well as direct and indirect fire, and were feeling the heat. Canadian troops sensed it and had started to exploit it. Later in the afternoon, this was all confirmed by my good friend Dr Rassoul [Zalmai Rassoul, Afghan National Security Adviser], who said the Taliban had not suffered so many casualties since autumn 2001 and their morale was very low. Conversely, he said that the people of the region were delighted and that most importantly they had discovered that NATO can fight every bit as well as the Americans – a turning point . . . The Canadians who died will have saved many, many other lives, without a doubt. I asked David to pass my thanks on to his officers and men for digging so deep into that well of courage, stressing that they must keep the initiative and press home their advantage. By the time I had done all this I had to hurry to a short but dignified repatriation ceremony for an Argyll killed in a suicide bomb two days ago.

Friday, 8 September

In a conversation with Ed Butler, I told him that I expected a qualitative change of approach. I also explained in more detail what he needed to do to get alongside the Helmand governor and persuade him of the merits of the plan for Sher Mohammad Akinazada's forces to relieve his troops in two of the district centres. It is part of a comprehensive theatre package that includes holding Pakistan's toes to the fire and a drug smugglers' amnesty scheme that Karzai and I discussed again yesterday. I also ticked him off for talking up the intensity of the fighting in Helmand in a media interview – 'particularly intense' – just when he should be talking up the superiority they have established. At the lowest tactical level this is certainly true. The two sides have fought themselves to a standstill and his troops still occupy their positions. If he was trying to set the conditions for the Taliban to claim victory plausibly when his troops leave the platoon houses shortly, he could not have done a better job. Typically, he took his bollocking with a wry smile. I cannot help but like him and he's a great tactical soldier.

Saturday, 9 September

Well, I thought I'd had everything possible chucked at me but now General Jones has told General Back that he is not prepared to let me leave theatre for a planned few days R&R before the children go back to school. At a NATO Chiefs of Defence meeting in Brussels, he had consulted Jock Stirrup, who had not hesitated to agree. I am, apparently, viewed as 'indispensable' and my departure at such a time would send the wrong signals (I understand there is a risk in this but believe it is manageable, given my outstanding team and the fact that Pres K is happy). I am upset, for Caroline and actually for me, too. I'm knackered and I would love to see Po and Pips for a couple of days.

Loyalty works two ways and I am now more determined than ever to fight for Karzai and the Afghans on my terms. I have established considerable moral authority with people here, all of whom are angry about the poor level of support provided to the Afghans, given the importance of success globally and the depths in which they found themselves – in large part because of Western neglect over the previous twelve years – in the autumn of 2001. Anyway, Caroline took the news superbly and, of course, I then felt more upset than she was. I realise how much I love and owe her.

Monday, 11 September

On reflection, my emotional response to being ordered thirty-six hours ago to postpone my R&R was over the top, a mark perhaps of too little sleep and rather a lot of pressure. It was probably the right call and I have quickly come to terms with my disappointment.

The morning was pretty routine. Intelligence reports on Taliban morale were encouraging but not uniform. Pressure on Panshway must be stepped up. Everyone is clear that this *could* be a decisive point. Certainly, the Taliban are viewing it like that and continuing to pour fighters into the pocket. By the end of today, for the first time, we had secured an appreciable amount of ground and the Taliban are getting weaker. They are still holding on to two of our objectives but by doing so they are playing to our strengths, proving what a totemic piece of ground it is for them from a propaganda perspective.

Ben F., who continues to impress, visited the battle today and reported poorly on some Canadians – LAVs [Light Armoured Vehicles] parked up idle, side by side; soldiers sunbathing; some more senior officers lacking in initiative and oomph, overcautious and failing to take opportunities;

plans being made at 0945 hours for stopping where they were for the night. This may not be representative; possibly a snapshot taken out of context. Either way, collectively the Canadians appear to have taken their first main objective, which is good. Ben is always hyper-critical, so I was pleased when he concluded by saying that they may, however, be getting the message. An ad hoc force of Canadians and Afghan National Army as well as a few Americans, under American Colonel Steve Williams, has crossed the river and taken the south-east side of the original objective. A combined Afghan National Army /US special forces unit has taken another, further west, inflicting big casualties on the Taliban in the process. The unit is ready to cross the river and take the last big objective tomorrow. At the same time, Canadian troops will advance from the north on a fresh axis, linking up with Steve Williams, who will press on from the east. The Canadian HQ is really getting into its stride and I have confidence in them.

The big coup is that the noble Ben F. has, without more than a gentle hint from me, which he probably did not need, kept the additional US company and two heavy guns in the fight. Despite the Dutch leaving – for at least four days to escort a convoy – we probably still have enough to succeed.

Saturday, 16 September

Just as I was leaving for bed, I was asked to approve a top Taliban target. It all looked well within the rules but it's a huge responsibility; if it goes well, fine. But do I really know for certain that a woman will not walk into the house in question just as the aircraft drops its ordnance? Rather unreal, this power of life and death. I do my best to exercise it scrupulously within the rules but they are a guide only at the end of the day. This target is a very bad man and taking him out would surely save British and Afghan lives and make our task on behalf of the Afghan people that much easier to achieve.

Monday, 18 September

Woken at 0530 hours to clear another sensitive target. Some clever and very resourceful work had gone into this and I was content to give it the go-ahead. After trying to get a bit more kip, I read in the morning update file that a district in Farah has been taken by the Taliban. Disappointing. Breakfast at the UK residence with Stephen's Deputy Michael Ryder and Major General Chris Wilson (Karl's British deputy). Discussed the Helmand situation and the UK's poor record of delivery; all agreed UK provided lots of input and associated brouhaha but no output.

Tuesday, 19 September

Well, one of the best days of the tour; genuinely hugely humbling. I set off early for the south spending the day initially with the British in Helmand. Most of the time, I was in Kandahar, starting with a trip to the Canadian brigade HQ before moving with David to the scene of the fiercest fighting, followed by a visit to Canadian troops at FOB [Forward Operating Base] Wilson. Then it was back to Kandahar airfield for, among other things, a visit to the hospital to meet the wounded from yesterday's suicide bomb.

My abiding memories of the day are: the air of resigned frustration among British middle-ranking commanders, complemented by typical soldiers' humour and the obvious bravery of them all; the understated eloquence and sheer professionalism of US Colonel Steve Williams, who had gone from a broadly administrative job at Kandahar Airfield to brilliant command of an ad hoc battle group that had had a decisive impact on the southern flank of Operation MEDUSA; the sophistication and skill of the Taliban's defensive positions and their obvious determination to hold on to them at all costs, pouring in reserves when they should have seen the futility of it and pulled out, leading to many hundreds of dead and their biggest defeat since 2001; the cheerfulness, mixed with relief, of the Canadians I met at FOB Wilson, and their enthusiasm for following up their achievements; the emotional men of B company 2 Royal Canadian Regiment, who had put in an outstanding performance during the battle, tragically marred by a platoon losing four KIA and fourteen WIA in a suicide bicycle bomb three days later; the humour and courage of the Canadian wounded in the field hospital, and their willingness to talk to me, however much it hurt, as I sat beside them, holding their hand or, if they were too bandaged, whatever bit of skin I could touch; and the sense of purpose and resolve I detected in a tired but victorious David Fraser. He can now leave Afghanistan at the head of a rightly proud Canadian contingent, who had been sorely tested but come up trumps. It could so easily have been different. I am hugely proud of my Canadians and owe David much.

I gave the wounded their stripes and joked about the girls they would have flocking to them, only too conscious that, in one case at least, he would be very lucky to walk again. The bomb had killed a cow 70 metres (77 yards) from the explosion, huge ball bearings about 1 cm (just under half an inch) in diameter ripping through anything in their way in a claymore type arc. The men's body armour undoubtedly saved many lives.

Thursday, 21 September

I am writing this in an HS 125 (a small RAF passenger jet) somewhere over Baluchistan on my way home to Germany for a few days leave . . .

As I sit here looking back over the period since I assumed command of the south, I feel reasonably content. The situation is more stable today, set fairer than I could have hoped would be the case even two weeks ago when things looked pretty grim. We have given the Taliban a sound drubbing and proved to the country that we can beat them. Indeed, I have never been hugged by so many men with beards in my life. We have established the ADZ concept and are set to introduce it within weeks; the

Auxiliary Police are an accepted necessity and are also on track; we have a tribal solution running in Helmand that could prove the basis for similar schemes elsewhere; the Pakistanis are at last showing some signs of genuinely recognising that the Taliban are as much of a threat to them as to Afghanistan; we have got funding and agreement on the Special Force that, played well, could tip the military balance in Helmand and then more widely; and, through the amnesty scheme, we have the basis for dividing at least some of the drug lords from their Taliban allies, although there is some way to go in putting the details together on this.

Above all, we have created, against the odds, a mechanism for coordinated and timely government in the PAG and it, like the ADZs, is now an accepted part of business in Kabul. To add important icing to the cake, under huge pressure my troops at every level are doing superbly well; and the media are still, cautiously perhaps in some cases, giving us the benefit of the doubt. All in all, a satisfactory few months. However, plenty more to do yet. Stage 4 – the point at which I assume command of the whole country and which, we are now being told, Rummy has agreed for 5 October – is the next big challenge while bedding in all our initiatives for the long term.

FOURTEEN

Afghanistan III – Four Stars and the Whole Country Under My Command

The third and final section of my Afghan diary features the conflict between me and General Jim Jones, Supreme Allied Commander Europe, over his decision to constrain my freedom to speak to the media after some unfortunate misreporting of earlier interviews. During this phase of my command, we were still keeping the pressure up in the MEDUSA area, and the rumbling over the Musa Qala deal in Helmand continued.

I sensed a gradual cooling of my relations with President Karzai, who seemed to think, wrongly, that I had 'gone over to the other side' following a visit by me to Pakistan. While I had a close relationship with most of my American civilian and military colleagues, I strongly suspected that one or two were briefing against me by the final weeks of my tour.

Among many others, we entertained Prime Minister Blair, the British Foreign Affairs Select Committee, the new US Defense Secretary Robert Gates, and Dan McNeill, the US General who was to succeed me as ISAF commander.

In my final weeks in Kabul I succumbed to a severe case of pneumonia. It nearly killed me. I had to be flown back to Europe to recover. In the event, it turned out to be caused by severe whooping cough. But I was back on my feet in plenty of time to hand over to General McNeill in the first week of February 2007.

Tuesday, 3 October

Princess Anne arrived – single-minded, brave and tough with a delightfully warm side that breaks through intermittently. Her husband, Tim Laurence, was with her and it was good to see him again. On and off had to look after them for the rest of the day, including escorting them to the palace in the evening.

Thursday, 5 October

Well, I am now responsible to Pres K for the security of the whole of Afghanistan. Quite a challenge, and if I pause too long to think about it, I may get a little worried. But, I don't and won't – thick, unimaginative or clever, I'm not certain. Now a four star, too; lots of nice messages and e-mails. The parade seems to have been a great success – short and dignified; speech seemed to go down well and Pres K on excellent form. After the formal bit, he asked if he could speak to the troops on parade, which was a great touch and went down very well with the boys and the audience. After the ceremony, took him round the HQ, and then a press conference.

Saturday, 7 October

To the Ministry of Tribal Affairs for a tiring four hours with tribal elders from RC East, the last of the five regional commands to come under me. It was actually the best of these events so far and the overriding messages were: corruption/poor governance will not be tolerated much longer; Pakistan is the source of their ills and what are we going to do about it; we need security – empower us – and we need some visible reconstruction and development to keep people sweet. Interestingly, there was a real little spat shortly after my arrival when we were still in the Minister's office. A newly appointed 'Deputy' minister walked out in a huff because he had not 'approved' the elders who had been invited to meet me. He objected to the fact that elders who might not like him had been invited – pretty typical of the country and a problem I need to discuss man to man with K. If he does not recognise that this sort of thing is destroying his moral authority, we will have a problem soon.

Sunday, 8 October

After lunch, back to camp for a number of office calls and a phone call from General Jones, who wanted to know if I was seeing Musharraf during my imminent visit to Pakistan, clearly hoping the answer would be no. I explained that there was a possibility and that if he asked to see me, I could hardly say no. Misunderstanding completely the authority and influence of wartime theatre military commanders, the Secretary General has obviously told Jim Jones that only he should have a relationship with Musharraf. He does not understand the dynamics of this region; if Musharraf sees me, it is because he wants to hear from the man responsible for the security of Afghanistan, who is actually doing the business, rather than politicians, who in practice have insufficient depth of knowledge and commitment, often appearing more focused on their own organisation's or country's agendas than on improving the lives of the people of the region. They must learn to trust and empower people in my position to work on their behalf to broad policy direction and to stop constantly interfering in the detail. Anyway, Jim Jones was content with my line but wait for more on this!

Sunday, 15 October

Called David Fraser and told him he needed to get things moving faster in the MEDUSA area or risk giving ground back to the Taliban with all the hugely negative propaganda that would engender, not to mention the security implications. Sadly, some of his contingent have lost their enthusiasm to get stuck in and we need to ginger them up again. One CO is weak and should have been sacked during MEDUSA. Still, all is not lost yet and I have great confidence that the Canadians can get this right and prove a final point.

Tuesday, 17 October

Got back to be asked to clear two more special forces detention operations. Both contain risk but the prize was well worth it in both cases. I am conscious, though, that I am asking good men to take huge risks with their lives. If I did not genuinely feel this campaign as a whole, and the individual operations within it, were fully justified, I am not certain that I could do this job.

Wednesday, 18 October

Quickly to see K, who started the discussion by giving me a hard time for being too objective about Pakistan. Sources tell me that he thinks I went over to the other side while on my last visit. I stuck to my guns and argued back, telling him that if we did not work with them, at the current rate of decline in relations, the only logical outcome was war of some kind. Pakistan had acknowledged that the Taliban was a joint problem and we had to sort it out together. This shut him up and we agreed to talk about it tomorrow. Gerhard Back is visiting and I took him along with me. He sat bemused by the openness of my discussion with the President.

Thursday, 19 October

Late lunch in my office, before an unpleasant phone call from General Jones over a subject that I suspected would excite people. A couple of nights ago I gave an interview to the Pentagon Press Corps, a high-powered group of principally US journalists. I was asked why the situation had deteriorated since 2001, a frequent question to which I always give a similar answer. Despite great work by the Coalition, it was not sufficient to achieve a sustained effect, and the international community as a whole had not approached the reconstruction and development needs of Afghanistan with the sense of urgency that could meet the people's expectations. The Taliban had slowly exploited the resulting vacuum and this year it had reached a new pitch. The *Washington Post* had headlined this as me criticising the Coalition effort as insufficient and too passive. General Jones, who had not taken the trouble to read the transcript, had been got at by the Dutchman and Rummy and clearly had not tried to defend me or place the interview into context, either in terms of what I actually said or in terms of the overall success of our media and general campaign. He, essentially, has banned me from speaking to the media without his consent. I said this was not sustainable, to which he agreed, and we agreed to review it on his visit next week. I also said he should read the transcript and get our political leaders to look at the balance of media reporting and not isolated, misinterpreted/quoted articles. I may be wrong but I put his reluctance to stand up for me down to the fact that he has no operational experience at theatre level and therefore has little feel for the pressure.

Later in our video teleconference, General Jones worried me further when he tried to claim that there was no reason for him to badger for more troops because we, in theatre, had not asked for any. What planet is he living on? I had done nothing but stress this point for months, including directly to Rummy. This was an issue that Back raised privately yesterday. He tried to persuade me that it was not worth asking for more troops because it was clear nations would not provide them. I said that I could not agree. When it went tits up in a few years' time, the politicians would simply say that they were following military advice; no one had asked for more. I said apart from the integrity issue, did he want such opprobrium? Clearly that was a powerful point because he said that, on reflection, he would after all raise it with the Supreme Allied Commander.

I have taken risks, and will continue to do so, but it looks as if I am going to suffer for it despite our success against all the odds, although I do not think this is understood for one moment by our senior leadership or political masters. If modern generals feel that they are going to be constantly second-guessed by distant people with their own agendas, so that they cannot use their instincts to conduct the full orchestra to achieve effect over time (especially given the intense media and political oversight they suffer), does this mean the end of the art of generalship as we know it? If so, it is not for me. Finally, just as I was about to crash out, I was asked to approve a US special forces detention operation in a difficult area. I let it go ahead, conscious that a bungled operation resulting in civilian deaths could finish me. I have to do what my judgement tells me is right. The target has killed countless people, Afghan civilian and ISAF soldiers alike. I cannot go wobbly now; this is a war that must be won and leaders like this target are irreconcilable. Fingers crossed.

Friday, 20 October

Woke to the good news that last night's operation had been successful: well done the US special forces. Had a good lie-in and then off to the gym for an excellent workout in which I imagined the treadmill was composed of all my favourite superiors – very refreshing.

Saturday, 21 October

Saturdays and Sundays are good; my superiors will be at home with their families or girlfriends/boyfriends. Only a major issue will persuade them to get to a phone to complain at me for something us poor sods are trying to achieve on their behalf but may have got a little wrong. As I sit and write this just before midnight, prior to another six hours in my scratcher if I'm lucky, our luck has held! Average day: started with recording a Happy Eid message for the Afghan people and then went on to a series of office calls. My first visitor was an obviously highly political Canadian three-star General, equivalent of the UK's Chief Joint Operations, i.e. the officer responsible for the actual conduct of national operations. Patently lacking any operational 'feel', I got the bleating I so often get from national reps about how, in this case, Canada is the only nation doing a proper job and what are the others doing to help? I explained just how much we all, and especially the Afghan National Army (at a time when the international community is supposed to be shielding them in order to let them develop and train), were doing. I also had the temerity to remind him that Canada volunteered for the most important province and were full of hype at the time about their leadership role. They should have thought then about how to sustain it. Canada is doing a lot but I just wish they would make an effort to understand the overall picture, and place their problems/efforts in a bigger context. The UK, of course, is no better. Anyway, I will continue to do all I can to ease Canada's burden, however self-inflicted, ensuring they remain my tactical main effort and thus get the lion's share of my limited assets.

My morale was lifted at a good command group dinner where I could relax with some really good friends. I am conscious that I'm not that happy at the moment, due I'm sure to the nagging feeling of not being fully trusted by my superiors – after all we have achieved for them against the odds. Anyone else and any other HQ would probably have succumbed by now, either to defeat or to starting an all-out war. We have steered a route through tremendous challenges and are today the most respected and trusted organisation in Kabul. Do they know even half of this, and if they do, do they care? Anyway, bollocks to the pusillanimous, ignorant and cravenly political lot of them. This great team and I can continue to look ourselves and the Afghan people in the face, knowing we have done the right thing.

Monday, 23 October

At the JOC [our Joint Operations Centre from where I exercised command over all ISAF forces] I discovered that the US CJSOTF [Combined Joint Special Operations Task Force i.e. US special forces not directly under my command] had threatened to bomb a group of suspected Taliban near Musa Qala, even though my team had explained that they were there probably to parley with tribal elders and their deaths would cause a huge problem of strategic scale. Apparently, the US officer had said if we did not have the stomach to kill them, they would simply declare it a CJSOTF target and bomb them regardless!

Wednesday, 25 October

Post-Eid lunch with Pres K at the palace. Dr Spanta (whom I cannot help but like despite his open hostility to Pakistan, over which we disagree) and Wardak were there, plus K's advisers. The mood was solemn because of a report of large numbers of civilian casualties in a small battle south-west of Kandahar. The figures could be as high as sixty or seventy. K was really worried that this would undermine much of what we are trying to do. He is right; the heart of our cause is that we offer hope, and we care for civilians, whereas the Taliban offer despair and care nothing for civilians. We agreed to conduct a joint investigation and to be entirely honest. The Taliban were attacking us from among the civilian population, knowing what our response risks. It is very cynical but clever. We then went on to discuss Pakistan and what our approach should be.

Thursday, 26 October

Met with a German special ambassador, who seemed to take things on board but was concerned about ADZs in the north, where he claimed they were not really necessary. He had not appreciated that this concept is not just to do with development and security but rather about unity of effort and campaign coherence. I think he got the message but it's worrying that no Kabul-based German has sold it to him; worrying but, from what I discovered later, not surprising. At a reception this evening, an unpleasant German Colonel who works for the Senior Civilian Representative was talking with the same German special ambassador and another German diplomat about how the operation was far too dominated by the Brits, how they did not appreciate what the Germans were doing in the north and generally having a real go at all we were doing. I will have to do something about him. We only know because a British soldier on duty at the main door to the reception speaks excellent German and overheard the lot! He had the gumption to get the message to me.

Friday, 27 October

General Jones is visiting and I went down to meet him from a helicopter after his latest trip. He seemed to have had a good day. I briefed him on the Kandahar incident and he seemed strong and sensible over it. He had a meeting to go to but as he was leaving I was asked to rejoin him so that I could help him speak to the Secretary General, who is in Washington and needed to know more about the incident. The General thrust the phone into my hands and I summarised the current position, giving some useful lines to take. The Secretary General seemed genuinely grateful and went in to see George Bush armed, should it come up in discussion and afterwards with the media. He has since sent a message to say he has enough information for now, so it must have worked. If only the three of us could work like this every day, it would be quite a combination.

Saturday, 28 October

To the President. Not that much genuine bonhomie evident. I have got to know him well. He was, by Afghan standards, reserved. Noticeably, he started by giving us a gentle enough ticking off (by Western standards) for the recent collateral problem. Before he did this, the media were ushered in and filmed the lot. I told him clearly that he must explain and defend us or nations will lose faith in him. As much as we regret civilian casualties, the fact is we are under attack from Afghans and are dying for his country. He needs to stay on the team and not play Afghan politics with us. Rassoul [Zalmai Rassoul, Afghan National Security Adviser] understands and I will use him to reinforce the message. Predictably, he also went down the usual Pakistan rabbit warren, looking for excuses for our joint failings.

Monday, 30 October

An excellent PAG chaired well by K. Afterwards, he asked Tom [Koenigs, Special Representative of the Secretary General], Ron [Neumann, US ambassador], Stephen [Evans, British ambassador] and me to adjourn to his office. He wanted to discuss one or two very sensitive issues, including how the government should respond to a truce overture from one of the most serious of his/our opponents, Hekmatyr [Gulbuddin Hekmatyr, leader of the Hezb-e Islami party]. We all spoke up for a positive response, with no conditions, in an attempt to sow the seeds of dissension between Hekmatyr, the Taliban and other armed groups, as well as to show to more moderate opponents that there is an alternative for them. I said that he would have some ticklish political issues to resolve, a thought not mentioned by the diplomats. Afterwards, Rassoul had a private chat in which he said the point I had made was a key issue for them. Hekmatyr had killed a lot of Afghans and many in the country would be very hostile to any deal with him. Rassoul also told me of an MP from Kandahar with whom my troops had a relationship, who was harbouring Taliban. I returned to HQ and ensured that my J2 [Chief of Intelligence] and J3 [Chief of Operations] were in the picture.

An effective thirty-six hours for the military side of the operation. Yesterday, about 75 Taliban were killed in Oruzgan and today about 60 were killed and 20 wounded in Zabul. It does show that there are plenty of Taliban around but with this scale of casualties, we may just buy enough time to establish the ADZs.

Key thought: we cannot be beaten militarily and we have the capacity to do much good, but can we synthesise the two? The PAG is vital, and I'm keeping my fingers crossed that there are no sizeable civilian casualties to undermine our efforts.

Tuesday, 7 November/London

I did a short background interview with my ever-serious but good friend Nik Gowing (BBC) before walking across St James's Park to see Tony Blair. This was the first time I had met him properly and I can now see why people enjoy working for him. He is very personable and makes one feel important. We had a proper two-way conversation and focused on the key issues affecting the future of NATO as well as the campaign in Afghanistan. Agreed that he should take a strong line at Riga (the imminent NATO summit) with those nations who are failing to help in the south. They should either agree to provide troops or spend money there in lieu. We also talked about Pakistan and the lines he might take with both Musharraf and Karzai on his forthcoming visit to Pakistan and Afghanistan. The meeting ran over my allotted time but I had the cheek, to which he responded enthusiastically, to ask if we could have a photo together. He suggested that we go next door to the Cabinet Room. Simon, my ADC – who couldn't get over the fact that Tony Blair treated him with such courtesy – took three photos of us. and For the third one the Prime Minister suggested that I sat in his chair while he stood behind me as my adviser – 'the military coup' he called it to much amusement all round!

Thursday, 9 November

On arrival back at Kabul at 0500 hours, I had a briefing from Johnny Bourne (my new Military Assistant, who is shaping up well after the departure of the understated but effective and likeable Felix Gedney) before unpacking and trying to get some sleep for a couple of hours. Then it was back to the grindstone. All pretty positive other than for the anticipated letter from the politically wobbly Supreme Allied Commander, directing that I am essentially not to engage with the media without his express authority. This has even extended to the post-tripartite press conference [representatives of Afghanistan, Pakistan and NATO/ISAF had a meeting every four weeks or so], something desperately needed if we are to persuade a sceptical Afghan public that Pakistan is working with and not against the government of Afghanistan and Coalition forces. This is crazy stuff and I told General Jones's principal Military Assistant, Colonel Steve Meier, that I was not at all happy and hinted strongly that I would find it difficult to continue under such undue and unwise interference in the execution of the campaign. It's back me or sack me time I think, and I have a call booked with General Jones tomorrow, when I will pursue this key issue.

Tuesday, 14 November

A visit from Richard Dannatt, who appeared tired, perhaps unsurprisingly to be fair after a very long journey. Disappointingly, he could not spend long with us, much to the sadness of my more senior officers, who have worked hard here and wanted a bit of time with their chief. Whilst I can understand why, given that he is an ex COMARRC who I know understands the importance of the theatre level, he remains very Helmand-centric. If Richard is like this, with his refined military instincts, what hope for others in the MoD? All that said, it was good to see him and we parted on characteristically positive terms.

Thursday, 16 November

To parliament. I had been asked to address the upper house some time ago. Understandably, Daan [Daan Everts, Hikmet Cetin's successor as NATO's Senior Civilian Representative, who had a hotline to his fellow Dutchman, Jaap de Hoop Scheffer, the Secretary General] jumped on the bandwagon. I did not fear the competition so agreed to take him along with me. We arrived to a cordial greeting. I was asked to speak first and got in a lot of our key messages. Daan's speech was rather lacklustre but he made some telling points. I was then asked to take questions, which I proceeded to do for the next two hours or so! It was one of the most exhausting things I have done for some time. Some of the questions were long and complex, made the more so by the need for translation. Some of my audience, many of whom were well-known warlords and drug barons, bought off by the government by being made senators, were aggressive in their style, although I have discovered most mean little by it. I was asked everything from questions about civilian casualties on the one hand through to explaining the slow delivery of reconstruction, and why are we losing after five years, on the other. Impassive most of the time, when I left at the end, they became far more friendly, coming up to shake my hand and thank me, even the most aggressive of my questioners. So, I hope it went well and that a mutual respect will have been established while getting some key messages across. Daan was asked not one question, so towards the end I deflected one of a political nature to him. He misunderstood it but it gave me a break for two minutes, so I was content.

Friday, 17 November

A visit from Major General Frank Kearney, the reassuringly capable and likeable US special forces commander, to discuss the recent spate of civilian casualties caused by his men. They have done a great job overall but one or two of them are letting the rest down. He is pressing criminal charges against one officer and a Sergeant. We agreed that he needs to revisit their training and get them better to appreciate the environment in which they are operating, to understand that it may be wiser to let their enemy go if the alternative is killing him in cold blood in a market place. Frank gets this in spades but the US Army is trying to turn round a culture that is built on the very successful 'warrior' ethos needed to win conventional wars, and it will take time.

Sunday, 19 November

A day totally and rightly dominated by visits to Nuristan and Kunar Provinces in the far east of the country. In the latter, we were within 2½ miles (4 km) of the Pakistan border, the steep mountain ridge that demarcated it emphasising the problems the Pakistan Army has controlling the people who live there. Much of the time was spent in a helicopter with the very game Ron Neumann and Ben Freakley, our principal military host – a long day but well worth it. The scenery on the eastern border is stunning, literally breathtaking on occasions – fast-running rivers in steep ravines, tree-lined mountain slopes with snow-capped peaks, through to wide and fertile river valleys. In Nuristan, I attended the opening of a new US-led PRT [Provincial Reconstruction Team] and had to make a short speech in front of a hundred or so elders, all of whom had walked for up to 20 miles (32 km) to be there. Governor Nuristani (his family hails from the province) was with us, a charismatic but some say politically weak figure, who has spent much of his life in the USA. He fought against the Russians but has not done too much since. However, the elders were very much onside and hopeful of the future. Just before the speeches, I was asked if I wanted to cancel or delay the ceremony because some insurgents had been reported in the next-door valley, intent on attacking us. I said we should carry on but the ADC could join the US local protection party to try to earn a medal, an offer that brought a cheerful smile to Simon's boyish face. After we left, an Apache reported sighting a group of twenty or so youngish males moving rapidly towards the PRT but, if they were the Taliban, they had missed their quarry by some margin.

Monday, 20 November

The Prime Minister landed at Kabul and I went to our football pitch to meet him off the helicopter. He greeted me warmly and we had a good office call for about thirty minutes. We discussed the key issues and confirmed what lines he should take with Karzai: Pakistan and Afghanistan must work more and more closely together; K must deal more energetically with corruption; and the international community must produce much better coordinated and speedier reconstruction and development. Blair was pleased to hear that there was some real military progress being made and accepted my claim that while we had certainly not won, we had managed to stabilise the situation against many odds. Nigel Sheinwald and a rather passive Jock Stirrup were present, neither really adding much to the conversation. I found myself agreeing with Blair's instincts and I think vice versa: good or bad? Would I have ordered the attack on Iraq, given the importance of the relationship with the USA? Who knows –

luckily, not something that will keep me awake at night. From my office I walked him to the gym to meet a selection of UK and foreign staff officers and for some photographs. He was in good form and genuinely pleased to meet Sandy Gall (veteran former ITN news reader and Afghanistan expert) and his daughter Carlotta, his wife Eleanor being away in Mazar. Much to Sandy's delight, I had invited them both to meet the PM, a small gesture of my respect and affection for him. From there it was off to the palace.

It all went well, although Blair and Karzai had a genuine one on one, which frustrated Sheinwald and Stephen Evans but did not worry me. I just had a lot of fun with my Afghan pals, gossiping and pulling each other's legs. The great men emerged and off we trudged to a rather tame press conference. Sadly, Blair did not get the lines I had rehearsed him in quite right – that we had come through a necessarily difficult summer but in the last two months there had been a huge reduction in incidents so that now we could start to do all the good things we really wanted to do – but he was not too bad. From there to lunch; usual excellent fare and atmospherics generally good except when Karzai had his customary rant about Pakistan.

Tuesday, 21 November

James Driscoll, who has taken the irrepressible Chris Boryer's place as my second military assistant and is equally excellent, back-briefed me on a request (order?) from Tony Blair to act as a go-between between Musharraf and Karzai over a sensitive piece of intelligence that, if we could unlock it, could trigger a big increase in Pakistan anti-Taliban activity. Quite cloak and daggerish and sounds rather interesting.

Thursday, 23 November/Islamabad

A good flight over the Hindu Kush – looking fantastic with early snow on all the peaks and some of the high valleys. Landed at Islamabad shortly before Chinese President Hu, who is here on a state visit. Rather hilariously, the police allowed me – but not, for some reason, Daan Everts, which I found mischievously amusing – to drive down the secured route into the city a few minutes before the presidential motorcade. Thousands of people were waiting to greet the president. The signal for his arrival was a lot of police cars and outriders, which also accompanied us, so as we drove by, bands started playing, balloons were released, schoolchildren waved flags and horses started to prance. I waved back regally and told my party that this is what I expected on all such visits from now on! I hope the crowds did not disperse before President Hu drove by.

Tuesday, 28 November

A knackering day, bitty with no single theme except the need constantly to explain to a range of people – visitors, Afghans, ambassadors – what we are trying to achieve and what their role might be. Successful I think, but wearing, and sometimes highly repetitive, for me not for them, I hope. I go into automatic mode, the same lines and arguments, but it's so important they understand. I fear my weariness with it all might come through but I think I warm to my act and keep that risk at bay.

A visit from the House of Commons Foreign Affairs Committee – a good group who asked some sensible questions. Gisela Stuart (Labour MP for Edgbaston) stood out; she listened and her interventions were spot on. At the end, she compared me to Tony Blair – worrying?! A session with local media – quick pitch followed by lively and helpful Q and A – was followed by lunch with them but I cut it short to meet with our 'war artist' Brendan Kelly. He has been commissioned to paint the leading players, including Karzai, in a group of some sort. I spent well over ninety minutes having my photograph taken and wandering around the camp with him, looking for the right light and backdrop. Rarely has a single person out here had so much of my time; hope he felt honoured.

Wednesday, 29 November

The afternoon picked up apace with a useful discussion in which we examined with an intelligence expert what other players think of me, Pakistan and the much discussed Musa Qala deal. I know the US have been briefing against the latter and the expert is in part reflecting their typically black-and-white view.

My successor Dan McNeill (Commanding General, US Army Forces Command) arrived on a recce. We had an hour together by ourselves, discussing the whole range of key issues. This was followed by another excellent briefing from James Bucknall. with me and others piping up as necessary. From there we took him to dinner with my command group, which he seemed to enjoy although he is rather typically slightly ill at ease in company. My view? A really good guy and undoubtedly a very capable soldier, but will he have the vision and impetus to get above the tactical fray and play his part on the wider stage? Time will tell but his instincts are good.

Sunday, 3 December

In Kandahar during the morning, a UK logistic convoy was attacked by a suicide bomber. Mercifully, at the time of writing, no fatalities but three wounded, which is bad enough. The President expressed an interest and I was asked to ring Dr Rassoul. I had a problem getting the context and necessary minimum detail out of my JOC [Joint Operations Centre] so ended up ringing Jerry Thomas (Commander 3 Commando Brigade Royal Marines and Ed's successor as Commander Helmand Task Force. I know him well as he was my Chief of Staff when we served in Joint Forces HQ together). True to form, he had all the facts and we agreed to sort out the passage of information from top and bottom. I then rang Rassoul. After the bomb, a British soldier had fired into some civilians, thinking they were Taliban and part of the ambush. Understandable perhaps, especially as the bomber had killed up to six civilians, but our man sadly added another one killed and six wounded to the tally and his actions were not acceptable. A cock-up from which some lessons need to be learnt.

A good secrets brief at the UK Intelligence cell that confirmed Pakistan is definitely beginning to have some effect on the Taliban and that the Musa Qala deal is, at worst, a neutral issue to date in terms of who is gaining most from it.

Saturday, 9 December

A slightly delayed meeting with the President over Helmand. Michael Ryder is the Chargé d'Affaires in Stephen's absence on leave. The two of us were ushered in to find that Ron Neumann, US ambassador, had been invited to attend. This was a major error on Karzai's part and it understandably upset Michael – big brother umpiring as their major ally got a bollocking. This was especially unfortunate as – and I had the temerity to point this out at the meeting – the US may have been behind the problem under discussion because of their dislike of the Musa Qala deal. Tony Blair, with much pushing from the Embassy, had stressed to Karzai on his recent visit that the sacking of the Deputy Governor of Helmand, Sheer Mohammad Akunzada's brother Amir, would be a good thing and fast. K had agreed but he sacked the Governor, Mohammad Daoud, at the same time. He did this to keep the delicate tribal balance in Helmand intact but he had failed to explain to London, via the Embassy, what he was doing. Whitehall is in uproar; 'their' man being treated in the same way as his 'undesirable' deputy. Ryder, realising that he was not getting anywhere, got pretty angry with K. After some fruitless and increasingly ill-tempered debate, K said, 'I had not realised that Afghanistan was not a sovereign nation,' and suggested we call a halt to proceedings. Ron and Michael left but I stayed on for about thirty minutes, mending fences and doing my bit for the FCO, persuading K not to carry out his threat to declare Michael *persona non grata*. I explained that in part this was because of London's obsession with Helmand and their belief that they effectively called the shots there. I think much of this was a little reminder by K to the UK that we did not! But, it went further than K intended; he said he was 'baffled' at how much of a fuss the UK was making. Disingenuous perhaps but, I think, truthful, too. This will run a bit, with Blair threatening to ring Karzai on Monday. I suggested a compromise whereby Amir Mohammad Akunzada was sacked tomorrow and Daoud was selected for an important new post on Tuesday. This will give the UK the space and excuse they need as long as K can handle the tribal side.

Tuesday, 12 December

Long but satisfying day spent travelling to and back from Kandahar for the Southern Region PAG. I first suggested this to Pres K in August. Four months late but we've done it; sums up the speed of things in Afghanistan but it's all progress. It was a great success, though, and I could not be more chuffed. A real sense of purpose and solidarity was evident round the room. We all, Afghans and the international community, have got to know each other really well through the mechanism of the PAG and we are genuinely working well together. K was in good form and led us well. I was asked for my views on a variety of things, provoking Chris Alexander into quipping good-humouredly that PAG stood for Please Ask the General. He denied leaking this to the *Economist*, although his British assistant Arabella Philimore looked less certain. Ron Neumann made the only comment that I had to push back on – generally he spoke very well – which was to suggest that we should warn people of a difficult time ahead next year. I said that we must talk up achievements and prospects for now, while planning among ourselves for an upsurge in violence again next year, or people will seriously question whether they are right to support us. K agreed.

Wednesday, 13 December

Two years I have now dedicated to this job, shouldering a huge amount of responsibility and influence. I have received no real direction from my country and, it often seems, precious little support. Indeed, I usually hear from the leadership only when the last Supreme Allied Commander or the Dutchman complain about a media issue. Tony Blair is the only one to have actually thanked me properly. I reassure myself by recalling that I would not be the first British General serving his country in exotic lands who felt this way, Wellington and Slim being but two others. My uncharacteristic sensitivity may be aggravated in this era of high-speed communications by a capital or superior's ability instantly to interfere, whereas historically they had little choice but to trust the deployed General. Anyway, Rob Fry's successor as Deputy Chief of the Defence Staff reported in a phone call that he was having a very difficult relationship with CDS and was facing the sack. Poor chap, I have always found him competent and very helpful. He also knew nothing about a post-tour role for me. I said that I needed to know in order to plan, either way. Then two more visitors and dinner with them. It's now 2230 hours and I still have another hour's work to do.

Thursday, 14 December

Busy day and I'm going down with a proper bug. It's hanging around my throat – hurts to cough – and I need to keep it off my chest. Anyway, a day dominated by three events: an excellent battlefield tour of the final drive on Kabul in November 2001 with the man who commanded it, General BK (General Bismullah Khan, now head of the Afghan National Army and an increasingly good friend and comrade in arms) combined with visits to the Governors of Kapisa and Parwan provinces; video teleconference with the new Supreme Allied Commander Europe General Craddock (US Army General Bantz J. Craddock); and dinner with a number of Afghan and international community guests nominated by my Command Group. It was pretty exhausting and not what I should have done, given I felt unwell. Craddock seemed sensible, modest and genuinely keen to listen to us. He visits here on Saturday so we shall see.

Saturday, 16 December

Got up from what seemed like my deathbed to spend a couple of hours with General Craddock. What a breath of fresh air! He is normal [!] and actually listened and took advice from those of us who know this country best. What a shame to be leaving shortly – we could have made a great team.

Thursday, 4 January 2007

I write this sitting at home in Germany. It's been a long, debilitating couple of weeks. I went downhill and by Tuesday, December 19th, I reluctantly agreed to go into hospital. The system swung into business and I found myself a not too casual observer/participant in the medevac [medical evacuation] process. I was sent by helicopter – my biggest concern was being dropped from the stretcher at the time of this move – to the French role 2 hospital, where I spent the next nine days feeling pretty sorry for myself. I had developed a complicated form of pneumonia and had quite a struggle fighting it off. Day after day, I felt no better and the charming Doctor Emmanuel Sagui, who took brilliant care of me, conceded, as I grew stronger, that he had been pretty worried. Constant muzz in the head and huge weakness. Never been seriously ill before and never want to be again: character forming, though, and I am sure it's left me the better man (I think!). Low point was when the French padre asked Simon Briggs what religion I was as the medical staff had warned him that he may have to deliver the last rites. I told Simon to thank him but to tell him to bugger off as I was not intending to die. That said, on the 26th, having thought I was improving a bit, I collapsed unconscious in the shower – much running around and drama – but at last, thirty-six hours later, like flicking a switch, I started to feel better. On the evening of the 29th I was helicoptered to the US field hospital at Bagram and six hours later found myself in a huge US C17 aero med flight direct to Germany, the UK being unable to help, rather typically.

Tuesday, 9 January/Pakistan

In a hotel in Islamabad. An excellent BA flight – they really are hard to beat in the round and I trust them, their engineering and pilots – and we found ourselves landing ahead of time at 0530 hours. Did not sleep really, four-hour time lag; watched film, had a very good meal and dozed fitfully for an hour or so before having breakfast. Met at the airport by a Pakistani Major General, two Brigadiers and my usual Gunner regiment. Sped off to the hotel where I had a second breakfast with Colonel George McGarr – an old friend and my Chief Liaison Officer in Pakistan – before sleeping for a couple of hours. Then went shopping for an hour for a suit and things for the family, before going up into the hills above the city and having lunch. By 1530 hours, it was all beginning to catch up with me and I realised I was not fully recovered. The doc in Germany had said it would take a month and he may be right. We returned to the hotel and I had a bit of a kip.

Rang Caroline first. I love her so much and need to finish in Kabul as planned. She has been brilliant; cared for all the wives, especially the soldiers' wives, earning their affection and respect in the process. Ably helped by some others in Rheindahlen, she has also started a wonderful charity for Afghanistan (the Afghan Appeal Fund) and earned the admiration of many.

Wednesday, 10 January/Pakistan

My first day of real work for the best part of three weeks. Not demanding by normal standards but by the early afternoon, I had had enough. Started with a useful session which included a rather bleak read-out on ISI [Pakistan's leading intelligence agency] involvement with Taliban leaders. It is a mixed picture, though, and dependent on different people in different regions responding in different ways to direction from President Musharraf. A top insurgent might have been arrested if it were not for ISI interference. This was hugely frustrating but mitigated in large part by their apparent assistance in an operation that resulted in the death of Mullah Omar's number two (Taliban leader), one Mullah Osmani.

Thursday, 11 January/Pakistan

The most troubling thing that occurred today was an attempt by Major General Ben Freakley to send a letter direct to General Hyat – Ahsan Saleem Hyat, Pakistan Vice Chief of the Army Staff and *de facto* Army chief, given Musharraf is president. A cross-border incident last night resulted in a large number of Taliban deaths and Ben's letter was hugely critical of the Pakistan Army's role in this, and made a number of demands. I think he's gone temporarily loopy; he is a tactical commander and has no right to communicate on such issues with the chief of the Pakistan Army. It was also unbalanced and inappropriate. I do not know if he had any sanction from his US superiors but I forbade the letter to be sent to Hyat and ordered its withdrawal. I also told James Bucknall to find out if

Karl Eikenberry had approved it. I suspect not, but if he did, I am going to hit the roof with him as well as Ben.

Friday, 12 January/Pakistan

An excellent day dominated by a successful hour spent with President Musharraf. We now know each other well enough to get straight down to constructive, honest talking. He remains firm about not responding to President Karzai's outbursts but is nevertheless determined to go ahead with Pakistan's own solutions, including the mining and fencing of parts of the border, if the international community and Afghan government cannot do something about it. I emphasised the importance of the two leaders and their key ministers getting together in order to understand the issues better, develop a proper dialogue and address problems jointly. I suggested again that a JAPAG (Joint Afghan Pakistan Action Group), or something like it, must be formed. Last time he was ambivalent but today he was enthusiastic, even proposing that I should be the international arbiter. I said that this would depend on Tony Blair, and President K, obviously, but that if I could serve, I would be happy to do so.

Sunday, 14 January

Back in Kabul. A couple of farewells before I was driving the well-worn route to the presidential palace. President K was clearly genuinely concerned for my health but I was able to reassure him that I was well on the way to recovery. I thanked him for his kind messages and gifts. Then we got down to some serious business. He confirmed that there was huge and damaging scepticism about UK motives, among them that we were more sympathetic to the Pakistanis than the Afghans, and were doing deals with the Taliban. I strongly rebutted all this, calling to witness our excellent record, and included for good measure my criticism of his apparent inability to come to terms with, and exploit, President Musharraf's desire to mend fences. After that, he showed real interest in my meeting with Musharraf, and seemed convinced of the need to get together. I gave him a non-paper on the case for a JAPAG and for the first time he seemed to understand its significance and potential benefits. He said he would like to see Tony Blair to discuss the UK's stance on the region and I agreed to facilitate this, suggesting it coincide with his visit to Italy and mine to London in mid-February, to which he readily agreed. We discussed Musa Qala and again I powerfully recalled the facts – it was his and Governor Daoud's deal, not mine; I had refused to redeploy my troops from the town for a period of four weeks in order to ensure the deal had stuck. He looked a little bashful and I rammed home my point by criticising a close ally for actively undermining the British position and misrepresenting our role and motives. We shall see whether I achieved the effect the UK and I need; fingers crossed.

It's become clear to me that persons unknown have been briefing against me to Pres K. While most have been fantastic friends and supporters, I suspect certain Americans resent my influence. They were already actively undermining the Musa Qala deal. Much talk in Kabul of a British 'conspiracy', difficult to pin down but I can feel it, palpably – the atmosphere is different from that of a few months ago.

Tuesday, 16 January

I had a short period catching up on e-mails and admin, together with a couple of short farewell calls, before receiving Secretary Gates and the usual large party of hangers-on. I found him receptive and a listener, as well as personable and likeable. I had been warned that Karl E. and others had been critical of NATO at a briefing for him earlier in the morning. I decided that I needed to make it clear to Gates what a difficult situation we had inherited from the US and how ISAF had succeeded in stabilising the situation once we had taken over. I did not pull any punches and, for a while, I thought that General Peter Pace – the US Chairman of Joint Chiefs and the only other person in my office at this stage – was going to reprimand me in some way. He did not look too pleased but I relaxed the atmosphere by thanking and congratulating the USA for all they were doing (a sentiment I genuinely feel).

I also reassured them that we had advanced plans for our Spring Offensive, we would not cede the initiative to the Taliban, and stressed that when examining progress, they should base their assessment on the situation post-August 2006 and not simply tot up the total number of incidents in 2006 and simplistically compare it with the lower number in 2005. I emphasised that while we may, post MEDUSA, have stabilised the security situation, we should not expect the same combination of circumstances to exist in 2007. And anyway, we should plan to win this winnable campaign, not just be content with stabilising the security situation. The latter was not a tenable aim in the medium term as it would not satisfy the peoples' needs and we would lose their consent to what we were doing. While the Afghan government and international community needed to do more, we the military also needed to put more effort in now to ensure success and to give the Afghan National Security Forces time to reach the required standards. He said all the right things, although Peter Pace, while being supportive of the need to reinforce success, told me candidly that the recent decision to build up US troop numbers in Iraq was going to make this very difficult. I sympathised with him and he laughed ruefully. I escorted the party to their waiting helicopters and saw them off. The feedback was that I had been rather 'bold' but had achieved the aim. I was more than content with this, having learnt that, for some reason, people in Gates's position remembered briefings only if they recalled the person giving them.

Wednesday, 17 January

Some short office and phone calls and then a farewell office call from the wonderful Italian ambassador and his musically talented deputy. He was extremely complimentary about what we have achieved, saying we would leave a lasting legacy. He pondered whether I was really a 'hugely talented politician masquerading as a soldier' or 'a hugely talented soldier masquerading as a politician'. I told him that modern generals had to be both soldier (primarily) and 'politician' but only in the sense that they had to be able to wield political influence and have the courage to act in the political environment.

Thursday, 18 January

We put on dinner for the French hospital medics as a big thank you for all they did for me while I was in their care. What was astounding was the news from Dr Sagui that I had been suffering from a severe form of whooping cough, which Caroline had tried to warn us all about some months ago. I am going to give my medical staff a very hard time about this tomorrow. If Caroline had been listened to, I could have avoided being nastily ill for many weeks and the others who are suffering, including some children in Germany, might have avoided what is a very unpleasant illness. Anyway, the gallant and conscientious Dr Sagui and his dedicated band of doctors and nurses clearly enjoyed their evening and expressed astonishment that my fellow generals and I had not only invited them to dinner but also were so hospitable. I was very proud of my small team of multinational senior officers – James Bucknall, Emilio Gay, Steve Layfield, Dickie Davis, Richard Nugee and Nick Pope, to name but some. As I watched them enjoying a bit of banter with the French medics, not for the first time I reflected how incredibly lucky I am to have such men here with me.

Saturday, 20 January

Another average day in Paradise but quite a lot quietly achieved. Started with a good-natured update meeting at which I had the pleasure of thanking a genuinely 'Great American', Colonel 'Chuck' Waggoner for all he has done here. Chuck has piloted our very impressive counter IED programme and is single-handedly responsible for saving many, many lives. He is a wonderful, generous-hearted man in the true tradition of the USA.

After a useful PAG, back to camp to continue tidying up my list of outstanding issues and to dictate my Change of Command speech to my wonderful Military Assistant 2, James Driscoll. I am sending James home a few days early to look after his wife, who is a bit low while expecting their first child; James feels very guilty about leaving us before the end of the tour, almost in tears I think. A wonderful, loyal, dedicated man but I'm lucky enough to have more like him.

Tuesday, 23 January

An agitated General Sati (Chief of General Staff Pakistan Army), on the phone. It would appear that the US may have dropped a bomb and used artillery against suspected insurgents right up against the border with Pakistan. The result was one Pakistani soldier killed and two wounded. I suggested, and he agreed immediately, that there should be a joint investigation with HQ ISAF membership (this to reassure them that the US would play by the rules, sadly). Ben Freakley did not like this proposal but was wise enough to do as he was told. I had another call later in the day with General Hyat, who was grateful for my prompt and constructive direction. I await the outcome of this investigation with interest, fearing that this time the US have pushed their luck too far.

Wednesday, 24 January

My last conference call with my five subordinate commanders; again good stuff and I told them at the end that one reason I am optimistic about the future is because, when I watch and listen to them, I am filled with confidence. It was a good opportunity, as it was meant to be, to hear how we can help them and for me to give a little extra direction and guidance on the key issues and explain what is happening at the strategic level.

I had the huge pleasure of making an award to a local Afghan guard and an interpreter who between them had overpowered a suicide bomber at the gates of the US camp they helped guard. I presented them with a signed certificate, one of my coins (these are specially minted for commanders to award to deserving soldiers and civilians) and $150 each in cash. I have no doubt that the latter counted most, but what selfless bravery – humbling, a word I use frequently in this troubled land.

Representatives of the ICRC [International Committee of the Red Cross] came to bid me farewell. We have enjoyed a close and constructive relationship to our mutual benefit. They remarked how refreshing it had been to be viewed from the outset as helpful and not as 'enemy forces'. They thought that only the US, from a policy perspective and not the soldiers on the ground, now seemed to have a major suspicion of them.

Thursday, 25 January

In the evening we held our farewell dinner – a pretty grand affair by Kabul standards and we were very pleased with the turnout. Everyone who was anyone here seemed to have accepted our invitation and the atmosphere was buoyant and positive. Ex-President Mujadeedi, who is pretty ancient, arrived back from China in mid-afternoon and insisted on attending, much to his wife's annoyance so he told me. He is a wonderful man and, although I do not agree with some of his views, I revere him as

Above: Kabul, 4 May 2001. General Gerhard Back hands the ISAF (International Security Assistance Force) flag to me on my assumption of command.

Right: Tony Blair visits my headquarters in Kabul. Behind him is Jock Stirrup, Chief of the Defence Staff, and behind me is the British ambassador, Stephen Evans.

Left: With President Karzai.

Opposite page left, top to bottom: With Hikmet Cetin, NATO's senior civilian representative in Afghanistan, at a press conference in Kabul; Lieutenant Colonel Stuart Tootal and the Secretary of State for Defence, Des Brown; at one of many meetings with tribal elders.

Opposite page right, top to bottom: Donald Rumsfeld and I share a joke; Tom Tugendhat; with General Wardak, Afghan Minister for Defence; Staff Sergeant 'Shep' Shepherd MBE, my close-protection team commander.

Above: Planning our autumn offensive with General Bishmullah Khan and General Kayani.

Below: Change of Command Parade, Kabul, 4 February 2007. From left: General Dan McNeill, President Karzai, DR.

Above: A routine 'Chiefs' meeting. Clockwise from left: Nick Houghton, DR, Mark Stanhope, Stephen Dalton (back to camera).

Left: With Ed Llewellyn, David Cameron's chief of staff.

Right: With David Cameron, in the Cabinet Room.

Below: Working at home.

Above: Joking with an honour guard. Garrison Sergeant Major Billy Mott, who became a good friend, is to my left.

Right: The Queen and I enjoying the Jubilee parade, Windsor 2012.

Below: British armed forces to the rescue, Olympic Stadium 2012.

Above: Aung San Suu Kyi and I, Myanmar 2013.

Left: Visiting air crew who were operating over Libya, Italy 2011.

Below: Chairing a multinational Libya planning meeting, London, June 2011.

Top: Entertaining my US and French counterparts (left to right) Mark Stanhope, Mike Mullen (US Chairman of the Joint Chiefs of Staff), DR and Edouard Guillaud (French Chief of the Defence Staff).

Right: Corporal 'Dil' (left) and Warrant Officer 2 Julian Tranter.

Inset below, right: My farewell lunch at Downing Street, July 2013.

Sailing has been an important part of my life since boyhood. Caroline and Pippa at the British Kiel Yacht Club, Germany.

Left: Joanna and me.

much as every Afghan does. He made a short speech in which he told the hundred or so guests that I was the first commander of the International Security Assistance Force who understood the Afghans and could talk to them as an equal. It was pretty humbling and I felt, rarely for me, a lump come to my throat. Ron Neumann insisted on standing up, too, and made a strong and emotional speech about our work here together and how much he will miss me, presenting me with a certificate of appreciation for my efforts. And I made a speech in which I thanked a number by name and all collectively. I also took the opportunity to talk up our progress and express confidence for the future. It seemed to go down well and certainly led to prolonged applause. Afterwards, too many people came up to thank us for all we had done and say how very sorry they were that we were leaving.

Monday, 29 January

Helicoptered off for a meeting with General Craddock, who was more relaxed and less on his dignity than his predecessor could be – a real delight to be treated as an equal. I had the best part of an hour with him alone, discussing the key issues. He is the first American who seems to have a balanced view about Musa Qala – amazing. Then it was off to the palace for an emotional presentation to me by K of Afghanistan's most prestigious medal, followed by a really good debate over a range of issues, including Pakistan.

Back to camp to do some catch-up work, pose for a photo with my excellent Irish Army contingent, and then off to dinner with the visitors. Just before I was about to ask them all to sit down, General Craddock surprised me by asking for silence and making a very complimentary speech before presenting me with the NATO Meritorious Service Medal, together with the citation. I was bowled over, not anticipating it for one instance.

A good dinner was complemented by some excellent informed

discussion. At the end, I made a short speech, thanking General Craddock for his strong support and wisdom before asking him to present NATO campaign medals to four of our civilians, which he did. Then he gave me the finest pair of brass binoculars I have seen, together with a wooden box to keep them in, complete with an engraved brass plaque on the front, recording the occasion. I only had a pretty standard ARRC clock to give him in return but he seemed to appreciate it. I departed for my scratcher feeling thoroughly humbled by a day of unexpected recognition from both the Afghan government and NATO.

Thursday, 1 February

Operationally all quiet, but for an attack on the US Eradication Force (poppy-destruction team) in Helmand. I had warned them of the consequences of eradicating when the conditions remain unsettled. We will now be drawn into an additional conflict, which will not be easy to handle. Amateurs in national capitals will have the gall to regret the deaths of their soldiers, ignoring the fact that their misguided policies have yet again contributed directly to them.

Saturday, 3 February

Unsurprisingly, a busy final day. I held my last Commander's Update Afghanistan (CUA) meeting in the splendid new Combined Joint Operations Centre that the impressive Brigadier Nick Pope (in charge of command and control issues) and his team of signallers have done so much to bring into service, despite the lack of active support from the headquarters above us. After that, I spoke to the whole headquarters, ISAF 9 and 10 personnel, to congratulate and thank them and boost the confidence of our successors. Then I went to see the unsung heroes, visiting the cookhouse, the barbers (had a quick haircut, too), the shops and the gym, to thank all the staff for being such valuable members of the team.

A short chat with Egon Ramms (Commander, Allied Joint Force Command Brunssum) was followed by a private 'one-on-one' with General Wardak [Afghan Minister for Defence]. He was in sombre mood, concerned that he could not work with Dan McNeill. I talked the latter up and this seemed to improve morale. We then reminisced about what we had achieved together in the last nine months. I do have a huge admiration and affection for him, and look forward to hosting him on a visit to Germany or the UK in due course. Towards the end we were joined by Egon Ramms but I left after a while to move on to a farewell discussion with President K, grateful to be able to leave the rather cautious and unsubstantial discussions of two men just starting to get to know each other.

Pres K was in good form, although I detected some anti-UK sentiment (not directed at me I believe) amid the warm wishes and congratulations on an excellent job. I stressed, finally, the need to engage constructively with the Pakistanis and described the active cross-border measures explained to us a few days ago by General Hyat in Pindi. This seemed to please him, although he was more interested in a speech made yesterday by Musharraf that contained some 'anti-Afghan' sentiments. K ignored the many positive sections. Daan Everts and Egon joined us after a while. The discussion was conducted in friendly tones although Daan noted subsequently how, when talking about Pakistan in apparently moderate tones, K's body language revealed his hostility to that country.

Sunday, 4 February

I write this on board a US C17 transport aircraft heading home to Germany. Nine months ago I assumed command of a very different operation from the one I bequeathed today to my American successor. Have we done as well, or as much, as I had hoped? I think so and probably more, given the absence of any reserves of note, other than a plucky Portuguese light infantry company. So we achieved the military task given to me: NATO expansion across the whole of Afghanistan, in the process taking NATO into a new era for the Alliance – actually conducting and fighting, successfully, a land campaign. This alone is pretty dramatic. The Taliban chucked everything they had at us on MEDUSA and we gave them a drubbing, close run thing that it was. At no time could we relax, but had to work hard to maintain the initiative through innovative, nationwide Alliance/Afghan National Army joint operations, like OQAB EAGLE, and regional equivalents, such as BAZ TSUKI.

Of course, in Kabul, as the many diplomatic guests at today's Change of Command Ceremony emphasised, it is for our involvement in a range of, strictly speaking, non-military activities that we will be best remembered: the PAG, the ADZ, the creation of the Auxiliary Police, and our emphasis on reconstruction, development and improvements in governance. A number of people, privately and in speeches, have emphasised that I am as much politician as soldier and only thus have we been able to make the difference that they claim we did. My star certainly lost some of its lustre in President K's eyes over the last six weeks, because of his belief that I was too close to Pakistan. That is a shame but I stand by my actions and my advice to him. He has a weakness here and I will tell Tony Blair to advise him to become more open and balanced in his approach, while remaining sensibly cautious.

On this plane, I sit surrounded by some outstanding people without whom I could have achieved nothing: James Bucknall, Johnny Biggart, Simon Briggs, Nick Pope, Dickie Davis, Bill Aldridge, Bill Bailey, Dudley Giles, Steve Eden, Ralph Woodiwisse, Peter Copeland, Regimental Sergeant Major Campbell, Sergeant Green, Pod, Fergie, Shep, 'Brian' and Jonesy are just some. I could go on and there are many, many others, including Regimental Sergeant Major Colin Howard, Chris Boryer, Felix Gedney and Mr T, who have already left for home. How very well served I have been and our nation is. Do they, do the government, really understand what a priceless asset the British Army is? I doubt it, and over time the quality people who achieve these miracles and who allow us to do things other armies could not contemplate, will go, unloved and underpaid.

Whether anyone else ever reads this or not, I must for my own benefit also record my deep thanks and admiration for the thousands of allied servicemen and women I have had the huge privilege of commanding, and of their Afghan counterparts whom I have grown to respect and admire. Despite occasional frustrations, I must thank in particular the USA without whose generosity of spirit and commitment to freedom this noble enterprise – yes, with all its inadequacies – would have no hope of succeeding. Having met many, I now know what the term a 'Great American' means. And close behind the USA, comes the UK, Canada and the Netherlands, who, together with plucky Romania, volunteered for the most demanding roles in the south of Afghanistan and whose armed forces have proudly come of age in the process. Most important, though, are the Afghan people, the vast majority of whom have made it clear they do not want a return to the cruelty and hopelessness of Taliban rule. They and those fighting on their behalf in their armed forces are the true heroes of this tale. As has happened to so many before me, these people, with their quixotic blend of cruelty, generosity, courage and wisdom, have got into my bloodstream, as has their country, its splendour and contradictions reflecting the people so well.

This morning was a blaze of press interviews – I was able to tell a much gentler Alistair Leithead (BBC Correspondent) that we had attacked and killed the Musa Qala Taliban leader. I emphasised that this whole episode was a success, not a failure, pointing the way to a balanced approach aimed at empowering people, not categorising them simplistically as friend or foe. This was followed shortly afterwards by a dignified parade in which K, Egon Ramms, Dan McNeill and I each made speeches. K was less effusive than I suspect he would have been two months ago but kind nevertheless. I made a pretty good show (I think). Egon made a very long and tedious speech that sounded as if it had come out of a doctrinal pamphlet, but towards the end he was very complimentary about the

ARRC and my own role, which was good of him. He pointedly warned Dan that it was necessary to engage at every level and not just the tactical, while welcoming and wishing him luck. Dan's speech was commendably short but said little. At the end, like he did at October's change of command parade, K went round the troops on parade and shook hands with everyone. It was a nice touch that we all appreciated. I then accompanied him to his car, holding his hand for a long period in the process. He said he was looking forward to seeing me in London. I may be wrong but at the point we said farewell, he looked rather wistfully into my eyes and I sensed a rekindling of our relationship of last summer and maybe just a little doubt about my departure. Dr Spanta was full of good cheer and said my speech was 'fantastik' in his very German English.

Many people came to say goodbye – many kisses from bearded men. Wardak was emotional but we both know, God willing, our friendship is so strong that we will see each other again in better circumstances.

Soon it was time to board the waiting helicopters to be whisked off to the C17 waiting at Kabul airport. Once we had reached cruising altitude, a few of us popped a bottle of my favourite Moët and quietly toasted the end of this adventure, which none of us would have missed, despite its privations and long absence from our loved ones. The flight is estimated to take seven and a half hours, so we should arrive in Germany at about 1830 hours their time. I could be at home with my darling Caroline before 2000 hours – what a wonderful thought. The next two weeks will be full of presentations, talks and meetings with eminent people but, for now at least, the pressure is off.

FIFTEEN

Operation ENTIRETY and Chief of General Staff

When I returned from Afghanistan and had fully recovered from my bout of pneumonia, I went back to Rheindahlen for what would turn out to be another year as Commander Allied Rapid Reaction Corps. My initial duty was to report to my NATO bosses in Brussels on my tour in Kabul. I was to find that I was better received in the Belgian capital than I was in London, where the reception within the Ministry of Defence was lukewarm at best, or that's how it felt.

In Brussels, at breakfast with the NATO Military Committee, my host was Canadian General Ray Henault, Chairman of the Committee. General Craddock (Supreme Allied Commander Europe) joined us and was extremely complimentary about the work we had done in Kabul. Afterwards, I spent thirty minutes with Jaap de Hoop Scheffer, the NATO Secretary General, with whom I again struck up a sensible relationship. This underlined how well we could have got on during my days in Afghanistan, were it not for Jim Jones (former Supreme Allied Commander) and Gerhard Back (Commander Joint Force Command, Brunssum) inadvertently standing in our way. Today, the relationship between the ISAF commander and his political bosses is much closer, and rightly so. Especially in this era of high-speed media, a deployed commander must know his political boss and understand what makes him tick – and, dare I say it, vice versa. It's a team effort.

For my formal address to the North Atlantic Council, it was a full house – 'standing room only for you, Dave,' as one US General put it. A number of side rooms were linked to the council chamber by video conference. I reminded my audience what the Alliance had achieved and spelt out what more now had to be done. 'It is ours to lose,' I said. Success in Afghanistan was within our grasp, I argued, should we want it badly enough.

After my speech I took a number of questions. They all came at once, requiring me to write them down, which is the peculiar way they go about it in the Council. I ended up trying to answer something like twenty questions consecutively, which meant many good points were left unaddressed. All the ambassadors opened their question with a compliment, some exaggeratedly so. The most marked in this respect was Victoria Nuland, the US ambassador, who had been a consistent supporter of what I was doing.

I drove to Mons for an excellent lunch with Craddock and his senior staff, giving them a detailed briefing, and was back in Rheindahlen by the early evening, feeling the pace. I remember thinking how relatively unpressured I found my job in Kabul in comparison to days like this. I think that's because I like being my own boss and do not feel the pressure of events as long as I can control the outcome, or at least persuade myself that I can. I often tease Caroline that my blood pressure at home is much higher than it is on operations because, in my terms, I live a more stressful life at home. On operations, people broadly do as I tell them and I have few, if any, domestic problems to resolve.

Later that week, the wives at Rheindahlen gathered to give Caroline a surprise breakfast in our mess. More than eighty of them were there. They showered her with presents, a wonderful bouquet of flowers and a Commander's Commendation, which they had persuaded me – with huge pleasure on my part – to donate. Caroline played it just right and it was clear that she was held in the highest regard and affection by them. This was a tribute to her compassion, hard work and courage in tackling the few among our superiors, and sadly some of the support staff in Rheindahlen, too, who had not understood that our families must come first.

On Friday there was a church service to give thanks for the safe return of the Headquarters and for a job well done. This was followed by an excellent, unassuming, medal parade at which I gave a short speech aimed as much at thanking and congratulating the families as the officers and soldiers. That evening we all attended a dance where morale was high – it was a great way to part company, for leave in some cases and new postings in others.

The following week, I was back in London. The high spot was assisting Tony Blair at No, 10 in looking after President Karzai and his entourage. Karzai could not have been more friendly, while Blair was attentive to what I had to say, picking up on some of my key themes at his press conference. My driver, Sergeant Spencer Green, brought Caroline to No. 10 and she was heard to observe how peculiar it was to watch her husband standing on the steps of Downing Street with the Prime Minister, saying goodbye to the President of Afghanistan. Afterwards, I was dragged back inside for a final discussion with Blair's team of advisers. I remember thinking I would not miss this sort of thing, for a while at least.

I was a bit disappointed with my reception by the Chiefs, who did not ask me to brief them collectively, which, frankly, I thought was remarkable, given the nature of what I had been doing in Kabul and Britain's continuing commitment in Afghanistan. I spoke to them individually – to Jock Stirrup, Chief of the Defence Staff, and Richard Dannatt, Chief of the General Staff – but I had to book those office calls myself. It seemed clear to me that there was a lack of enthusiasm to hear my view in the MoD. I think perhaps I had been just too troublesome and my criticism of British tactics in Helmand had probably not helped, nor had my keenness to emphasise that there was a long, hard road ahead before success would be ours in Afghanistan.

My reception in other capitals was warmer. In particular, two visits stand out. The first was to Portugal, where the entire Portuguese Para Commando Brigade, from whom my single reserve company in Afghanistan was drawn, marched past with no other spectators present. It was bizarre and flattering at the same time to have 5,000 men on parade in front of just me. Afterwards, we had a terrific reunion and many of the soldiers spoke to me individually, which was a great pleasure. The other visit that stands out in my memory is to Australia. I had many friends there including the Chief of the Defence Force, Air Chief Marshal Angus Houston. Caroline was included in the invitation, which was typical of Angus's thoughtfulness. To return to thank a country that had stood so solidly behind me, and more than punched above its weight in military terms, was a real joy. We could not have been treated more generously and listened to with more care.

At around this time, Richard Dannatt informed me that he would like me to be the next Commander in Chief of the Army's Land Forces Command, a posting that would mean being based, for the first time, near our home in Wiltshire. This was an exciting prospect and a demanding job. The bulk of the Army would come under my command, presenting a great opportunity to influence all aspects of Army life – doctrine, training, preparation for operations and morale. In the meantime, I still had some months to go at ARRC and I maintained a keen interest in what was happening in Afghanistan. From a training perspective, it was important to recover our more conventional war-fighting skills, which we did through a series of demanding exercises. These and the occasional foreign trip kept me busy, and that year at last allowed us, as a family, to enjoy life in Germany, a country we had grown to like over many years of living there.

I was very honoured in July 2007 to receive a knighthood for my command in Afghanistan. I was told this was the first operational knighthood since the Second World War. It also made me rather guiltily realise that my efforts as Commander of ISAF had not gone unnoticed in London, whatever impression I formed at the time. In December, we were honoured again with an impressive farewell parade in Germany at which General Craddock and other senior NATO officers came to say goodbye.

I had been made an acting four-star General in Afghanistan, a rank I kept for a while on my return before reverting to my previous rank of Lieutenant General. Arriving at Headquarters Land Forces at Wilton, just west of Salisbury, to take up my new post, I was promoted to substantive General. Along with the job came the privilege of living in the elegant and historic Bulford Manor, parts of which date from the sixteenth century. The house had been acquired by the Army when it bought Salisbury Plain in 1898 and has recently been under threat of being sold off as part of defence cuts.

By the time I got to Wilton I had been thinking and breathing Afghanistan and operations for a number of years, but in my early forays as Commander in Chief, I soaked up a widespread feeling that the war there was little more than a passing distraction and there was no need to re-orientate existing plans around it. At a certain level and above, some officers were in denial that Afghanistan was a proper war. So were many civil servants. It was very clear to me that it *was* a war and I argued that we had to treat it like one, with the commitment and passion that implied. I realised that, however good my officers were individually, I was dealing with an institutional problem.

I put on my thinking cap and a few days later called my key people together.

'We've got to get the Army on a war footing,' I told them.

The new approach was to be called Operation ENTIRETY. I set out what I said would be a major shift in our thinking, to turn towards Afghanistan, not away from it. Everyone was sold on the idea and the meeting ended with a new sense of purpose.

Shortly afterwards, my Military Assistant, Lieutenant Colonel Ian Mortimer, came back in with a worried look on his face.

'General,' he said, 'you are a very important man as Commander in Chief.' I thanked him for the compliment. 'But,' he added, 'we've been talking and agreed that you're not important enough to declare war on your own.'

It was a good point. Possibly that was going a little too far, so I came up with another way of conceptualising what I wanted.

'Tell them,' I said, 'I have thought about it, and we won't call it a war footing. I'm putting the command on a *campaign* footing.'

And that is what we did. It meant from that morning onwards, our main effort was Afghanistan. Until then, people were talking about doing conventional war-fighting exercises before concentrating on Afghanistan. Now those priorities were reversed. A campaign footing meant everything was focused on looking after our troops in Helmand and making sure they were properly trained and equipped. That decision probably saved lives, and embarrassed London, where too many people at the Foreign Office, the Ministry of Defence and the Permanent Joint Headquarters were still stuck in no man's land, somewhere between Iraq, Afghanistan and preparing for World War III. My two key subordinates in HQ Land Forces, Lieutenant Generals Graeme Lamb and Nick Parker, were especially helpful in implementing this change of policy. They had told me that something was wrong and once I changed tack, I was able to let them get on with it. It helped that the three of us were close friends, something that made a serious business enjoyable, too.

As Commander in Chief, my job was to run 75 per cent of the Army and to implement policy and budgetary priorities agreed by the Chief of General Staff and the Army Board, of which I was a member. There is no doubt that I should have referred my decision on Operation ENTIRETY upwards, but I had been trying to make Afghanistan our main effort for a year or two and I decided to act unilaterally. I did not tell Richard Dannatt. He did come down to Wilton to discuss it, and pointed out that he would like to have been consulted, but he supported what I was doing.

I had great respect for Richard, who went through a period when he was not convinced that I should be his successor as Chief of the General Staff. He had a plan to go for a younger man, arguing that he and I were too close in age. But one way or another the merits of my case were impressed upon him and we worked through it. Richard eventually confirmed that I would be his successor in September 2008 and would take up my new post in the summer of 2009.

That left me the best part of a year to prepare. I used the time to reinforce the change of direction we had made with Operation ENTIRETY and went round ruthlessly checking that people had my Intent on that and were following it. Surprisingly, I needed to be very firm with some people to get my message across.

One of the things I first detected to an annoying degree in this large headquarters I now found myself commanding, was how difficult it was to pin down who was actually responsible for a decision and its subsequent execution. Often it would transpire that different people had responsibility, accountability and authority for a problem and, worse still, it often sat with a committee so no one individual had a decisive role. This was the antithesis of how the Army operated in war, where these three functions would always be aligned in a single individual. It made for a rather sloppy process in which people would endlessly debate issues and commission studies before decisions were taken, usually by yet another committee. We seemed to have absorbed the worst of civil-service practice.

I found this frustrating and strove to introduce the type of dynamic decision-making process based on individuals that we enjoyed on operations, which made us so effective. To bring this home to my staff, I coined the term 'ARA Principle' in which the process of resolving every issue had to pass the test of whether it aligned accountability, responsibility and authority in a single person. I am not sure this achieved too much but I embarrassed a few people and it was a useful reminder to many that they wore uniform and were not 'suits', our pejorative term for civil servants.

The ARA Principle was something I returned to with a vengeance when I was Chief of the Defence Staff (CDS), during the so-called Levene Reforms process. Lord Peter Levene was asked by the Secretary of State, Liam Fox, to review the non-operational decision-making structure of the MoD and how it related to the single services. I was very clear that this was an opportunity at last to introduce Lord Mountbatten's recommendations of the early 1960s. He had proposed then that the CDS should exercise full command of the armed forces, rather than attempting to do so through the moral authority he possessed as chairman of the Chiefs of Staff Committee. On a good day this might suffice but often, as Mountbatten ruefully recorded on more than one occasion, it did not.

This was largely because the individual single-service Chiefs answered constitutionally to the Secretary of State for Defence and not to the CDS, thus allowing them to play one off against the other.

I failed to persuade Levene of my case, although, being the highly intelligent man he is, I believe he might well have agreed if it had not been for three circumstances. Firstly, Fox liked his own ability to divide and rule, and was disinclined to lose it. Secondly, the civil service, who were the driving force in the secretariat established by Levene for the duration of his study, were strongly hostile to my proposal. They feared it would unite the armed forces through the authority of the CDS in a way never hitherto achieved and make them much more influential in the running of defence as a consequence. This argument was cleverly summed-up by the then Second Permanent Under Secretary in the MoD, Jon Day, a good friend of mine. He mischievously claimed that doing as I proposed would make the CDS the most powerful military figure since Cromwell. No one really knew what the hell Jon meant but it sounded ominous. So my proposal had little chance thereafter. The third reason was that the single-service Chiefs themselves wanted to preserve their direct relationship with the Secretary of State, fearing the loss of status and influence my proposal implied. In the event, they were removed from the Defence Board, the MoD's management commitee on which they had hitherto sat, so much of this happened anyway. But it did so without being compensated for by the CDS being given full authority over their services and thus welding them into a single force of huge influence.

I gave up the battle but not before Peter Levene agreed the creation of a new 'Armed Forces Committee' (AFC), chaired by the CDS, on which sat the Chiefs and the Permanent Secretary as well as other senior civil servants. This achieved much of what I was after but not the revolutionary step I, and I am sure Mountbatten all those years before me, was seeking. Interestingly, when discussing this issue with David Cameron, it became clear that he had not realised that the CDS did not exercise proper command of the single services, a common misconception. In the Strategic Defence and Security Review (SDSR) process, for example, the CDS had the most influence, but he was not necessarily decisive. He could not deliver a single agreed solution for politicians, although in due course we got much nearer this through the new Armed Forces Committee. Indeed, Jock Stirrup, when discussing his relative lack of authority as CDS, reminded his critics that he did not command the services but was rather a *primus inter pares* (first among equals). This is not the case on operational issues in which the CDS exercises command of all deployed forces.

Of course, being Commander in Chief, and Chief of the General Staff after it, had its lighter moments and fulfilling compensations. For Caroline and me, the best of these was when I was asked to become the Colonel Commandant of the Brigade of Gurkhas. I had first come across the Gurkhas on an exercise in the jungle in 1971 and had the privilege of commanding elements of them in East Timor, Sierra Leone and Afghanistan. But to be given such an honour came out of the blue. Under the expert guidance of the then Colonel Brigade of Gurkhas, David Hayes, we soon learnt to feel at home among these feared fighting men and their delightful families. As Colonel Commandant I was also chairman of the Gurkha Welfare Trust (GWT). We travelled to Nepal on a number of occasions to visit the Trust's highly efficient and impressive field arm, the Gurkha Welfare Service (GWS), and watch the staff perform its demanding work. Through its network of smart outposts in some of the most inaccessible places in Nepal, the GWS ensures that retired Gurkhas and their widows receive their pensions as well as improving the lot of local people through education and water projects. We loved our visits and made lifelong friends with the outstanding men of the GWS and their wives.

As well as our GWT work, supervised in a bishop-like manner by retired Colonel William Shuttlewood, and advised by a thoroughly committed group of largely civilian trustees, we enjoyed our visits to the units that make up the brigade, whether in the UK, Brunei or, in my case, on operations in Afghanistan. The Gurkha soldier, properly commanded and led, is as efficient, fearless and loyal as any in the world. A cheerful grin, great hospitality and kindness are their hallmarks. The United

Kingdom owes our Gurkha soldiers and their families a huge debt of loyalty and I hope we never forget it.

Among other appointments, I was proud to be the Honorary Colonel of my own regiment, 3rd RHA. I loved visiting them and their families, by now based in Germany, to hear all they were doing and to discover standards were as high as ever.

One sadder moment that came about during my time as Commander in Chief Land Forces was when I was required to give evidence at the Old Bailey trial on espionage charges of my former interpreter in Kabul, one Daniel James, a Territorial Army Corporal attached to the Princess of Wales' Royal Regiment. Thanks to a tip-off from the Americans it had emerged towards the end of my tour as Commander ISAF that James had been secretly passing information about NATO troop movements to the Iranian military attaché in Kabul. He had been working for me using his fluent Farsi and his knowledge of Dari and had done a reasonable job. He was especially useful during the early months of my tour until I realised that many of my interlocutors in Afghanistan spoke good English.

Born in Tehran as Esmail Mohammed Beigi Gamasai, James had come to England in his early teens and lived a colourful life that occasionally made him the butt of jokes among his army colleagues. In evidence, I described him as a 'Walter Mitty' character who always sought a bit more in life. He had run a salsa club in Brighton and worked at various times as a nightclub croupier and a bouncer. He had also been a keen body-builder. His job for me was to translate my speeches, something he did often with more gusto and hand and facial gesture than I thought necessary. On a number of occasions I had to remind him to remember that he was, 'not giving the speech, just translating it'. I had no reason to suspect that he was up to no good, but I did notice that he seemed overkeen to try to short-cut the promotion system. He tried to convince me and others that he should be moved up to the rank of Sergeant, something I would not allow unless it had been approved through the normal channels.

James's betrayal was embarrassing for NATO and I was angry that our vetting procedures had not picked up signs that he could be suspect. Although he had accompanied me to some high-level meetings, I was confident that he would have been party to strategic information only, not operational detail. Clearly, however, that strategic insight may have been of interest to Iran. At the end of his trial, James was sentenced to ten years in prison after being found guilty of 'communicating information useful to an enemy'.

While I had disagreements with my military superiors, even as I climbed the ladder towards Chief of the General Staff, I often had a rapport with my political masters. The best of them could see the logic of a well-argued position and could cut through all the objections when they needed to. In the early spring of 2009, John Hutton, who had become Defence Secretary the previous autumn and whom I had got to know, decided he wanted an away-day out of London to discuss priorities and, in particular, Afghanistan. Much to the annoyance of the current generation of Chiefs, he did not invite them to the meeting to be held at the Joint Services Staff College at Shrivenham in Oxfordshire. He focused instead on the next generation, waiting in the wings, including me.

Richard Dannatt was understandably apoplectic about being sidelined and I could understand his feelings. Jock Stirrup seemed to have gone along with it because he, too, was focusing on the next generation, having found the current Chiefs an awkward bunch who did not get on with each other particularly well. Hutton was keen to hear my point of view, which would have been more difficult had the incumbent Chief been present.

On the day, in the old library at Shrivenham, the political editor of the *Sun*, George Pascoe-Watson, was invited to take part in one session. We were debating how well the government and military were presenting to the British public the progress of campaigns such as Afghanistan, for which public support and political will were vital, especially with casualty numbers increasing. At one point the discussion boiled down to whether the conflict in Afghanistan amounted to a war or not. The very fact that we were debating that seems somewhat ridiculous in retrospect. I argued forcefully that it *was* a war – I knew it was because I had been there commanding NATO troops and I knew what we were up against and the scale of the effort we were putting in. Against me was a senior civil servant in charge of defence policy, who was saying that he could not accept that it was a war, something that he defined in terms of old-fashioned mass movements of opposing armies. I got pretty stroppy about this and could see that Hutton was sympathetic. Then Pascoe-Watson was asked for his view.

'I'll tell you this,' he said. 'The General's right. You guys better think it's a war, with everything that's at stake, or how do you think the British public is going to stomach what's happening, if it's not that important?' I looked across at the civil servant and thought I couldn't have said it better myself.

As I prepared to take on the job of head of the Army, I have to admit that the prospect did not fill me entirely with joy. The weight of political pressure on someone of that rank is huge. A twenty-four-hour-a-day job, it's capable of sucking much of the fun out of life. For the first time, I could see that this was going to be a hard grind. Even as Commander in Chief, I still felt I was my own boss. But as Chief of the General Staff you are knee deep in politics and you can easily become ground down by bureaucracy and by the endless need to discuss and justify everything.

I arrived in London to succeed Richard Dannatt in August 2009 and Caroline and I took over the flat that came with the job in Kensington Palace. I should point out that this was not grace and favour residence. We had to pay a substantial whack of mortgage by way of rent on it. But that flat was a big bonus that helped me keep life in perspective while doing a busy job. We lived in a wonderful part of London and could go for runs or walk our dog Poppy, a border terrier, in Kensington Gardens. It was a great privilege and pleasure to live where we did. I am a firm believer that people in tough public-service roles need a plus point for their families and, for us, it was that flat.

That said, I had a sixth sense that living there could become controversial.

I insisted that the MoD properly examine alternatives. This they did but after two months of scouring the market on their part we were informed that somewhere appropriate in Central London would cost the same as the Kensington Palace flat, especially as my security was included in the latter arrangement. We were duly directed to occupy the Dannatts' apartment.

With Operation ENTIRETY I had already signaled my priority. As a new member of the Chiefs of Staff Committee, I brought that approach to centre stage. Jock Stirrup, the CDS, declared that Afghanistan was our main effort and I made sure that our civil servants were working in line with that priority. I emphasised to Stirrup that we should listen more to the senior theatre-level commander in Afghanistan, and a little less to the Helmand Task Force commander, who tended to be preoccupied with the tactical detail of that deployment. Lieutenant General Nick Parker was Deputy Commander of ISAF by this time. I was pleased to note that his views rightly started to influence decisions in London although it was not until I took over as CDS that Parker's successor, Lieutenant General James Bucknall, finally took part in a weekly video teleconference with Kabul. In this way we were at last beginning to take proper notice of the people who were helping to drive the campaign as a whole, working alongside the likes of US Generals Stanley McCrystal and David Petraeus.

I assumed command of the Army in what was already the run-up to the general election of May 2010, when a new Conservative-Liberal Democrat coalition government was to take office under the leadership of David Cameron. When I joined the Chiefs of Staff Committee, we were all well aware that a major review of defence spending was in the offing after the election, whoever won it. The Strategic Defence and Security Review (SDSR) was announced straight after the election and published the following October. After much haggling, the SDSR delivered a 7.7 per cent reduction in real terms in military spending.

The build-up to the Review generated a classic inter-service battle as each component of the armed forces fought its corner against the cuts. I was active in promoting the Army's case, making speeches at the Royal United Services Institute, Chatham House and elsewhere, some of which made the front pages. While playing a constructive role in designing our armed forces for the long term, I was very clear that we had to succeed in Afghanistan before we worried too much about what might come along next. It was not a case of either/or. Afghanistan, I believed then – and still do – is central to our security and the reputation on which some of that security is based. I was clear, too, that whatever the shape and size of our armed forces, they had to include a respectable land component, because ultimately battles and wars are won on the land where people live, not on the sea or in the air. Politicians and many others had been seared by long drawn-out entanglements in Iraq and Afghanistan, and this was not an easy case to make. But I was determined that poorly executed coalition campaigns should not lead to the lessons of history being ignored.

In early September, on just my third day in the new job, I found myself quite unexpectedly back in No. 10, by then under the leadership of Blair's arch rival, Gordon Brown. I was summoned by the Prime Minister's office and arrived the following day feeling a little under-prepared. I was ushered into his office and spent over an hour with him. We talked a little bit about military business, but much of it was devoted to literature and his recently published book *Courage: Eight Portraits*, which featured profiles of, among others, the Burmese pro-democracy leader Aung San Suu Kyi, Robert Kennedy and Nelson Mandela. It was a fascinating discussion. I said to myself, 'Why on earth am I sitting in No. 10 having this conversation with the Prime Minister?' In retrospect, I am convinced that Brown was on a charm offensive. He was basically signalling that we could work together and that he did not want to have the problems he had experienced with Richard Dannatt, with whom he did not get on.

Within three weeks, Brown and his wife, Sarah, followed up with an invitation to Caroline and I to lunch at Chequers. There we had a useful discussion about world affairs, as well as Afghanistan and troop numbers, and he listened to me. While you could sense the hard edges of a personality scarred by the cut and thrust of frontline politics, I found Brown charming and intellectually engaged. Sarah was no less so and took Caroline on a fascinating tour of Chequers, including the room where Lady Mary Grey (younger sister of Lady Jane Grey) was once imprisoned.

Interestingly, Brown had lunch or breakfast with the Chiefs every six months or so, to talk about what was happening in defence or Afghanistan. In comparison, David Cameron has had less formal interaction with the Chiefs as a group, preferring to see them on an individual basis or in the case of the Chief of the Defence Staff, through the medium of the National Security Council.

A number of my close military friends and I are of the view that not all Tories – I exclude David Cameron – are as close to defence and the armed forces as they profess to be. We often found that Labour politicians were generally more interested in what we had to say and in involving us in their decisions. They seemed to have an intrinsic respect for officers in the armed forces whereas the Tories could be less receptive. 'If you have any brain, why join the Army?' sometimes seemed to be the view.

In the event, I had just over a year as Chief of the General Staff, which I regret. Despite the pressures I have described, I enjoyed most of the job immensely, especially the impact I could have on morale. To visit troops in Afghanistan or round the country or in Germany was very rewarding. These were your people. They looked up to you and had an innate respect for their Chief, however bad or good you were.

The conduct of the Strategic Defence and Security Review, which was published in October 2010, involved endless meetings as we traded ideas and defended our respective turfs. I was not only fighting the Army's cause but, as a member of the Chiefs of Staff Committee, I was helping Jock Stirrup to synthesise a complex multi-dimensional negotiation. I had my own meetings with David Cameron after he became Prime Minister and with his chief of staff, Ed Llewellyn. Notwithstanding decisions about such things as the number of maritime patrol aircraft we should have, which was important because the size of that programme affected everything else, there were two key issues as far as I was concerned. One was the size of the Army and the other was the difficult question of what to do about aircraft carriers.

On manpower, I was passionate in my defence of the Army as it was then constituted, but I accepted that the country's economic plight meant the Army should bear some of the pain and come down from 102,000 to 95,000. I was content that we could do that and still meet our obligations, most importantly in Afghanistan. What my critics probably don't understand is how much worse the result might have been without the fight put up by my fellow Chiefs and I, including, importantly, Jock Stirrup. Liam Fox, who was Secretary of State for Defence, fought hard, too, once a red line he had drawn himself looked like being crossed. But other members of the government, including George Osborne, the Chancellor, and Nick Clegg, the Deputy Prime Minister, even back in 2010, were prepared to cut the defence budget and thus army numbers even more. This did not happen ultimately because of the ally we had in David Cameron. But even so, we will end up with smaller armed forces than many people, including me, think is wise.

A year later, since the defence programme and available money were still out of kilter, it was decided that further cuts would be necessary. This manifested itself in a new, mini Strategic Defence and Security Review, known as the Three Month Review. The first results of this were announced in July 2011, by which time I had been Chief of the Defence Staff, succeeding Jock Stirrup, for nine months. Another significant reduction in expenditure had to be made and the eyes of the bean counters were focused again on the size of the Army, despite the original cut that I had agreed as Chief of the General Staff, which, give or take, had been confirmed by my successor, General Sir Peter Wall. The question was how to do this without imperilling important capability. Liam Fox set up a team to examine the scope for growing the size and utility of the Territorial Army (TA) in a way that would compensate for a further cut in the regular Army. The members of the group were its chairman Nick Houghton, Vice Chief of the Defence Staff, Tory MP and TA officer Julian Brazier and my old friend Lieutenant General (Rtd) Graeme Lamb.

Fox knew I might be difficult over this, so he ensured I could not play a central role. In fact, it wasn't a bad idea to bypass the normal Ministry of Defence bureaucracy and inject some fresh thinking, although I retained a scrutiny role as·chairman of the Chiefs of Staff Committee. But the motor for this project was Nick Houghton's team, operating largely outside the normal Ministry of Defence process. As Chief of the Defence Staff, too late in the day, I realised on this one that, yet again, I had responsibility without power.

The team came to the conclusion that the regular Army could be reduced to 82,000 while at the same time the Reserves would be expanded to 30,000. This would be a more active Reserve force than hitherto, with bigger operational and training commitments, but the issue for opponents of this scheme is that for many years we have had a problem finding these people. We were now requiring more of them at an age when many have other priorities, young families and careers for example, than being in the Army Reserve. Reservists' new obligations would also place greater pressure on their civilian employers, especially small businesses that could ill-afford to lose key people for the twelve months that was being proposed.

I understand the principle behind the new Reserves concept, but I remain concerned that without a massive input of additional resources, thus in part defeating the object of the exercise, it will be difficult to deliver this re-balancing of regular and Reserve strength. Interestingly, Nick Houghton, when briefing the National Security Council on his proposals, included the need to prove their practicability before the scheme was adopted. The government decided to push it through regardless of this sensible precaution. Not for the only time, as we walked back to the Ministry of Defence from No. 10, Nick said to me, 'My good nature has been taken advantage of.'

I am sad to report that progress to date on recruitment of Reserves has only underlined my concerns, though I wish the new regime well. David Cameron and the government have put a lot of political capital into the scheme but I fear they will need to match it with more financial capital, money that will be taken from other parts of the defence budget.

On the thorny issue of aircraft carriers, back in 2010 I could not bring myself to accept that we needed to build two, vast new ships of the Queen

Elizabeth class, as we are now doing, to replace the old Invincible class. I couldn't see the justification either from a cost point of view or in terms of the extra capability the new ships would offer. In a perfect world it would be great to have them, but given a fast-shrinking defence budget, the relative impact on the rest of the defence programme, including the rest of the Navy, was too much. My advice to the Prime Minister was that we should build two new ships of the Invincible class or a modern equivalent, and keep the existing carriers going, with their excellent Harrier jets, until the new ones were ready. The irony of what has actually transpired is that the new carriers are routinely likely to have no more than ten to twelve fixed-wing aircraft on them, which is the same as the Invincible class, instead of the thirty for which they were designed, because of cost issues. I discussed these options with Cameron and he agreed with me that it made little sense to go for the bigger version.

When it became clear that it was already too late to axe the first new carrier, HMS *Queen Elizabeth*, which had been commissioned under Gordon Brown, I argued that we should scrap plans to build the second one, HMS *Prince of Wales*. I proposed we should enter into an arrangement with the French whereby they would have one carrier at sea, and available to us, while ours was in re-fit and vice versa. Instead of the second carrier, I argued that we could have five new frigates for the same money. After the Strategic Defence and Security Review was published we did explore the notion of a tie-up with the French at an Anglo-French conference at Lancaster House during my first weeks as CDS. This may yet come to fruition because we probably won't have the money to commission the second carrier anyway.

My suggestion on frigates was tapping into the clear schism within senior ranks in the Navy between those who wanted the new, bigger carriers at all costs and those who thought the price was too high in terms of the inevitable reduction in the size of the overall fleet. My hopes in this area were dashed by some clever footwork by Mark Stanhope, the First Sea Lord. He told Cameron that there were no suitable frigate designs that could be built in the time frame required. Cameron suggested that we build frigates similar to those being sold at the time to Oman. Stanhope invoked the row over Snatch Land Rovers in Afghanistan, which had been found to be seriously wanting in their ability to protect troops from IED attack. He described the ships going to Oman as 'snatch frigates' – the toxic implication being that whoever ordered them would be accused at a later date of not looking after our sailors properly. There were also objections about the frigates' ability to cross the north Atlantic in a gale in winter and their lack of an anti-submarine capability. David Cameron and I chuckled about why anyone would want to take them across the Atlantic in winter, but we gave up the struggle and the Strategic Defence and Security Review confirmed both carriers would be built.

Stanhope won the day on carriers but the fighters and launching systems they were to carry was another big area of disagreement. Liam Fox not only wanted the new carriers, he was insistent that they should be fitted with a catapult launching system for their aircraft. Catapults and arrestor wires – 'cats and traps' in the trade – are a sophisticated and expensive way of launching and retrieving fighter jets, and the system to be fitted in our new carriers was of a new and unproven design. Cats and traps do have the advantage of being able to handle aircraft with a greater range and weaponry payload than the alternative Short Take Off Vertical Landing (STOVL) system used on the Invincible class. With this there is a ramp on the deck of the carrier and the planes take off under their own power. When they land, they have to hover to do so. The cats and traps version is vastly more expensive but the advantage in capability it offers, in the region of 10 to 15 per cent, is marginal and, in straitened times, in my view, cannot justify the cost.

Fox's determination to install cats and traps was estimated, even at the time of the Review, to add another £800 million to the carriers' cost. That estimate was to prove conservative. This was because HMS *Queen Elizabeth* had to be redesigned and re-engineered to take the catapult and then those modifications had to be applied to HMS *Prince of Wales*. Fox was passionate about defence and was absolutely convinced of his own judgement, arguably to a fault. He wanted the best and saw maritime power as being the key component in Britain's future defence posture. As Chief of the Defence Staff, I accepted the inevitability of the new carriers, but I argued strongly with him about the case for cats and traps. He could not be dissuaded and I lost the argument.

When Philip Hammond took over from Fox in October 2011, I told him at our first meeting that I believed we had made the wrong decision on carrier variants. The cats and traps version was going to be more expensive still than he was being told and, I argued, would distort the shape and size of the armed forces, including the Navy. By that stage, defence insiders were talking about an additional £2 billion required for cats and traps. Not only did it involve changing the design of the carriers, it also meant ordering a new variant of the F-35 Joint Strike Fighter plus retraining the Navy to use the new launch and retrieval system.

Hammond listened to me but we didn't take it any further then. Whatever else one could say about Hammond – high on IQ but less strong on EQ soon became a popular description – he is ruthlessly logical. I could tell that he had hoisted in my concerns. Three weeks later I had another meeting with him.

'Why are you the only person in this building who is telling me that we have taken the wrong decision on carrier variants?' he inquired.

I said, firstly, that I believed that Bernard Gray, the new Chief of Defence Material, who was in charge of procurement at the Ministry of Defence, shared my view. Secondly, I told him that the decision on cats and traps was being affected by 'group-think' and inertia. A decision had been made, it had gone through the mill and people could not tolerate the thought of re-opening it.

To do Hammond much credit, in May 2012, courageously supported by David Cameron and the government, the decision to revert to STOVL was announced. It was presented as being principally because of a concern that the Joint Strike Fighter version designed for use with cats and traps was beset by delays and would not be available until 2023. But the more important underlying reason was as I have described.

A subsidiary issue on aircraft carriers was the fate of the Harrier jump jets that Fox persuaded everyone should be sold off to the US Marine Corps. We were in a bizarre situation, divesting ourselves of the ability to fly planes from carriers, despite having identified it as a critical capability. We were deciding to pour billions of pounds into creating a new version of that capability but acquiescing to an eight-year gap before the first of the new ships would come into service. The Ministry of Defence needed to find the money for the new programme and so decided to get rid of the existing one to help pay for it. Fox was, paradoxically and conveniently, convinced that we could survive without Harriers or carriers in the interim, neither of which were available to us during the campaign against Colonel Gaddafi in Libya. But it was more the flaw in his overall logic that I, and I have to say many in government, including Nick Clegg, questioned.

I slowed down the sale of the Harriers as much as I could by quietly countenancing a much longer and more drawn-out process of transfer to the Americans than Fox had envisaged. My hope was that a decision would eventually be made to revert to STOVL on the new carriers. In the meantime, we could keep that capability alive by having a few Harriers that we could operate from HMS *Illustrious*, the last of the three Invincible class carriers still in service. The Navy was more than happy discreetly to go along with this. Indeed, they were probably doing it anyway, as was the Air Force.

I admit that I was being mildly insubordinate in trying to delay the sale. When Fox discovered that not all the Harriers had been sold, he instructed that his direction on this was to be implemented immediately. I think he realised this was a backdoor route to preserving STOVL, which he was dead against. Either way, the upshot is that the UK will be without this vital capability, which is so important that we are spending billions on it, for eight to ten years.

SIXTEEN

Chief of the Defence Staff

I took over as Chief of the Defence Staff (CDS) on 29 October 2010, having been the first person selected for the post to be subjected to what amounted to a job interview, conducted by David Cameron and his deputy Nick Clegg. Nick Houghton, who succeeded me on my retirement in July 2013, was by then the only other candidate and I had a clear sense that many in the establishment, the civil service and the Ministry of Defence favoured him as a safer pair of hands. I was told by well-placed friends that I was seen 'as too much my own man', outspoken on big issues such as Afghanistan and defence cuts. I am sure some people held this view.

The interview was Cameron's idea and there were just the three of us in his office at No. 10 as I responded to questions about my leadership style, my career history and what my priorities as head of the armed forces would be. I was particularly concerned to put a marker down on Afghanistan and the importance, as I saw it, of countries such as Britain not surrendering to the temptation to cut and run once our combat role was over. I made it clear that I was committed to Afghanistan and wanted to finish the job properly. This was to be a theme that ran through my tenure as Chief of the Defence Staff over the next three years and the cause of some tension between the government and me.

In the end, the choice of who should get the job probably came down to a matter of personality as much as anything. I actually rather enjoyed the well-informed discussion the three of us had that day and, despite the job's trials and tribulations, am enormously grateful that Cameron and Clegg saw beyond the Whitehall gossip and gave me such an opportunity. Of course, much as I was delighted to be selected, it meant ending my stint as Chief of the General Staff after only fourteen months. I left a job that I had grown to enjoy knowing there was much more still to do.

As I prepared to take the reins from Jock Stirrup, I remember his advice. 'This job,' he said, 'is quite different from any other, and until you're doing it, you probably won't realise it.' He was spot on. There is pressure on you in many senior roles in the armed forces but as CDS there is no one else to turn to. Even as Chief of the General Staff you can always talk to the CDS, but as CDS it's just you and they all come to you. All the big problems end up on your desk and your better judgement is constantly being called upon. While the members of the Chiefs of Staff Committee, all of whom were good friends of mine, were an excellent sounding board, ultimately you have only the Prime Minister and the Secretary of State for Defence to go to. Often they will not want to hear what you are about to say.

A year after I became CDS, I went to the retirement parade in Arlington, Virginia of Admiral Mike Mullen, Chairman of the US Joint Chiefs of Staff. During his farewell speech, he remarked that only his fellow Chiefs of Defence – from nations big or small – knew about the sort of pressures he had faced as head of the armed forces. He added that his colleagues overseas had become, for him, sources of immeasurable wisdom, clarity and support. Everyone there, including President Obama, knew what he was saying about how tough it is to fight the corner of the services against the whims and wishes of politicians, especially in an era of defence cuts.

CDS is a busy and high-intensity role involving countless visits, speeches and engagements, all of which are an important part of the job. There was the occasional week when I thought to myself that I had too many government or state protocol events to attend, taking me away from my primary responsibilities. But these occasions, state banquets for example, were important networking and influence-making opportunities as well as a huge privilege. You quickly appreciate that they are all part of the job and you have to manage your time and make sure you prioritise effectively. My most treasured of such occasions were my audiences with Her Majesty the Queen. Twice a year, I had the opportunity to update her on how things were going in her armed forces, with just the two of us present.

In some ways, CDS is almost a marketing role for Britain. The job has a much wider remit than people might think, involving a lot of foreign travel, with trips to the Far East, the Middle East, Africa, Europe, Russia and the US, as well as frequent trips to Afghanistan and Pakistan. The head of the armed forces is required to play an important part in the British government's international effort. His programme is coordinated with key ministers, he is a member of the National Security Council (NSC) and he needs to understand the government's policies and strategy, and influence them. Domestically, it would be impossible to do it all without help. In Warrant Officer Class 2 Julian Tranter and Corporal 'Dil', my Gurkha orderly, we had two of the hardest working and most devoted people it is possible to find. Both became de facto members of the Richards family and always will be.

A big moment for me was my first Remembrance Day in Whitehall as CDS. As I marched out to the Cenotaph, having saluted the Queen as the head of her armed forces, I realised, really for the first time, the significance of the role I was fulfilling. I was struck by a sense of history, duty and the responsibility of the office I held. We were commemorating great men and women and millions who had died in the service of their country. For the next three years I would be the head of today's armed forces with who knows what challenges ahead. Our withdrawal from Afghanistan on terms that my predecessors would respect was definitely one of the biggest challenges I faced. Could my generation hold our heads up high in comparison with the standards set by my more illustrious forebears in that regard? Reflecting on this often made me feel somewhat stronger and bolder when it came to defending my turf with my political masters. I used to think, 'Would Alanbrooke have stood for that? Of course he wouldn't. There's no way round it, Cameron and Clegg need to hear this straight and true.'

Among the first acts of the new Conservative/Liberal Democrat coalition was the creation of the National Security Council (NSC), a cabinet committee designed to oversee all issues relating to national security, intelligence coordination and defence strategy. It had been set up partly as a return to collective government responsibility after the 'sofa government' of the post 9/11 Blair years. The NSC consists of a core group of ten ministers led by David Cameron and Nick Clegg plus senior officials. The only military man on it is the CDS. Routinely we met in the Cabinet Room in No. 10, but in my time, once a campaign or operation of some kind was under way, we tended to go downstairs to the COBRA room in the Cabinet Office, where communications facilities allowed us to talk to ambassadors and others using video teleconference.

I remember my first NSC meeting, when I was still enjoying a honeymoon as the new man. I was very much Cameron's CDS, with Clegg's strong backing, and he greeted me as I arrived and introduced me to the assembled company, who then banged on the table or clapped in a warm welcome. I thought, 'Bloody hell, this can't last.' I knew, as they did, that there were big issues looming that would test our collective patience to the limits.

David Cameron chaired the meetings, sitting in the Prime Minister's customary place in front of the fireplace. To his left was William Hague, the Foreign Secretary, and to his left Liam Fox, the Defence Secretary and subsequently Philip Hammond, and then me. There was no one to the left of me routinely but the space might be filled by people invited to particular meetings where their expertise was deemed useful. Opposite me were, among others, Simon Fraser, the head of the Foreign Office, who was not formally a co-opted member of the NSC but fought hard to become one and, de facto, did so. I think he was right to insist on it. Next to him was Iain Lobban, director of GCHQ, then the Director

General of the Security Service – at that time Jonathan Evans, now Andrew Parker – and then the Chief of the Secret Intelligence Service (SIS – MI6), John Sawers. Next to him sat the chairman of the Joint Intelligence Committee, Alex Allan – now Jon Day. All these officials were highly effective and it was a genuine privilege to work with them. Most stayed pretty much in their lane although Sawers, Day and I felt we had a remit to range pretty widely. Then came the other ministers, among them Nick Clegg, the Home Secretary Theresa May, the Chancellor George Osborne, the Chief Secretary to the Treasury Danny Alexander, the International Development Secretary Andrew Mitchell, subsequently Justine Greening, the Energy Secretary Chris Huhne – replaced by Ed Davey – Ken Clarke, then Minister of Justice, and finally Oliver Letwin, Minister of State for Policy and a powerful voice on the Council. The National Security Adviser was an important presence in the form of Peter Ricketts – then Kim Darroch – as was the Attorney General, Dominic Grieve. Behind David Cameron sat his *eminence grise*, aka his Downing Street Chief of Staff, Ed Llewellyn.

I am a great supporter of the NSC in principle. It was important to reset the practice of government after the distortion of the Blair years and no other body that met regularly covered the remit set out for the NSC. My frustration with it, which was evident throughout our discussions on Afghanistan and the conduct of the war in Libya, was that it tended to focus on the near-term and the tactical as opposed to the big foreign policy and grand strategic issues. The re-deployment of 120 men in a war in Afghanistan controlled by NATO, for example, should not have been a decision taken by the NSC or the Prime Minister, a point I once welcomed being made by Nick Clegg at an NSC meeting.

Some confusion has arisen about the respective roles of the NSC secretariat, chaired by the National Security Adviser (NSA), and the Chiefs of Staff Committee, chaired by the Chief of the Defence Staff. The NSC secretariat does not have the required experience, processes or skill to run a war, even one involving a major cross-government effort. However capable the civil servants in question might be, they have little training in the coordination and conduct of a military campaign. Yet, taking their cue from their political masters on the NSC itself, this is what they too often seek to do. If the NSC secretariat, under the NSA, are required to play this role, they need to develop the necessary skills and recruit the right people. Despite my offering Peter Ricketts and Kim Darroch a small number of military officers to assist them, this was consistently declined. Either the NSC focuses properly on the strategic level, devolving responsibility for implementation to the appropriate experts working faithfully to political intent and supervision, rather than micro-management, or it develops the right skills to run wars. Until this is sorted out, the full potential of the NSC will not be realised.

Sir Peter Ricketts, the National Security Adviser for much of my time as CDS, was both a good friend and close colleague. He generously agreed to me creating and chairing a powerful new committee, colloquially known as the 'Super Chiefs'. This consisted of the traditional armed forces Chiefs of Staff Committee plus the NSA, the heads of MI6, GCHQ, the FCO and DFID, as well as the Chairman of the Joint Intelligence Committee. It was an attempt on my part to reflect the realities of creating and implementing a military strategy in this new more complex environment in which civilian agencies play a key role in most military operations. John Sawers and Iain Lobban were powerful allies in this effort and I remain indebted to them both.

On the subject of Whitehall mandarins, individually and collectively I soon began to realise what an impressive bunch they are. Successive governments, and indeed the country, should be much more grateful to them for their intelligence, integrity and commitment than sometimes appears to be the case. I also learnt that it's much easier to criticise those in government, politicians and mandarins, than to actually do it. Something I would ruefully compare with how easy running complex military operations clearly appears from the comfort of editors' offices and academics' studies, especially with the benefit of hindsight.

That said, I came to realise many in Whitehall confuse policy goals or perfectly valid strategic waypoints with a proper joined up strategy. Some people, especially many politicians, do not like feeling hemmed-in by a strategy, disliking the term grand strategy in particular. I understand this so started using the term 'strategic handrail' to persuade them of my case; something that could be used as a guide to the future direction of the country and its priorities thus allowing people like me to devise a plan to meet its objectives. I would remind people that Singapore is what it is today because it had a clear national strategy, or plan, that, while sensibly veering and hauling around its direction of travel when necessary, the Singaporean government stuck to robustly from the moment that great statesman Lee Kuan Yew first devised it. In many respects this difference of opinion between what is policy and strategy lies at the root of the friction between the MOD and FCO. It has made me wonder if Whitehall should not develop an additional breed of mandarin trained for modern day challenges. The NSA, for example, would be a 'securicrat' rather than a diplomat, a powerful leader with a deep understanding of how to turn policy goals into joined-up strategic plans. There are senior servicemen like General Sir Nick Carter who would fill the role well and Sir John Sawers and Mark Sedwill would be equally good.

In terms of the pattern of my own contributions to meetings, I guess, together with John Sawers, you could describe me as a dose of reality. We both had a reputation for speaking truth unto power and trying to consider problems on a wider canvas than some others around the table. I could be grit in the ointment, and the background of cuts to the defence budget meant there was often an underlying tension in the debate about what we were being asked to do and what we could deliver. But as CDS, you couldn't keep complaining about lack of resources and I understood why government expenditure needed curbing to avoid the huge strategic risk of economic meltdown. When a sensible opportunity arose, I would remind the Prime Minister about the realities of a smaller defence budget, but then got on and did my best to achieve the government's legitimate goals. 'I am not going to say that you have made life difficult for us, Prime Minister,' I would say. 'You certainly have, but we can do it. We'll manage this somehow, but it has to be militarily sensible and we may well be able to achieve what you seek only with allies, or in a different way from how you envisage it.'

The traditionally cooperative approach adopted by the armed forces when asked to mount operations on behalf of the nation by governments that often have little feel for what is involved, carries risks other than simply military ones. For one, it undermines the credibility of our case in the battle for more resources and better equipment. Our bluff can be called if we keep pulling things off that we said beforehand would be in the 'very difficult' box. One day, though, a CDS will sit in the NSC and have to tell the Prime Minister of the day that we cannot deliver what has been asked for. As it was, during my time in the post, more than once I found myself resisting the politicians instinct to intervene in a crisis, scarred as I am by ill-thought through or poorly resourced operations. Often government ambitions had to be tempered by the harsh reality of what was feasible. But in Cameron, I had a Prime Minister with whom one could have a proper debate and who was prepared to modify things if the case was well made.

In an era when the leaders of the Western world have fretted over intervention – the shadow of Srebrenica and Rwanda always rightly hangs over the debate – I often found myself trying to shift the focus of discussion about what to do, to that old-fashioned concept of vital national interests. Given the political realities of the day, it was inevitable that governments such as Cameron's would react sympathetically to fledgling democratic movements in traditionally authoritarian nations in the Middle East and the Gulf as the Arab Spring swept the region. 'The people have spoken and we must respond,' was usually the starting point. But when the people spoke, it was often only a tiny minority who came out on the streets. And how representative were those people? Were we always backing the right ones? At one point, I went so far as to postulate supporting Bashar al-Assad, the embattled Syrian president, in order to bring the humanitarian crisis to a halt more swiftly, and reduce the long-term risks from militant jihadism. Of course, that was never going to happen but, from a point of view of hard-nosed realpolitik, it helped focus our minds on what it was in Britain's interests to do. On a visit by Vice President Joe Biden of the USA, David Cameron remarked during our discussions that I was, as he put it, 'a big state man'. I agreed with him. I told him I was worried about the way the state system was breaking down and some states were fracturing. I was not that concerned about the danger of state on state warfare – it was unlikely in the short to medium term, we were part of what is still the most successful military alliance in history, which is stronger than most people realise, and, barring the risk of the law of unintended consequences kicking in as a result of ill-thought-through foreign policies, we should have sufficient warning. My issue was with creeping anarchy and the rise of Muslim extremists and other violent non-state groupings. They could have a security impact on a global scale and we needed a grand strategy – by no means only military in nature – that brought like-minded states together, including Russia, to deal with them.

When I started the job, the big items on my desk were Afghanistan, the future of NATO in a post-communist world, European defence cooperation, particularly with the French, rumblings in Buenos Aires over the Falklands, the continuing problem of Islamic extremism and Al-Qaeda and dealing with the consequences of the Strategic Defence and Security Review. No one saw the Arab Spring coming, even though it was just weeks away.

When the spark was lit in December 2010 – in the form of self-immolation by Tunisian street vendor Mohamed Bouazizi – we all went off for Christmas none the wiser. But in the New Year began a phase of revolutionary transformation in the Middle East and the Gulf, the long-term consequences of which are still difficult to read. As protests swept through Tunisia, Yemen and then Egypt, among other countries, an upsurge of opposition to the dictatorial rule of Colonel Gaddafi in Libya brought the crisis firmly on to my agenda. This started with widespread street protests against the regime, which responded with lethal force, and within a few days armed resistance to the government had developed in

Benghazi. This quickly deteriorated into a complex and multi-dimensional civil war, pitting often poorly equipped rebels against the armour of Gaddafi's army, supported by mercenary fighters from such places as Mali. It was clear from early on that Gaddafi was determined to use all means necessary to stay in power.

To start with, our involvement in Libya was limited to the conduct, in February 2011, of a successful Non-combatant Evacuation Operation (NEO) in concert with other nations, principally the French, Americans, Egyptians and Turks. It was ably commanded in Britain by Air Marshal Stu Peach, Chief of Joint Operations at Northwood. At that stage, there was nothing more than loose talk about further involvement. Anders Fogh Rasmussen, NATO Secretary General, made it clear that he did not consider the situation in Libya to be a direct threat to NATO or its allies and he did not envisage military action. We did, however, look at what military options might be open to us – the imposition of a no-fly zone, inserting peace-keeping forces, providing force protection for a humanitarian relief operation or an airlift. But in the background there was increasing alarm at the brutality of Gaddafi's response to the uprising, and by early March, David Cameron was becoming concerned about the threat to the people of Benghazi. The feeling was that the West could not stand idly by and allow Gaddafi to inflict terrible vengeance on the people of Benghazi, who had dared to defy him. This hardened politically into a collective determination not to let the city fall and to intervene to protect the population of eastern Libya generally.

I started to look at military options and quickly came to the conclusion that we had to involve NATO, and the Americans. I insisted in the NSC and with David Cameron that any military campaign in Libya had to be a NATO operation. Some around him were quite attracted to the idea of it being an essentially Anglo-French operation – something President Sarkozy was advocating – but we could not have done it with the French alone. We needed the Americans alongside us, particularly in the critical areas of command and control and surveillance/intelligence, and for NATO to take responsibility. I was instrumental in ensuring this did happen.

The Americans, of course, did not want to get involved. They were squeamish politically about getting drawn into another conflict after Iraq and Afghanistan, and were concerned about other commitments in the region. Mike Mullen was quite embarrassed about it but, with justification, his view was that the bigger strategic risk lay with Iran, whose nuclear weapons programme risked plunging the Gulf into war. He did not want to become strategically unbalanced by a heavy involvement in Libya. I was of the same view. One of my concerns was that we could not move against Iran and Libya at the same time. So we ended up with the Americans leading on Libya, as it were, from the rear, but they still played a vital role, especially through their intelligence and logistical assets.

Did Barack Obama play a clever hand on Libya? I am not so sure. The Americans did drop some bombs but I think he came out of it weakened because the Arabs were left confused. Qatar, UAE, Jordan and Egypt, among others, all wanted Gaddafi dealt with decisively but they saw the US equivocating, not leading. American dithering provided an opportunity for Britain and France and we took advantage of it. This was particularly so in the case of the French who, despite the agreed NATO plan, rather typically launched their initial air attack four hours earlier than the rest of us.

Once it was agreed that military involvement of some sort was required, the next battleground was the nature of it. I was clear from the beginning that curtailing Gaddafi's air power alone through the imposition of a no-fly zone would be insufficient to make a decisive difference. But, while I was sure he would agree, for some reason I had a hell of job trying to convince David Cameron of this. The key point in my view was that very little of the death and destruction being meted out to opponents of Gaddafi's regime in the centres of fighting – Zawiya, Misrata, Zintan and Benghazi – was being inflicted by air assets. The more important weapons were his tanks and artillery and we needed to have authority to be able to hit those targets from the air and create what is known in military parlance as a Ground Control Zone.

During the build-up to the coalition intervention, I had lunch with David Cameron at Chequers and explained my thinking on this. Perhaps he was not listening properly or I was just explaining it badly but I could tell he did not appreciate the importance of what I was advising. Indeed, the next day in the NSC he was still talking about getting UN approval for a 'no-fly zone'. I reminded him of our conversation of the previous day and made the point that if we were going to get involved in Libya, we should 'clout, not dribble'. I made equally ineffective progress with the Foreign Office on this point. In the end, I resorted to phoning my American counterpart, Admiral Mike Mullen, who immediately appreciated the need for a wider mandate, and when the UN debated it, thanks to the US delegation in New York, authority was given under the rather vague 'right to protect' doctrine to hit targets on the ground. UN Security Council Resolution 1973, passed on 17 March 2011, imposed a no-fly zone over Libya but also authorised all means necessary to protect civilians and civilian-populated areas.

Two days later, to complete the first mission – albeit in the wake of the French – our Tornado GR4 pilots pulled off an amazing feat of airmanship, flying all the way from the UK, conducting three midair refuelling operations on the way, and one more on the way back. We had no aircraft carrier available, although our planes were later able to fly from bases in southern Italy. (The absence of a carrier is an interesting point given the confidence with which people in the Strategic Defence and Security Review debates had argued that we could do without them while we awaited the new ones. We managed it, but a carrier would have made life a lot easier.)

As a result of my discussions with my French counterpart, Admiral Edouard Guillaud, it became obvious that we needed some means of influencing events on the ground. We both spent a lot of time with the Qataris and the Emiratis persuading them of the need for what was effectively a proxy land force. I knew we were getting authority to use maritime and air elements, but I also knew we would never have British boots on the ground, not that I wanted them, especially given our commitments in Afghanistan. I went to Qatar and to the Emirates to help them set up an operational theatre-level headquarters, and during the campaign we were in constant touch, advising and assisting them. They had excellent contacts inside Libya and we got a lot of information about what was happening on the ground through them. They inserted some of their own people to help direct the opposition. The role of these Arab forces deserves credit in the coalition effort to bring an end to the Gaddafi regime. We deployed some liaison officers of our own. They played a limited but useful role. Later there was also a small number of advisers deployed in an ad hoc headquarters in Benghazi and then in Misrata.

Operation ELLAMY – the British component of the campaign – ebbed and flowed. The threat to Benghazi was lifted and the battle for Misrata continued for months. We constantly reviewed targeting and other options to increase the pressure on Gaddafi, aware of the risk that the war could settle into a protracted stalemate. The Royal Navy and other coalition navies imposed a maritime exclusion zone so the regime could not use the coast to resupply its forces in the east. There was considerable political pressure to get Gaddafi himself, to have him made into a legal target, something the politicians viewed as a quick route to finishing off his regime.

This was another source of tension with the government. It was my responsibility to make sure that what the armed forces did was legal as well as militarily sensible, and I was clear that Gaddafi should not be targeted unless he was in a military complex or another setting where he was helping to direct the war. To start doing otherwise is a very slippery slope. In May, I was asked about this by a BBC reporter as I left No. 10. I said that in my view Gaddafi was not a legal target, adding that I did not want to discuss it further. I recall that this led to David Cameron reproaching me along the lines of 'You do the fighting, I'll do the talking.'

A key moment in the Libya campaign came when we made the switch from focusing the main opposition military effort from the eastern half of the country to the west. The rebels in Benghazi had become proficient at protecting their city but they did not have the military cohesion, or the support of the people, to move westwards. A huge gap exists between Libya to the east and Libya to the west, both in geographical and tribal respects. I realised that the long haul from the east was not going to work – or at least that it might work but that it could take a very long time – and I was well aware that there was an impatience to get on with the business at hand. I recommended that we should switch the emphasis to the west. This was agreed and I spoke to the Qataris who focused arms, leadership and advice on the rebels in the west, where there were better fighters who were fiercely determined to bring Gaddafi down. From the air, we concentrated on Tripoli and on using our bombing raids to open a corridor for the rebels as they moved towards the capital.

On the day Gaddafi was killed, I was in a meeting and got a text from Lieutenant General Simon Mayall in the Gulf. Mayall, a three-star plenipotentiary, was Britain's military representative to the Arabs. His role – Defence Senior Adviser Middle East at the Ministry of Defence – was one I had personally fought for, believing it to be vital that I had someone dedicated to our military relations with the Arabs. He was in a meeting himself, in Qatar or the Emirates, when the moment came. 'It looks like we might have got him – the big one,' he wrote. Qatari Major General Hamad Al Attiyah, a great friend of mine, had received a message from his people in Libya that Gaddafi had been trapped as he tried to flee, and had been killed.

The Libya campaign underlined that well-directed proxy forces can be a powerful alternative to Western boots on the ground, an issue that would come up next in the context of Syria. In Libya, the proxy option worked. The people inserted on our behalf were properly trained and supported, and provided the vital land component to go alongside our air and maritime inputs. As a general rule, a land component is absolutely vital for a successful military campaign. You will not win wars by air and sea alone. So if you are not prepared to put boots on the ground yourself, you have to find a substitute.

During the campaign, the political leadership showed considerable impatience to get the thing over with. David Cameron always wanted me to do more. Beyond sometimes having patiently to explain that some of this was not militarily feasible, the legal basis for any given option had to be carefully considered. Despite his impatience, Cameron absolutely understood this, but he was quite right to bounce things off me and put me under pressure. I had to explain that war is not straightforward, it is not easy and that we should never make the mistake of underestimating our opponent. I chucked quite a lot of these home-spun philosophies around and I could tell there were occasions when they all thought I was a bit off the wall, but I got my points across. This was David Cameron's big war. Understandably, he enjoyed the influence that came with it, and, although the long-term strategic outcome is still debatable, it was a tactical success. The campaign took slightly longer than he imagined it might, but actually it was relatively short and, in the end, we got our man. It was all the better that we did not do it ourselves and the Libyans dispatched him, albeit – and regrettably – without due process.

Overall, I would argue that David Cameron's leadership was highly effective. He was clear that we had to succeed and he held everyone's toes to the fire to ensure that we got on with it. He was single-minded about it. We had far too many meetings on Libya in the space of six months – and we were constantly getting into what I called the 'tactical weeds' as Cameron sought to micro-manage the campaign. At one point, I had to teach him about the concept of Commander's Intent and we enjoyed a lot of banter about this. I used to say to him, 'Prime Minister, leave the detail to me, just give us your Intent.' In a smaller meeting, I told him that being in the Combined Cadet Force at Eton was not a qualification for trying to run the tactical detail of a complex coalition war effort in Libya. He saw the funny side of that. When I retired two years later, Cameron presented me with a framed and signed copy of my Commander's Intent from Afghanistan. In his own hand along the bottom he had written, 'With thanks for always having my "Intent"!' I suppose you could say that Cameron's military and strategic inexperience is the risk that democracy takes in its choice of leaders but he proved himself to be a fast learner and was always prepared to talk things through.

In terms of our military contribution, the RAF in particular was outstanding in Libya, despite the pressure the campaign brought on limited manpower and aircraft resources. As a CDS from an Army background, I'd seen the Royal Navy at work in various places, including Sierra Leone where they had done great things. But Libya brought home to me the courage, fortitude, resilience and skill of our pilots. They would set off from their base in southern Italy not knowing where they were going – although they normally had a first target – then refuel in midair, which is no mean feat in itself. Then they would go and drop ordnance or whatever their mission might be, be re-tasked, get more fuel, head deep into the south of Libya, drop more ordnance, get more fuel and so on. They did this for days and they were sometimes in the air for more than seven hours, carefully de-conflicting their sorties with the aircraft of other coalition nations that were airborne at the same time. Our fast jet pilots distinguished themselves in Libya and this is not to forget the Army Apache helicopter pilots, flying off HMS *Ocean*, who also performed heroically during that campaign.

Since the war, Libya has stuttered. The strategic outcome is at best uncertain. We certainly understood the importance of post-conflict reconstruction after the debacle in Iraq, and we put in a stabilisation team as soon as the war was over to give the Libyans advice. But we underestimated the incoherence, even anarchy, of the tribal and militia patchwork that filled the vacuum left by the Gaddafi regime. In short, there was no one to engage with in Tripoli and it proved difficult to deliver outcomes on initiatives despite much enthusiasm and early visits by Cameron and Hague, who were greeted like heroes. I think we were relatively outsmarted in this area by the French and Italians, who know that part of the world better than we do. My own view is that the Arab Spring should have been the trigger for an international strategy of organisation, involvement and generosity on a par with the Marshall Plan that America deployed to help rebuild European economies after the Second World War. But you can only impose a Marshall Plan, or gift it, if the people concerned want to be helped, or are capable of being helped. If they are not capable, you have to put in the people yourself. If you are wary of doing that, and for good reason, it's a very difficult issue to get right.

While Libya has been a qualified success, our response to the civil war in Syria, which started in March 2011 while we were fully engaged on Operation ELLAMY, has never been satisfactory.

As CDS, I was outspoken with the government about the need for a more effective strategy. As I watched David Cameron become increasingly concerned with what was happening on the ground there – the destruction of rebel-held cities, massacres carried out by regime-supporting thugs, allegations of chemical weapons use – I became frustrated at the incompatible nature of our ends, ways and means. For me the first requirement was to contain the crisis, preventing it from spreading to neighbouring countries especially Lebanon, Jordon and Iraq. I pressed for a robust 'containment strategy', a no-brainer I thought but found that everyone was focused on events inside Syria and getting rid of Assad rather than on the risks of contagion from it. To my surprise, I was even asked by NSC staff what I meant by a containment strategy. This gulf in understanding was aggravated by a failure in some senior establishment circles to accept that the Sunni-Shia split was as serious as I and many experts viewed it. This did not help them see the regional implications of the fast deteriorating situation in Syria.

Her Majesty's Government's end, however much it was sometimes disguised, was the removal of the discredited Syrian President, Bashar Al-Assad. But our ways and means – indirectly helping the opposition with money and 'non-lethal support' – were not in line with that objective. As a result, we were left in the worst of all worlds. We, together with the Gulf Arabs, the US and the French, were doing enough to exacerbate the humanitarian situation by helping to prolong the war, but not enough to have the decisive impact that could end it. Given that our sole justification for getting involved was the right to protect a people not being protected by their own government, I saw our approach to Syria as inimical to our humanitarian purpose. In the summer of 2013, I even went to see Dominic Grieve, the Attorney General, to discuss this and raise my concerns.

While we – the West – dithered on the sidelines, the conflict became ever more complex and fractured with Muslim extremists increasingly taking advantage. The outcome now looks hard to predict but there seems to be every prospect that Assad will remain at the head of a rump Syria with other areas controlled by extremist groups, most notably ISIS, ideologically opposed to the West and to our friends in the region.

My own strategy, which I wrote in the autumn of 2011, was called 'Extract, Equip and Train' and was built around a plan to train a proxy Syrian Army that could provide the land component to be used decisively against the regime at a time and in places of our choosing, alongside air and maritime offensive action by Western powers. The idea was to extract tens of thousands of Syrian men and then equip and train them in bordering countries over a twelve-month period. At the same time their political leaders and administrators would be trained and prepared for office. This would all be part of a clearly signalled multi-dimensional strategy that would be carried out with some fanfare. It would be a decisive move by the West, designed to send an unambiguous signal to Assad's forces that, in the long run, they were going to lose. There was every chance that the deterrent effect of this plan would be enough in itself to end the war. Seeing inevitable defeat approaching would have a corrosive effect on morale among Assad's troops. It would also have the benefit of marginalising extremists. I argued that we should adopt a tough approach with Arab states and the myriad Syrian opposition groups, saying to them, in effect, that if they did not support this plan, they would forfeit any further Western help. Had my strategy been implemented in late 2011, we could have ended the war by the autumn of 2012 and certainly in 2013.

I made my proposal to Kim Darroch and discussed it with Marty Dempsey, the new Chairman of the Joint Chiefs, at a NATO meeting in Brussels. Most people accepted that it was the correct military strategy but no one had the appetite for the investment and scale of what was required. I never properly discussed it with David Cameron but I talked to his advisers about it, including Hugh Powell, Deputy National Security Adviser. Hugh was a leading defender of the approach we had embarked upon, claiming, perhaps rightly, that it was 'the most the market would bear'. He and others also said my plan would take too long to execute, misunderstanding that relative speed, or tempo, is what matters rather than speed itself. I could see the point about the scale of what I was proposing. It would involve thousands of coalition troops in training, a lot of material in weapons and ammunition and full cooperation with neighbouring states, including Turkey, Lebanon and Jordan. But I still believe, as ISIS occupies chunks of Syria and Iraq, that it was a better option than what has since occurred. Indeed, it would have prevented it transpiring. If our ends are as we claim, the ways and means to achieve them have to be of this order of effort and commitment.

On Syria I was viewed as cautious and too purist. This was partly because I made the point that if we were not prepared to adopt a comprehensive strategy, the next best option was to let Assad win – something that was politically unthinkable. I had no time for Assad and I could understand the moral indignation about him remaining in power and continuing to lead a repugnant regime that inflicted misery on his own people; but he posed no grand strategic threat to Britain. The old adage about vital national interests still works. It cuts through problems and muddle with absolute clarity.

Throughout the period of the first flush of the Arab Spring, we were heavily distracted by Iran and the possibility that war could follow an Israeli strike on Tehran's nuclear installations. Although the intelligence was mixed, there was broad consensus by early 2011 that the chance of the Israelis launching a strike in a bid to disrupt Iran's attempt to develop nuclear weapons was as high as 40 to 50 per cent. The view was that the Israelis would want the Americans to come in alongside them but if that support was not forthcoming, they would do it themselves anyway, hoping to provoke US involvement. The assumption was that the Iranians would not be able to take a strike of this magnitude lying down and would unleash war throughout the region, almost certainly blocking the key Straits of Hormuz in the process.

Whilst some well-informed people believed an attack was unlikely, the rhetoric coming out of Tel Aviv at that time was certainly consistent with an impending strike. From our point of view, we had treaty commitments with several Gulf countries and were bound to come to their aid in the event of an attack. We were not privy to the full detail of American contingency planning but at one extreme was the assumption – extremely remote – of some sort of invasion of Iran. Much more likely was a punishment strategy, principally involving air and maritime assets. We were very conscious of the fact that a wounded Iran could be highly dangerous and unpredictable and could inflict all sorts of damage on Gulf countries using its airforce, missiles and fast patrol boats. Dubai, Abu Dhabi, Bahrain and Qatar were all within easy reach. There was also the prospect of asymmetric warfare in Bahrain, Kuwait and the eastern coast of Saudi Arabia, where there are substantial Shia populations, as well as in Afghanistan. The closure of the Straits, possibly by mining, was a big worry but we were confident that it could be dealt with by the US, with our assistance, relatively quickly. The main concern was that the Israelis would have started a war the consequences of which were hard to calculate or anticipate. We assumed the Iranians would use every tactic in the book, having reached the conclusion that they would not be able to win in a conventional sense.

As CDS, the first thing I had to do was to get the Ministry of Defence to realise that intelligence suggesting up to a 50 per cent chance of war had to be taken very seriously. We had to assume that it was going to happen. So I said that, de facto, we were moving on to a war footing, which was not easy, given our limited resources and commitments in Afghanistan and then in Libya. I wrote to the Prime Minister to say I was concerned about Iran and that we were taking all the military measures he might expect. This involved putting forces at high states of readiness, focusing training on the tasks that we might be called upon to execute and preparing our logistics for deploying in the Gulf.

Our primary role in the first instance was to protect our own nationals in Gulf states and then help defend our allies from attack. Our fighter aircraft would have been capable of playing a role in any strike on Iran, but we were not going to be invading. We were mainly intent on maintaining the status quo in the region and allowing our Arab allies to survive a possible war.

My own view is that a grand strategic understanding between the West and Iran is worth actively exploring. The Arabs don't like the current stand-off and are worried about the durability of Western commitments to their protection. If a war can be avoided, that's a good thing. Do I trust the Iranians? No, not entirely of course. Like most countries there are influential factions who we would be naïve to put any faith in. But, we should in principle seek to do business with the Iranian body politic as a whole. The prize is worth the risk. They will probably end up with what's known as a 'breakout' capability. They won't have a nuclear weapon but everyone will know that they can get one in short order. That is the compromise that people, including the Israelis, may have to live with. Iran is a nation with a great history and a population of 80 million people, many of them very sophisticated. It is galling for them to be treated as a pariah state, even if their recent past suggests this is justified. It must be in our long-term interests to try to bring them back into the family of nations.

The CDS portfolio is varied and wide-ranging. While much of my time was spent focusing on operational commitments abroad – either fighting wars or anticipating them – there was a big item in my diary on the home front. The London 2012 Olympic Games, which turned out to be an outstandingly successful landmark event for Britain in the early years of the new century, had always been on my horizon from a security and defence point of view. But we ended up with a far bigger commitment than we had anticipated when the government asked the armed forces at the eleventh hour to supply servicemen and women to staff access points to the main Games venues. This happened after it emerged that G4S, the private company contracted to provide these services, was going to fail to deliver the staffing required.

My main concern in the broader security field was the danger of terrorist attack by individuals affiliated to or inspired by organisations such as Al-Qaeda. The biggest risk to the Games venues, we concluded, was from the air. The worst-case scenario was something like a 9/11-style takeover of an airliner that would then be flown into the Olympic Park in east London. We put in place concentric security rings around the capital to prevent that happening. We had the Rapier and other ground-based air defence missile systems deployed on open ground and on the tops of buildings – including some blocks of flats – sufficient to cover a 360 degree arc around the Olympic stadium. We also had Typhoon jets, on short notice to scramble, based at Northolt for the duration of the Games. We were worried about the danger of a slow-moving small aircraft that could suddenly prove to be a threat, and deployed a group of so-called 'air-snipers' to deal with that. These were a handful of Royal Marine marksmen who were trained to fire at the cockpit of a small plane while flying alongside it in a helicopter. On the water we deployed the helicopter carrier, HMS *Ocean*, to the Thames at Greenwich, we had Royal Marines patrolling the river in fast boats, and down at Weymouth, at the sailing venue, we had ships acting as an outer security cordon.

My biggest concern – which will come to fruition at some point – was the threat of a small Unmanned Aerial Vehicle (UAV), better known as a Drone, laden with a bomb. A tiny machine, about the size of a small model aircraft, could be fitted with explosives and flown at low level to a Games site from a range of half a mile, and then detonated among spectators. This is an extremely difficult threat to combat. It is possible to pick up small UAVs using radar but it is not easy to respond in time. The security services voiced their anxiety but said that those who might consider such a course of action did not yet possesses the technology to deliver a bomb in that way. Even so, we were on our guard.

The overall security brief of the Games was in the hands of Charles Farr, the director of the Office for Security and Counter-Terrorism at the Home Office, who was reporting to Jeremy Hunt, the Culture Secretary. Farr was working with a number of different agencies so the command and control aspect was quite diluted. As it became increasingly clear that G4S were well behind schedule in recruiting staff to man the security gates at access points to Games venues, there was a bureaucratic reluctance to concede that, collectively, they might have got this wrong. The upshot was that, very late in the day, David Cameron took the decision to bring in the armed forces to fill the significant gaps where G4S personnel should have been.

I appointed Nick Parker, Commander in Chief Land Forces, who was also the officer with responsibility within the military for homeland defence, to take on this ambitious project. Nick is an old friend and a hugely capable officer. He set to with great purpose. Calling up and deploying thousands of men and women at short notice was no mean feat. Some were due to go on leave, having recently returned from deployment overseas, including Afghanistan. As well as bringing order to some pretty chaotic command and control, Nick had to organise camps and other facilities to accommodate everyone, as well as ensure we had the right number of people in the right places. There was some grumbling but the vast majority of the servicemen and women involved thoroughly enjoyed this unusual role and most of them managed to see something of the Games, too.

It was a big operation put together in very quick time. G4S's logistics turned out to be haphazard and at one point we had up to 17,000 service personnel earmarked for Games duty to be on the safe side, although not all of them were eventually used. Virtually every Games venue was secured by soldiers, airmen or sailors and I think the forces gained considerable kudos, quite rightly, for what we did. It proved a wonderful opportunity to interact with the public and show what we could do. Parker's operation demonstrated our ability successfully to take on a complex task from a standing start, providing highly effective command and control, quality disciplined people and logistic assets where required and on time. The armed forces' great strength lies in our capacity to analyse a problem, plan a solution and then implement it under pressure. This is what we did for the Games.

Sebastian Coe, the chairman of the London Organising Committee for the Olympic Games, came to visit our operation. The two of us were filmed at a camp in Hainault Forest on the north-eastern edge of London that was the temporary home of 3,500 service personnel. We met the troops and were required to get on exercise bikes in the tented gym for the cameras. I was impressed with Lord Coe. He is personable, trusts people who work for him and is a good front man, who can be tough when he needs to be. He paid a fitting tribute to the men and women called up to help at what turned out to be a superb event. 'I really genuinely think that when we look back at these Games, one of the defining features will be the involvement and the commitment of our armed services. They've discharged their duties with professionalism, with humour and with grace, and that has really gone noticed in pretty much every corner of this project,' he said.

In the end, the Olympics went off without any major security incidents but we were ready and vigilant right to end of the closing ceremony and beyond.

A background theme during my tenure as CDS, but one that caused some alarm – unnecessary in my view – was anxiety over the security of the Falkland Islands. This was always going to be a particularly touchy subject with any Conservative Prime Minister and David Cameron was no exception. A disaster in the Falklands on his watch would have been toxic. As a result, he was, rightly, concerned to be assured that our plans were sound. My job was to address those concerns and get across to him and his ministers that there really was almost no cause for alarm.

Friction over the islands flared periodically. Critically in my view – and this was missed by some of my political interlocutors – such flare-ups were normally related to diplomatic moves at meetings such as the G20, rather than anything with a military flavour. Nevertheless, the issue would come up at meetings from time to time and some were exclusively devoted to the subject. I explained that while our own military capability in the Falklands had been transformed from what it was prior to the Argentinian invasion in 1982, at the same time the Argentine military had significantly deteriorated since then. Taken together this made a second attempt by the Argentinians to take the islands, or even some sort of symbolic invasion, an extremely remote possibility.

People often ask whether we still have the capacity to conduct the sort of operation mounted in 1982 to retake the Falklands. The question is based on a false premise. Our current strategy is not focused on retaking the islands should they be lost for a second time, but on preventing an invasion happening in the first place. If we think the risk is increasing, we can rapidly reinforce our already substantial presence on the island and in the surrounding sea, using the airfield at Stanley, which can take wide-bodied jets, and by sending fast surface ships and submarines to the South Atlantic. Our goal – and I believe it is realistic – is always to remain inside the Argentinian ability to land on the islands, and we have well-prepared plans to react if required. This is an effective deterence strategy but should for some reason it fail, our ability to defend the islands effectively is not in doubt. There are other dangers which could lead us to overreact, something that given the limited supply of international backing for our stance on the islands, we could ill-afford.

Since I have serious concerns over the way in which the West is extracting itself from Afghanistan, and because of the importance of the country to me personally, it seems only right to conclude my account of my tenure as CDS with it.

The cornerstones of the West's exit strategy were the NATO summits at Lisbon and Chicago in November 2010 and May 2012 respectively, both of which I attended. At the first of these, it was agreed that the Coalition's combat role would cease at the end of 2014. Setting a date was something that I reluctantly accepted. I could see its value in focusing people's minds on a proper process of transition, and in any case, there was a sense that this deadline would not necessarily be hard and fast. If elements of the Afghan armed forces were not ready to take on their assigned role, there could be flexibility.

Every leader who spoke, including President Obama, David Cameron and Australian Prime Minister Julia Gillard, wanted to do the right thing by Afghanistan. The collective determination was not to allow a repeat of what happened when the crumbling Soviet regime abandoned President Najibullah, who ended up being forced from power in 1992 as the country spiralled into a self-destructive civil war. In 2010, the 33,000-strong American troop surge was going into Helmand, so there was still a strong sense of resolve and commitment. I was reasonably happy, although I recognised that our job in the military was to make sure the politicians did not gradually lose this determination.

In Chicago eighteen months later, we heard many of the same sentiments but by then people were going through the motions. One could sense the hypocrisy, the difference between what was being said and what was likely to happen. There was no real affection for Afghanistan. People wanted out but didn't have the guts to say so. At Lisbon I took our political leaders at their word; at Chicago I knew I was up against it. There was going to be a struggle ahead and I was determined to ensure that we did not renege on long-term commitments to support Afghanistan with military training, financial help and assistance with civil government. I could see what was happening in Iraq, since reinforced by events there in 2014 as ISIS threatened the country's break-up and the creation of a terrorist caliphate, and was clear that the people of Afghanistan should not suffer a similar fate at their and our peril.

By then I knew that many politicians in Britain also no longer had their hearts in it. At that stage, we held regular briefings on Afghanistan for the government which proved a perfect opportunity to test the water. You could see that certain people round the table were losing patience and drifting into the position of my good friend Simon Jenkins of 'we just want out'. George Osborne had the state of the economy as a major pretext but I think politically he was increasingly out of step with a long-term commitment. Oliver Letwin was in the same camp (although he later became a supporter after visiting Afghanistan with me), Nick Clegg was ambivalent while William Hague said the right things but without passion. David Cameron was supportive but probed and tested all the time and was quite difficult. The rest were more or less neutral but there was no great enthusiasm among them for doing the job properly. I remember describing to a colleague after one such briefing what it was like walking into a room full of the most powerful people in Britain, knowing that not one person in that room wanted to hear what you were about to recommend. Not fun.

One of a number of critical issues was the question of how many British troops should remain in Afghanistan during the transitional phase. It was vitally important not to backtrack in this respect, in order to give our Afghan allies the best possible chance to prepare as they progressively assumed the lead for security. In my view, we were committed, through our pledges at Lisbon and Chicago, to remain capable of combat until the end of 2014. However, a plan put forward by the Cabinet Office, which the Ministry of Defence was forced to contribute to, envisaged us coming down to 3,200 troops by the end of 2013. This meant, effectively, we would be out of the combat role a year earlier than we had pledged, because, in my judgement, we would no longer have enough soldiers to commit to battle. The plan also had us getting out of Helmand completely by the end of 2014, which meant that we would have little prospect of offering any help to the Afghan Army after about March that year as our people focused all their energies on closing our base there and getting out in good order. It looked like a strategy to cut and run.

Helmand had become toxic politically by that stage. Our losses in the province and the continuing pressure brought to bear on our forces by the Taliban had sapped the collective political will. The Afghans were keen that we remain in an advice and support role and I argued that we should be prepared to do that, given our huge investment, both in terms of lives and material. But the prevailing view, despite a US commitment to provide for our security, was that we should retreat to Kabul and offer our advice and support from the relative safety of the capital.

I fought hard to retain 5,200 troops until Christmas 2013. I considered this to be the minimum required to enable us, on a sliding scale through the year, to maintain a combat role to the end of 2014. I made the case forcefully to David Cameron. 'If you insist on going to 3,200, you will not be honouring the commitments that you, Prime Minister, made on behalf of our country at Lisbon and Chicago,' I told him. That hit hard. In the end, to their credit, I managed to persuade ministers of my case. We kept sufficient soldiers there until the end of 2013, enabling us properly to support the presidential elections in Afghanistan in mid-2014 before progressively winding down.

There was a big debate, too, about our residual commitment. We had explicitly said we would do what was required as part of NATO's long-term support to Afghanistan, but the prevailing view in London was that we should be minimalist. I felt that was wrong. The Afghans genuinely wanted us, and needed us, in and around Kabul, at the very least. The plan was we should provide what was known as a 'Sandhurst in the Sand' – a military academy in Kabul predominantly staffed by British officers and funded to the tune of £75 million. After a high-profile sign-off by David Cameron in July 2012, this was opened to the first 270 cadets in May 2014. As useful as this may be, that college amounts to the main British contribution to Afghanistan's long term security. It means that by early 2016 our involvement in the country will be on a smaller scale than that of the Australians or the Italians.

When discussing this with the government, one of my arguments was that we were in danger of creating circumstances in which the Taliban could threaten to retake control. I made the point to David Cameron that this chicken could come home to roost in 2015, just about the time he would be facing re-election. I said that it would be tragic if, for want of a hundred million pounds each year, we allowed this to happen and missed the opportunity that I believe exists to help put Afghanistan permanently on the right course. The Taliban will struggle to overcome resistance from the Northern Alliance, which probably remains strong enough to stop them. But years more fighting would be disastrous for a people who have suffered enough, and an unnecessary indictment of Western efforts over the last thirteen years.

I do worry about those who argue that Afghanistan is no longer worth it. We should constantly remind ourselves what happened on 9/11 and not allow Afghanistan to fragment – it remains morally and strategically a vital interest for Britain and the West. Indeed, after Fusilier Lee Rigby's murder on a Woolwich street, the new head of the Security Service, Andrew Parker, said to me that the armed forces could be very proud that not one terrorist incident has been planned or executed from Afghanistan since we deployed there in 2001. Memories are short and we need to understand better the cunning and cruelty of those who yearn to repeat such horrors. In the long term, the Taliban will have to be brought into the fold somehow, although the 2014 presidential elections allowed the Afghan people bravely and decisively to remind us that they will not allow them back on the old terms. They are tired of years of conflict, and I am confident that new leaders on both sides will sit down together and say, in effect, let's make a deal, something I first advocated publicly in 2009. The Taliban will have explicitly to reject any linkages to Al-Qaeda and this will have to be carefully monitored. The regional context in which this dialogue develops is vital. India and Pakistan must behave responsibly as must, of course, the new government in Kabul, and the West must continue to foster the right climate. This support and encouragement is vital in sustaining the confidence of the people in the long-term outcome.

It was hard going on Afghanistan. There is no doubt that I was typecast as the stubborn one who would not give ground on commitments that few others were happy to support. It was, 'Oh, here he goes again,' and a consensus developed that this was a subject on which we were not going to agree. It was all very civil and polite. 'Morning, CDS, how are you?' 'Very well thank you, Chancellor,' and so on. But then the shutters would come down and you felt the hostility, not to me as an individual but to what I was saying. I sometimes used to think that if the Afghans or my soldiers could hear some of the most powerful people in Britain apparently failing to support what we were doing, it would be awful. I did say once, 'Really, if people could hear some of this . . .' On reflection, I realised that they were doing their job, testing my logic and recommendations to the hilt. The fact that I usually won my case does credit to them but it was certainly tough stuff. On one occasion, I took Nick Carter into a meeting in No. 10 when he was preparing to take up the job of Deputy Commander ISAF in Kabul. I thought it would be instructive for him to get a feel for the state of play before he left. As we walked back to the Ministry of Defence, after another session of verbal combat in the Cabinet Room, Carter remarked, 'I had no idea what you have been going through on our behalf.'

At various times during my long career I had been an outspoken junior officer and sometimes a quite controversial senior one. I maintained the pattern right to the end by agreeing to a proposal from one of my staff that there should be a change of command parade when I handed over the post of CDS to Nick Houghton in July 2013. This had not happened before and I know some of my colleagues thought it was all rather un-British, almost hubristic. This was not the case. There was a serious purpose behind it. And besides, the last thing I wanted at such a busy time was yet another parade and yet another speech to write, despite the helpful wizardry of my Military Assistant, Tom Tugendhat, with whom I had collaborated so successfully on many such occasions over the previous four years.

Until then the practice had been for the retiring CDS to leave without any ceremony. My predecessor, Jock Stirrup, for example, got those civil servants and military officers in the MoD who were available together for a short farewell speech and that was it. My view was that this was wrong, not just in terms of recognising Jock's personal contribution – which was immense – but more importantly in recognising that the overall head of the armed forces was retiring and handing the baton to a successor. In America, this is done with a full ceremony attended by all the senior military and political figures of the day, including the President, the Vice President and the Secretary of Defence. I didn't want to go that far, but I was determined to invest the moment with a more formal right of passage. It was an opportunity to ensure the armed forces, and indeed those in the country who were interested in such things, knew from the outset that a new man was at the helm, and a chance for the old one to thank and congratulate them for all they had done for him on his watch.

Despite a lukewarm reception to the idea in some quarters we did it, albeit in modest form. On a beautiful sunny day on Horse Guards Parade, conscious that the Duke of Wellington's office was to our rear, an immaculately presented tri-service guard from the Royal Navy and Royal Marines, the Army and Royal Air Force paraded for me and Nick. The Brigade of Gurkhas band provided the music. I had been their Colonel Commandant for five years and this touch, which I had not been made aware of, reflected how much thought my staff had put into the occasion. Caroline was there, together with Joanna and Pippa, who very brilliantly flew back from Malawi where she was working, getting in at six that morning. Taking a General Salute for the last time and having the privilege of inspecting some of the finest men and women in our armed forces was very emotional and I will concede a lump came to my throat. I really was about to conclude forty-two years' service.

The parade was attended by Philip Hammond, who made a very generous speech. I paid tribute to all three services and thanked the many individuals who had worked with me over the years, making special mention of the enormous contribution made by Caroline. This, in turn, was followed by a short speech by my successor, Nick Houghton. And that was it. The point had been made.

A number of overseas Chiefs attended, ranging from Romania to Malaysia and including my close friend Admiral Edouard Guillaud of France. Others, including my old pal Marty Dempsey from the USA, could not make it but sent senior representatives. David Cameron, on advice, decided not to come, which I think was a pity because he missed a chance to thank the armed forces and the senior officer corps – without whom, it is often forgotten, the armed forces could achieve none of the exceptional things they do – for their contributions in Afghanistan, Libya and even during the Olympics. The Prime Minister did, however, give me a very jolly lunch at No. 10, attended by some of my closest colleagues, which was exceptionally generous of him. At that lunch he presented me with a first edition copy of T.E. Lawrence's *Seven Pillars of Wisdom*, inscribed by him.

Among other events in my last days in uniform was, I admit, a quite poignant final lecture to the Joint Services Command and Staff College at Shrivenham and a rare convening of the Defence Council in the form of a big dinner for Caroline and me at Lancaster House. It was attended by all the Service Chiefs, political leaders and senior civil servants and their wives. Philip Hammond again spoke very warmly. I also had a final audience with the Queen, in which she was typically very generous.

The evening after the parade, we held a party for as many of my Military Assistants and ADCs, and their wives and partners, as we could get hold of. It was great fun, full of reminiscences and 'lamp-swinging' anecdotes. In a short and somewhat irreverent speech, even by my standards, I thanked them for everything. Without these people, I would not have done half of whatever it is I may have achieved and I owed them all a huge amount. Looking down on them from a rather precarious perch that our wonderful Gurkha orderly, Corporal Dil, had insisted I stand on, and with the comforting presence of Sergeant Major Tranter off to one side, it was brought home to me yet again what a wonderful bunch the British armed forces are and how fortunate this country is to have them. Rear Admiral Matt Parr, the senior of those there who had worked for me, spontaneously made a witty but powerful speech, generously thanking me, and Caroline, in return.

I knew I would have to retire one day. I had set out to be a soldier for three years and ended up doing forty-two, so I could rationalise it – there was no more I could do, it was time to leave – but in my heart, soldiering was all I had known. I didn't know anything else. And I loved it. Despite the tribulations of NSC meetings and difficulties with my NATO superiors, for example, I had loved the challenge and seemed to prosper in that climate. Initially, I didn't feel very much; it was still exciting and I lived on the fumes for a while. We still had our apartment in Kensington Palace, which was helpful because we were very kindly given plenty of time to pack up properly. I experienced all the usual little jolts that people go through who have been working with staff and then suddenly find themselves operating on their own again – getting into a car and realising I had to drive it, having to get hold of people on the phone myself and sending my own work e-mails, to name but three. I certainly had withdrawal symptoms and for a few months I flapped around a bit, wondering what to do and what it was I could offer. But then the phone started ringing.

The decisive moment in this transition to civilian life, which all career soldiers go through – often at a younger and more critical age in terms of their families and finances than I am – was watching the Remembrance Day Parade at the Cenotaph three months after I had left. There, on the screen, was my successor as CDS and the other Chiefs joining in a parade that I had been involved in for four years, and for a minute or two I felt quite empty. But then came a moment of metamorphosis. Suddenly, I knew I could put it all behind me and move on. My service life had been an enormous privilege that had gone on far longer than I ever intended. Now a new chapter was beginning. I don't talk about retirement but about my new career. At 62, I am enjoying the challenge and I think I have a few more years in me yet.

SEVENTEEN

Reflections

I have enjoyed my service more than I could have hoped. It has provided me with challenge, interest and the opportunity to make a positive difference to many people's lives from Northern Ireland to Afghanistan and many places in between. But ultimately the reason I have stayed the course is because of the people in our armed services. Their humour, camaraderie, integrity and selflessness are essential parts of service life and theirs is genuinely a noble calling.

The British armed forces are second to none. It is the people in them rather than the equipment they man that provides the battle-winning edge. Each service attracts more than its fair share of talent. We have everyone from a future king to the poorest member of the Commonwealth in our ranks and we are equally proud of them all. The courage and resilience they display, and the sacrifices they have made, and continue to make, are humbling.

I am in the debt of those from the United Kingdom and many allied nations who have fought under my command, and sadly, sometimes died or been badly injured doing their duty. To paraphrase Isaac Newton: if I have seen further, it is by standing on the shoulders of giants. I am acutely aware of how much I owe the people I have served with and frequently had the privilege of commanding.

And their success has been huge, not least in the impact our commitment in Afghanistan has had on choking off any attempt to export terrorist activity from that part of the world since 9/11. Along with the Afghan and Pakistani security forces, and allies from NATO and around the world, we have saved countless innocent lives and given the Afghan people hope. As we come out of Afghanistan, society must continue to recognise its service men and women, ensuring that they, and their families, who are such a vital element of military capability, are not disadvantaged for serving their country.

Speaking of families, I would like to thank my own, Caroline and our daughters Joanna and Pippa. Caroline little knew back in 1978 that she was marrying into thirty-five years of service and twenty-nine moves of home. She has been the rock on which my career has been based, tirelessly reminding me of my obligations to service families. She has done her duty every bit as much as I have, even to the point of publishing a book, *Afghanistan Revealed*, through her charity, the Afghan Appeal Fund, designed to raise knowledge and interest in Afghanistan.

Joanna works hard for what she believes in as an adviser to the Prime Minister. Loyal, rightly, to David Cameron but also, naturally, to me, she had an uncomfortable time on occasion as I sometimes rather vigorously fulfilled my role as his military strategic adviser. She steered a course through these periods with great skill and humour, while finding time to do a huge amount of charitable work in what little spare time she had. Pippa has my wanderlust and works for a British NGO in Africa. We wish we saw more of her and worry about the way she too frequently takes risks but we are intensely proud of all she does for some very poor people.

Non-partisan commitment to the service covenant is something for which our political leaders, from the Prime Minister downwards, deserve thanks. I would like to pay tribute to the political team for their efforts. We may not always have agreed – and indeed we had some robust confrontations in the National Security Council – but I have recognised, without exception, a genuine desire across the political spectrum to do the right thing.

I would like to say a particular thank you to Philip Hammond, my final Secretary of State, for his leadership. Our relationship was not always easy but I recognise talent and commitment when I see it. Our armed forces are in much better shape than many understand. Future

Force 2020 is the envy of many of my fellow Chiefs of Defence; and the UK Joint Expeditionary Force and Anglo/French Combined Joint Expeditionary Force will ensure Britain can fight effectively as part of a Joint Combined force, particularly with our French and other close allies, for many years to come. The Defence Engagement Strategy and the repositioning of the Ministry of Defence as a military strategic head-quarters have added to our ability to support the national interest around the world.

Throughout this book I have touched on some key issues that will confront my successors in the years ahead. Cyber war, in different guises, is already with us and needs protocols such as those that govern conventional conflict. Miniaturisation – especially small drones, explosives and weaponry – offers huge possibilities but poses many risks, too, not least in the hands of ruthless non-state actors. Very high-speed long-range missiles will pose a major threat to our surface ships, especially the new carriers, and war in space – an environment few realize is hugely influential on our way of life – is a very real possibility. Conventional bureaucracies and military establishments are uncomfortable with modern means of communication and need to understand and exploit them much better if they are to have any chance of remaining ahead of groups such as Al-Qaeda and its many offshoots. These are the groups that responsible states must now coalesce to defeat, putting their traditional rivalries to one side for the common good.

In this respect, I commend one final time Sun Tsu's most useful aphorism: 'strategy without tactics is the slowest route to success; tactics without strategy is merely the noise before defeat.' Vital national interests must be the arbiter of our foreign policy and the key deter-minant of our strategies, not the well-intentioned instinct to intervene half-heartedly on behalf of vocal but frequently unrepresentative minorities, whose exploits can lead to years of misery for unconsulted populations. Even a rapidly mounted humanitarian intervention must be rooted in a politically workable framework.

While I consider the greatest threat to our way of life is today posed by ruthless non-state actors, such as ISIS and Al-Qaeda, I remain a strong believer in the collective security offered by our membership of NATO. It alone, and not the European Union for many years to come, if ever, offers the solidarity, strength and reassurance that its member nations need in a crisis. The UK must set an example to other nations in our level of commitment to the Alliance. And while fully recognising the expense and opportunity cost of the Trident successor programme, on balance, given the unstable world we inhabit and until new technology makes it safe to invest in different solutions, I believe we have to have it.

It does worry me that Britain may be losing the appetite for foreign interventions, especially those involving significant defence commitments. One day there will be something that we really ought to do for other people – or in our own vital national interests – and if we miss the opportunity, we'll regret it over time. We need to keep asking whether we have the right people in charge, people who have the perspicacity to seize the moment and rise to the challenge; and whether we have the armed forces to be able to respond in a timely manner. Given the relative decline of all NATO countries economically and militarily, Britain, by 2020, will still be the second most powerful country in military terms in the NATO alliance after America. But that doesn't mean we have got sufficient military resources; a question that needs regular review.

So are we losing the appetite? I have some faith in the British people. I believe that where there is a good case and the argument is well made, they will support even expensive commitments, costly in both blood and money. I just hope that the government – or future governments – don't get themselves into a position where, when that moment comes, they are unable to act. That's the risk. It's all very well saying 'we're up for a fight' and then – and this is a judgement I have had to make more than once – finding you can't commit because you haven't got the forces, or you can't persuade your allies to come with you. Even if you know that you ought to be in there, you can't do anything, and it could become another Rwanda.

As for the painful cuts that continue to be made in the size of our armed forces, it is important to remember that Britain, like every other country in NATO, assumes it will only go into a major conflict with others. So as long as all of us collectively have got the will and the capability to intervene when required then cuts, however difficult, need not necessarily mean the end of the world as we know it. That's because collectively we are still going to be a lot stronger than any of the opposition, a point regularly made by the Secretary General of NATO Anders Fogh Rasmussen as he strove to persuade Alliance nations to work together on redesigning their armed forces. For these reasons I think a well-thought through, relative reduction in national capability, for sound strategic economic reasons, is manageable in the short term. That said, as the economy grows so must the defence budget. It takes very little time to remove a particular capability but a number of years to develop one. To me, the world looks pretty unstable and, with close allies, we should aim off for the worse case. A renewed commitment to devote a minimum of 2 per cent of GDP to defence after the next election would be the right start. Seeing the world as it really is, as opposed to what we wish it was, is now key.

It has been a privilege to advise the government as Britain's military strategic commander. Any failures have been my own but my successes have certainly come from a team effort. I have been immensely well served by my personal staffs and by the military and civilian teams who worked with me in the Ministry of Defence, the Permanent Joint Headquarters and in my subordinate commands, as well as by defence attachés and many others around the world. I would like to pay a special tribute to the men and women of MI5, MI6, GCHQ and the police forces of this country, including those in Northern Ireland, with whom many in the armed forces worked closely for so long. And I want to salute all those dedicated civilians across Whitehall, and our diplomats around the world, without whom the armed forces could not function and on whom we depend.

Finally, I would like to thank my fellow Chiefs of Staff for their support and friendship – Admiral Mark Stanhope followed by Admiral George

Zambellas, Air Chief Marshal Stephen Dalton, General Peter Wall, Air Chief Marshal Stu Peach, General Richard Barrons and General Nick Houghton. We are but the temporary custodians of one of the nation's most treasured assets – our armed forces. While successfully fighting wars and managing crises, financial and strategic, the Chiefs transformed each service to be fit for the future. They led with great skill, honesty and integrity, and deserve much credit.

It was with a great sense of privilege that I served Her Majesty the Queen and this nation for forty-two years as well as my comrades whom, on occasion, I had the joy to lead.

Acknowledgements

I was not intending to write a book after I retired. I am too lazy and had other ambitions, buying a boat and doing some sailing among them. Eventually, though, I succumbed to a combination of well-intentioned flattery and a genuine belief on the part of many friends that I had some sort of duty to record my experiences over a forty-two-year military career that, pretty uniquely by modern standards, included a number of interesting senior operational command appointments.

The military memoir is a well-established part of our nation's literary and historical culture. I hope this book finds a minor place in it somewhere. I have found the experience of writing it taxing but rewarding in equal measure. It was with mixed emotions that I was reminded how the satisfactions of army life are balanced by the loss and injury of friends and comrades and the shared pain of their families. The last five years were the toughest in this respect, although even this period, surprisingly, contained quite a lot more humour and quiet enjoyment than increasing responsibility might suggest would be the case.

The fact that I enjoyed my career as much as I did has little to do with me and everything to do with the people I had the privilege of serving alongside. In the pages that follow I have mentioned some of them by name. It would be quite impossible to record them all or the many events and incidents that make a soldiers' life so interesting, amusing and fulfilling, despite not always realising it at the time.

There are some people, though, whom I must mention here because they were a particularly formative influence on me. Within my family, my parents, Colonel Jim and Pam Richards, my brother Nick and sisters Jan and Sara and my cousin Nigel were especially so. Within the Army, well, where do I start? I can only brush the wave tops but I must mention a few. My first commanding officer, Lieutenant Colonel, later Colonel, Nigel Frend, without his knowing it, was everything I aspired to becoming, as was another early commanding officer, Lieutenant Colonel, later Major General, Brian Pennicott of 29 Commando Regiment. I owe them both a lot. Then there was Brigadier Brian Kenny, later General Sir Brian, who effortlessly, or so it seemed to me, personified selfless leadership of the type Sandhurst seeks to instil in everyone but rarely so fully achieves. Lieutenant Colonel, later Brigadier, Mark Douglas-Withers tolerated and encouraged me with rare wisdom and humour, as did a subsequent brigade commander Brigadier, later Major General Sir, Evelyn Webb-Carter. After I was promoted to General, higher-ranking officers continued to inspire and motivate me. Field Marshal Lord Inge, Field Marshal Lord Guthrie and General Sir Mike Jackson stand out. The latter in particular made a tough job fun and I will always be in his debt.

The list of these senior officers could go on and on while the number of private soldiers, NCOs, Warrant Officers, officers commissioned from the ranks and more junior officers whose company I have loved and who have taught me much is endless. They range from Gunner Trethowan, way back in 1971, through my RSM Warrant Officer Class 1 Richard Drewett and Quartermaster Major Bob Harmes in the early nineties, to Corporal Dil and Sergeant Major Tranter, who looked after me and the Richards family so well when I was Chief of the Defence Staff. The tolerance, loyalty, humour and professionalism of the British soldier, sailor, airman and marine is renowned and rightly so. I have benefited hugely from serving with the very best, officer and soldier alike.

Finally and specifically, I want to thank those who have helped and encouraged me to write this book. Major General (Retired) Nigel Richards, my cousin, and Lieutenant Colonel (Retired) Tom Tugendhat, my ex-Military Assistant, both very kindly read the manuscript and their observations were invaluable. The advice, expertise and encouragement given to me by Edward Gorman, the former Deputy Head of News at *The Times*, has been an immense help, and fun too. I would like to thank my literary agent, Charlie Viney, who first tried to persuade me to 'sign-up' three years ago and must have seen something in my life that I certainly did not; his perseverance paid off, or I hope it did! Simon Thorogood of Headline Publishing has been a quietly confident and efficient partner and friend who deserves special praise, as have many members of the Headline team who have made the process of writing a book much more enjoyable than it could have been. And I would like particularly to thank Sir Max Hastings for doing me the honour of writing the foreword. Despite all this help and encouragement, responsibility for the content as well as for any errors or omissions is mine and mine alone.

Last and biggest of my debts is to my wife, Caroline. Her advice and support has been vital as has her willingness to put up with another year of indifferent attention from a husband who had already given her too little over the previous thirty-six years. Perhaps now, we can go on that round the world trip, but perhaps not in a 30-foot yacht . . .

Index

Picture Credits